"I've studied boomers and the age wave for the past three decades; however, I also recognize the need to focus on younger generations, especially on the changing dynamics of gender relationships. In *The Future of Men*, Jack Myers confronts changing realities in society, culture, business, and more."

—Ken Dychtwald, PhD, author of *A New Purpose: Redefining Money, Work, Retirement, and Success*

"Jack Myers has done it again. This time he delves deeply into the current and future status of masculinity and what it will mean to 'be a man' in the decades ahead. The current fundamental recasting of gender roles is one of the most profound dynamics in the world today."

—David Houle, futurist, EvolutionShift.com

"Learn what it takes to be a real man. Whether you eat quiche or not, this book is a must-read!"

—Jeffrey Hayzlett, TV and radio host, speaker, author, and chairman of C-Suite Network

"It's no secret that gender roles are blurring, but discussion on the future of this evolutionary change has been minimal. *The Future of Men* is the guide we've needed to walk us through this shift from the macho man to the modern man."

—Sydney N. Fulkerson, author of *The Coffee Run: And Other Internship Need-to-Knows*

"From a world that worships the image rather than the reality, Myers tells us to ignore the images that have defined men in the past and instead embrace our sensitivity and become more empathetic. He's *got* to be good to pull this off! He is."

—Larry Kramer, former president and publisher of *USA Today*

"For years, in my work advising consumer marketers and the agencies that support them, I have looked to Jack Myers for insights on the media ecology and the consuming culture that feeds it. He has a way of packaging his cultural insights to directly assist the reader in business and in life at large."

—Kendall Allen, principal of Influence Collective

OTHER BOOKS BY JACK MYERS

Adbashing: Surviving the Attacks on Advertising,
American Media Council, 1993

Reconnecting with Customers: Building Brands and Profits in The
Relationship Age, Spurge Ink! / Knowledge Exchange, 1998

Virtual Worlds: Rewiring Your Emotional
Connections, Myers Publishing LLC, 2007

Hooked Up: A New Generation's Surprising Take on Sex,
Politics and Saving the World, York House Press, 2012

JACK MYERS

MASCULINITY
IN THE TWENTY-FIRST
CENTURY

INKSHARES

*Globally, and especially in Western cultures,
we are in the midst of what may prove to be the greatest societal
transformation in the history of humanity: the transformation
from male to female dominance.*

Published by Inkshares, Inc., San Francisco, California
www.inkshares.com

Edited and designed by Girl Friday Productions
www.girlfridayproductions.com

Cover design by Erick Montes

ISBN: 978-1-9417586-56
e-ISBN: 978-1-9417586-63

LCCN: 2015945416

First edition

Printed in the United States of America

Dedicated to

the idea that people of all genders and all nations
will reach the common conclusion
that we are all equal in God's eyes,
and due equal rights,
equal honesty,
equal opportunity,
equal accountability for our actions,
and equal pursuit of happiness.

There is no male counterpart to sisterhood.

With gratitude to all those who supported and contributed to my
personal growth as I wrote this book

And with great love for my children and grandchildren and future
generations with whom I share this as my legacy

CONTENTS

TV AND MEDIA: REFLECTING CHANGE, LEADING CHANGE

GENDER CONVERGENCE AND WOMEN'S STRUGGLES

THE FUTURE OF MEN

WHY I WROTE
THIS BOOK

The male gender as a whole is afflicted by an inborn sense of power and dominance over women that has existed since the caveman. There is compelling evidence, however, that the shift toward female power is far more pervasive than we realize and that male dominance is quickly fading. It's becoming very apparent that the future of men will be increasingly defined, dominated, and controlled by women. In this book, I share perspectives on the future of men and how men are affected and responding as women emerge from centuries-old cocoons and, like butterflies, soar to new heights.

Throughout 2012 and 2013, I toured the country speaking about the first generation of students to grow up with the Internet, who were born between 1990 and 1996—the millennial "bridge" generation I discerned and researched for my book *Hooked Up: A New Generation's Surprising Take on Sex, Politics and Saving the World*. When I shared the statistics on female versus male college enrollment (60 percent vs. 40 percent) and explained why these young Internet natives, especially women, were a powerful and positive force to be reckoned with, the most common audience question was, "What's happening to men?"

This question led me to a much deeper exploration into the emerging female power class and into the major trends and influences affecting men—how they are reflected in society, culture, business, politics, media, and advertising—and the implications for both men and women as this shift in control and dominance transforms roles and relationships.

As I wrote this book, I recognized how our society, culture, companies, and lives are permeated by inappropriate sexual activity, sexism, misogyny, and pornography—and how accepted this has become. I listened with more awareness as my male colleagues engaged in obviously inappropriate sexual banter and behavior, none of them considering that it was dangerous, painful, destructive, and offensive.

I also recognized an emerging cultural backlash in the media and among both male and female organizations that is polarizing gender issues and creating more distance between men and women instead of building healthier relationships and moving us forward on a path toward mutual respect and understanding. It became apparent that as society appropriately focuses growing attention on women's equality and issues, young men need an advocate and support as they navigate the challenging and confusing new world that the growing success of the women's movement is creating.

In *The Future of Men*, I consider the following questions:

- Where have all the real men gone?
- Why is the era of the dominant male ending?
- Who are the "real men" of today and the future?
- What is the future of relationships and sex, business, politics, education, media, and marketing?
- Where are we heading as a society, and how can we help men, especially young men and boys, find a path toward healthier relationships, self-awareness, and ultimately, becoming more functional and happy?

Jack Myers
September 2015

MEN: PAST AND PRESENT

CHAPTER 1

ARE EVEN THE GOOD ONES BAD?

Globally, and especially in Western cultures, we are in the midst of the greatest societal transformation in the history of humanity: the transformation from male to female dominance.

"All the good men are either married or gay. Otherwise they're fucked up." If you know any single women seeking a monogamous relationship with a man, you've certainly heard that sentiment. Many will even add, "And most of the married ones are fucked up, too!"

The shrinking number of heterosexual men who are emotionally functional and able to sustain a relationship built on truth is radically affecting the balance of power between men and women. Lack of supply is not creating high demand; instead, as feminism becomes an ingrained reality, women progressively take more and more control of their sexual lives, their careers, and their futures, unfettered by their needs and desires for male partners. Straight single men may find it easier to get dates and even have sex, but there are few women who are willing to accept most of them as prospects for long-term relationships (or even short-term ones). More and more, as personified in TV programs and advertising, women view men as a helpless and hopeless sex. In fact, a 2015 study from the international market research company YouGov described in the Independent Journal Review claims that women are more likely to end long-term relationships—as much as 84 percent of them were ended by the female partner!

Instead of trying to change men, as they once believed they could, women are progressively—and increasingly aggressively—taking control away from them. Women today are no longer willing to passively accept male dominance, deceit, aggression, and control. They will no longer stand by men who disrespect their love through infidelity or stay with men who are neglectful and detached and who fail to connect emotionally and share intimacy. A "good" man today is not defined by his conquests, power, or sexual dominion. These are the tenets of a dying race of dominant males, the parables of ancient rituals, and the requirements of an age that exists only in our own minds. Yet men and society remain ruled by these outdated beliefs, which remain deeply embedded pillars that stand firm against the rising tide of female power and leadership. They are men's weapons as men battle to retain their traditional roles and the right to do as they please without accountability, regret, or self-destruction. For too many decades, these pillars have remained solid, enabling men to hold forth against the tidal wave of women's advances and progress.

How many men out there believe they are acting in all the right ways, accepting total equality for women, and rejecting misogyny and sexual misbehavior while still engaging in stupid, chest-puffing male behavior without accountability? Oblivious to the dangerous and devastating implications of their actions, they believe that they won't be "outed" or that they will be able to lie or buy their way out of anything if caught. The Ashley Madison disclosures were just part of a growing wave of evidence that infidelity can no longer be protected behind a wall of secrecy. Comedian Bill Cosby has consistently refuted sexual abuse accusations since 2000 and continues to gainsay any criminal acts even after fifty women have come forward against him. Misguided and outdated attitudes are at the foundation of the belief system of male power and dominance rooted in almost all hierarchies, including family, work, church, sports, politics, education, and the arts.

As each chapter in this book will explain in well-researched detail, a power shift from male domination to female–male equality, and in many instances growing female dominance, is at the foundation of an upheaval that is now radically transforming society. The walls are tumbling and the floors collapsing under men's regime. Male masters of the universe can no longer use their physical strength, governmental authority, or financial control to dictate and rule over the position and privileges of women in the family, the workplace, society, politics, or culture.

Life and gender are intertwined and inseparable. Our gender education begins with our ancestral realities; it continues with our very first experiences with our parents, our siblings, and the men and women who raise and teach us. Our gender identity is at the very core of our being. It is also intimately linked to our sexual identity.

Sexual experiences and associations form fantasy worlds as we discover and experience what it feels like to be aroused. Do we connect or disconnect? Do we marry? Are we gay, straight, transgender, or one of the many other ways a person can experience gender identity? Are we enthusiastic about sex? Do we conquer destructive patterns in our relationships, or do they remain ingrained in our actions throughout life? Do we ever find true and sustainable love? Do we establish mutual trust in relationships and honor that trust forever? Do we achieve a sense of dignity, or do we act in ways that make others indignant toward us? Are we totally honest in our relationships, or do we follow the mantra of "deny, deny, deny"? Do we ever achieve true self-esteem, and if we do, have we earned the right to it?

Men and women need to be aware of and sensitive to the challenges these questions imply as traditional gender norms are uprooted and transformed. Men's and women's mutual commitment must be to understanding and interpreting new gender truths and to remaining open to change along the journey. They must begin to practice and teach a new mantra of absolute honesty, mutual respect, and trust.

A woman's power is in her intuition, experience, common sense, and her inherent desire to collaborate rather than fight. When women say, "I understand," they mostly do (unlike men, who are often clueless but won't admit it). Women are powerful—sexually, intuitively, and intellectually. Women view men through that prism, while men all too frequently view women sexually, seeing them as a collection of body parts. Women rarely, if ever, allow sex to take priority in their decision making without active consideration of the implications (even if that deliberation takes just seconds). The male sex drive is rarely informed in such a way; its role is to jump into action and perform. The libido takes up arms against rational thinking and fights off all obstacles to achieve its mission. When an inappropriate flirtation or fixation backfires, rather than backing off as he should, the man may continue to march forward, undeterred until the mission is carried through to fruition or declared abortive.

No matter where the male sex drive may center its attention or how aggressively men may assert their physical power and dominance, men are being progressively outmaneuvered, outsmarted, and outresourced by women. This is the genetic and historical reality that men must understand, accept, and embrace if they are to have a positive and productive future in a world in which women are at least an equally dominant force.

The last generation of "traditional" males is now in their late twenties. The first wave of Internet natives is just entering their adult years, heralding a new age of gender relationships that have different role models, a history born with the Internet, and new guidelines for behavior. This generation is dismissing customary gender definitions as irrelevant; conventional male/female roles are shifting. The first generation of "future men" is a more evolved species (though still in its formative stages). The future man recognizes, respects, and relates to the growing dominance of women in many areas of society, culture, relationships, family, and business. Yet these young men are also confused by the conflicting realities that put them in the crosshairs between traditional definitions of masculinity and emerging behavioral expectations. It will take decades, but we are in the midst of an irreversible transformation: women are gaining power and influence as traditional roles and expectations disappear and new gender norms evolve. This is the story of *The Future of Men: Masculinity in the Twenty-First Century*.

CHAPTER 2

THE FUTURE OF MEN: JUST THE FACTS

Man has been the dominant sex since, well, the dawn of mankind. But for the first time in human history, that is changing—and with shocking speed.

—Hanna Rosin, "The End of Men," the *Atlantic*

"The End of Men" was a shocking, controversial, and newsworthy headline when the *Atlantic* published it in July 2010. The article wasn't as depressing as the headline, but it did outline extraordinary changes in societies throughout the world—changes that have made life more difficult for the generations of men who were raised believing certain fundamental ideas about their place in family, business, culture, and society. The article goes on to say that, since the 1970s, our "postindustrial society" (one with a much lower percentage of jobs relying on size, strength, and stamina) has dramatically reduced the percentage of men who are the dominant sex in their families and workplaces.

Women's increasing success and men's diminished role is so profound that parents in industrialized nations such as the United States and South Korea who once preferred male babies now prefer girls, and parents in developing nations such as China and India are slowly but progressively making the same shift.

Rosin's article doesn't forecast whether the trends of the past four decades will continue—specifically, whether men can acquire the skills needed to succeed in a postindustrial economy. These skills are predominantly female-associated and include social intelligence, verbal aptitude, self-control, and as Rosin put it, "the ability to sit still and focus."

A study by Caliper, a talent management company, indicates that women demonstrate higher team-building skills and are, in general, better team players. Men are considered better at delegating; women generally excel at collaboration and group effort. Men have a tendency to want individual success and power; women score higher when it comes to persuasive skills. The article, "How Men and Women Differ in the Workplace," in the Fiscal Times suggested that women are more willing to look at all sides of a situation, which leads to better persuasive techniques. "He Said, She Said: Communicating Between Genders at Work," from Business Know-How details how women are more supportive of others in positions that are equal to or below them. Women give compliments; men give evaluations.

Sheryl Sandberg, chief operating officer of Facebook and author of *Lean In*, offers additional insight into the management styles of men and women. During an interview on *60 Minutes*, she was asked how men and women attribute their success. Sandberg stated that men are likely to credit their success to themselves, whereas women will give credit to others and downplay their strong points. When asked how she credits her own achievements, Sandberg responded, appropriately enough, with, "It is attributed to a lot of things, some of which really are luck, working hard, and help from others."

A study conducted by the Stanford Graduate School of Business showed that women who are able to develop the male qualities of assertiveness, confidence, and aggressive behavior—and who know when to use these behaviors—have more success in business. The interesting finding was that the success was not as much based on developing masculine traits as it was on controlling those traits. These results broke success into sections:

- Women who had masculine traits performed one and a half times better than masculine men did.
- They performed one and a half times better than women with a feminine business style.
- They performed three times better than masculine women without the ability to control the appropriate use of assertiveness or aggressiveness.
- Most important, these women did two times better than men with a more feminine business style.

If the positive skills of men and women can be combined, there are obvious benefits. A rapidly growing number of corporations and organizations will be positioned to capitalize on these benefits as women's corporate and economic power increase.

"Of the 15 job categories projected to grow the most in the next decade in the U.S., all but two are occupied primarily by women," wrote Hanna Rosin in her *Atlantic* piece. "Indeed, the U.S. economy is in some ways becoming a kind of traveling sisterhood: upper-class women leave home and enter the workforce, creating domestic jobs for other women to fill." The fast-growing "female" occupations referenced include child care, home health assistance, and nursing. The only "male" occupations on the list are computer engineering and janitorial work.

Since 2000, the number of manufacturing jobs has dropped from roughly eighteen million to twelve million, according to the Bureau of Labor Statistics. In a future with far fewer manufacturing jobs, education will become even more important. A 2012 US Census Bureau report revealed that in 1970, men had nearly a 60 to 40 percent overall edge in all college degrees. That same document shows that today and for the foreseeable future, women are earning about 60 percent of bachelor's and master's degrees. Women's increasing advantage in high-growth occupations and on college campuses has transformed society. Bureau of Labor Statistics data show that in 1970, women earned roughly 27 percent of family income in the United States.

Today, as told in the *New York Times* article "They Call It the Reverse Gender Gap," in many large American cities, single women between the ages of eighteen and twenty-nine without children earn an average of 18 percent or more than single, childless men in the same age group.

That doesn't mean "the end of men," but it does mean the end of a male-dominated society. A key question for organizations and for male–female relationships is whether the social and emotional challenges that result from these new realities will negatively influence men's effectiveness in business and progressively erode their traditional dominance in the corporate hierarchy.

The trend toward higher-earning women has already transformed the institution of marriage. "Increasing numbers of women—unable to find men with a similar income and education—are forgoing marriage altogether," wrote Rosin, who noted that the percentage of thirty-to-forty-four-year-old women who aren't married increased from 16 percent in 1970 to 40 percent in 2010.

WOMEN TAKE CONTROL OF EARNING POWER

No matter the field, the wage gap between men and women is still significant. Even men without a degree still make substantially more per hour than women. This unfortunate truth persists despite women going to college more often and even doing better in school than men. On the fiftieth anniversary of the 1963 Equal Pay Act, the *Huffington Post* published a study showing that women are still making only seventy-seven cents for each dollar that a man makes. In other words, a better-qualified, better-educated woman was still only worth about three-quarters of a man in 2013. Furthermore, a woman, on average, makes a total of $11,084 less than a man per year, despite women's rising education rates.

This leads to another socioeconomic factor that some experts haven't yet discussed. The Pew Research Center reported that single-mother households are earning over $10,000 less than single-father households, creating a significant income disparity.

Although the wage gap between men and women is closing, it's important to note that men are still on the top and likely will be for a while. Despite regulations and laws that enforce equal pay between the genders, experts believe that it will be up to forty-five years until women are making the same amount per hour as men. This is not a situation that is expected to change overnight; men will not suddenly become lower income earners than women. But some economists point out that incomes among millennials are shifting in favor of women and make a compelling case that within just a few years there will be a reversal of income disparity between genders, with millennial women outearning their male counterparts.

The job losses stemming from the 2008 recession and its aftermath are still reshaping American culture. According to Bloomberg, 95 percent of net jobs lost during the recession were middle-skilled jobs. *CNNMoney* put the total number of jobs lost at around 7.9 million, and *Forbes* said 78 percent of those were lost by men. At the same time, there has been a 12 percent increase in employment in female-dominated fields such as education and health services.

A Bureau of Labor Statistics analysis of the recession showed that the unemployment rate peaked at 10 percent in October 2009, which is the highest it has been since the 1983 record of 10.8 percent. Unemployment did not affect men and women equally, however, leading some to dub the recession of 2008 "the mancession." Mark J. Perry, professor of economics at the University of Michigan, wrote in "The Great Mancession of 2008–2009" that by August 2009, 11 percent of men were unemployed compared with 8.3 percent of women. The 2.7 percent difference was the greatest employment rate gender gap in US postwar history. A similar gender unemployment gap exists today, especially among millennials, and is likely to increase during this decade and beyond even as total unemployment shrinks.

This shift in traditional male and female roles is a permanent reality. The mancession of 2008 may have forced the situation, but it was and continues to be compounded by the growing educational superiority of women and the resulting effect on families, careers, politics, business, culture, and society.

A 2011 census noted that one in three preschool children spend more time in their father's care than with any other caregiver while their mother is working (most of the fathers work at least part-time). Researchers Ilana Demantas, from the University of Kansas, and Kristen Myers, director of the Center for the Study of Women, Gender, and Sexuality at Northern Illinois University, conducted in-depth interviews with men who lost their jobs during the recession. Depression and feelings of worthlessness were common among the men as they were forced to confront a shift in gender roles, said a Live Science article on the study. However, many stayed positive and took pride in taking on more housework, the researchers reported. Myers is quoted in the article saying, "None of these men would say they're feminist, but they're doing the best they have [sic] with what they have . . . They see it as fairness." Myers observed that this contradicts earlier research.

Jeremy Adam Smith, author of *The Daddy Shift*, thinks fathers need to embrace the option of becoming stay-at-home dads, which he believes "represent[s] a logical next step of fifty years of family change, from a time when the idea of men caring for children was inconceivable, to a new era when at-home dads are a small but growing segment of the population. This is the 'daddy shift' of the title: the gradual movement away from definition of fatherhood as pure breadwinner to one that encompasses capacities for both breadwinning and caregiving."

HOW ARE MEN FARING IN THE MODERN WORKPLACE?

The future of men in the workplace appears grim. We may look at these statistics and forecasts and, justifiably, ask one crucial question: how extensive will the changes in the workplace be? In other words, will women dominate the workplace from top to bottom as men did for centuries, or will the glass ceiling that has historically stymied women from attaining the highest-level positions in the workplace persist? From this question spring countless others, including the following:

How are men faring in various occupations in the business world?

Five of eight industries with the largest projected wage and salary growth, according to the Bureau of Labor Statistics, are the traditionally female-dominated health care and social assistance industries.

Are men of all family income levels losing ground to women, and are women advancing because of economic necessity?
    Yes!

Are men losing as much ground in executive suites as they're losing in mid- and junior-level offices?
    Not yet, but in business categories such as media and advertising, women are slowly capturing more executive positions, and the shift toward hiring women into more senior roles appears to be inevitably advancing.

What are the trends in business school enrollment, and how will they affect the future of the business world?
    The trends are clear. The percentage of female enrollees in business schools is increasing across all professions, as cited elsewhere in this book.

Are men more apt to be and succeed as entrepreneurs or are women shedding the stereotypes that they are more interested in security and less willing to take risks?
    There is less information about this, but anecdotal evidence suggests that young women are more likely to be hired by entrepreneurial start-ups and are more likely to be successful in their roles. Silicon Valley and Silicon Alley investors are actively seeking more female-led ventures, and organizations such as Kay Koplovitz's Springboard Enterprises are providing a catalyst for these organizations. Springboard boasts that it has helped generate $6.6 billion in funding for 562 female-founded companies, leading to eleven initial public offerings (the first sale of stock in a company to the public).

Are the commonly accepted beliefs that men are more effective leaders still true, or have women demonstrated that they are equally or more effective as leaders?

As reported in this book, there is strong evidence that public companies with three or more female board members are outperforming those with male-dominated boards. There is a growing body of research proving that the qualities required for success in a modern organization are more typically associated with women, such as collaboration and multitasking.

Are men adapting to changes in the workplace, and, if so, how?

Yes and no. It depends on the man and on the organization and its culture. More important, how do we support young men who are just entering the workplace and empower them to reject old boys' network traditions and embrace the female-dominated and multicultural reality they've experienced throughout most of their educational lives? And how do we educate and train "old-school" organizations, executives, and employees to embrace the looming power shift?

Will men need to become less traditionally masculine to succeed in the business world? For example, will they need to become more empathetic and willing to join support groups and share their feelings, or are old boys' networks still a safe route to success?

The old boys' network remains entrenched in many corporations and industries, but its membership is declining, and it is no more relevant today than the all-male golf club. More to the point of *The Future of Men*, the business world needs to develop a new model for successfully welcoming young men into corporate hierarchies. The men's version of women's mentoring groups needs to be created, and such meetings cannot be allowed to devolve into nights out at the strip club and conversations about sports and sex.

What changes will men need to make in their management styles to succeed in a business world that will have a far higher percentage of women than in the past?

See Chapter 21.

Will men become more apt to forsake business and career opportunities because of family commitments than they have in the past, and will women become less likely to prioritize their families?

Many men and women are choosing to embrace less traditional family roles, and many are being forced by economic realities to shift their priorities. The goal of this book is to share the new societal dynamics that make questions such as this not only inappropriate but irrelevant and outdated. Our culture is transforming as male and female roles become interchangeable and interlaced. The biological truth of womanhood no longer defines a woman's role in the family or in business. The idea that career opportunities and family are in direct opposition is offensive.

Are parents, particularly fathers, increasing their expectations of their daughters because of societal changes, and are they putting more or less pressure on their sons to become more ambitious and successful as they've fallen behind in the classroom?

It's inappropriate to generalize, but several experts point to increasing parental pressures on women to advance educationally and less pressure on their sons to excel in either sports or school. Reasons relate to the increase in female-led single-parent homes, a shift in youth sports that de-emphasizes winning, an increase in single-parent homes, and educational realities that favor women. A 2014 article in the *Atlantic* analyzing the difference in boys' and girls' school performance pointed out that "these days, the whole school experience seems to play right into most girls' strengths—and most boys' weaknesses."

Finding answers to many of the questions about men's future in the business world is often difficult, but one thing remains crystal clear— most of the available research looks at the issue from the perspective of "why aren't women doing better?" The US Department of Labor's Bureau of Labor Statistics, for example, has a section on women over several decades, but nothing on men. Numerous academic, business, educational, and professional organizations take the same approach.

The Bureau of Labor Statistics produced a report in February 2013 detailing the number of men and women in the US workforce from

1970 through 2011, how much money they made, how many hours they worked, and how each gender fared in various occupations and industries. The document, entitled "Women in the Labor Force: A Databook," stated the following:

- About 62.3 percent of the American workforce was male in 1970. That figured declined to 57.6 percent in 1980, 54.8 percent in 1990, 53.6 percent in 2000, and 53.1 percent in 2011. (By the time this book is published, it's reasonable to expect the percentage of women in the workforce will slightly exceed that of men.)
- The percentage of men with work experience declined from 84.3 percent in 1970 to 69.3 percent in 2010, while the percentage of women with work experience rose from 52.7 percent in 1970 to 58.5 percent in 2010.
- The percentage of working wives who earned more money than their working husbands increased from 17.8 percent in 1970 to 29.2 percent in 2010.
- Full-time female employees earned 62 percent of what full-time male employees earned in 1979. By 2010, the female-to-male earnings ratio was 82 percent—$684 versus $832 weekly. The gap has closed even more since then.
- Women's-to-men's earnings ratios were higher for blacks and Hispanics (91 percent for each group) than whites (82 percent).
- Education is a major factor in women's progress in the business world. Women with a college degree earn roughly twice what women with only a high school degree do. Women ages twenty-five and up earned a median of $998 weekly in 2011 if they had a college degree but $554 weekly with only a high school degree.
- The percentage of women with college degrees increased from 11 percent in 1970 to 37 percent in 2011, while the percentage of women who didn't graduate high school plunged from 34 percent to 7 percent.
- Men are losing more ground in white-collar professions than blue-collar professions, partly because of the higher percentage of educated women in the workforce. Although men

constituted 53.1 percent of the overall workforce in 2011, they made up only 49 percent of people in management, professional, and "related occupations."

The 2012 Bureau of Labor Statistics "Employment Projections" report stated that seventeen of the thirty occupations that are forecast to have the fastest employment growth from 2010 to 2020 require at least some college education. Hanna Rosin's article declared that women already dominate in twenty of these categories. Biomedical engineers—the third-fastest growing occupation—as well as event planners, interpreters and translators, market research analysts, family and marriage therapists, physical therapists, audiologists, health educators, cost estimators, medical scientists, mental health counselors, and veterinarians all require at least a bachelor's degree. "Occupations that typically need some type of post-secondary education for entry are projected to grow the fastest during the 2010–20 decade," stated the Bureau of Labor Statistics document. "Occupations classified as needing a master's degree are projected to grow by 21.7 percent, followed by doctoral or professional degree occupations at 19.9 percent, and associate's degree occupations at 18.0 percent."

"Women in the Labor Force," produced by the Bureau of Labor Statistics in 2011, noted that 86 percent of architects and engineers, 66 percent of physicians and surgeons, 95.7 percent of pilots and flight engineers, 75.8 percent of chief executives, 68.1 percent of attorneys, and 66.1 percent of computer systems analysts are men. However, men are projected to have a decreasing majority in the future, partly because the percentage of male students in professional schools is significantly lower than the percentage of male professionals (roughly half of today's law and medical students and about 58 percent of business school students are men, according to "The End of Men") and partly because male-dominated professions are expected to have far less job growth than female-dominated professions.

In addition, eleven of the twenty industries with the largest projected wage and salary declines from 2010 to 2020 are manufacturing industries, which have historically been dominated by men. Five of the eight industries with the largest projected wage and salary growth are the traditionally female-dominated health care and social assistance industries.

Economic crises tend to accelerate changes in the workplace. "Jobs created in recent recoveries looked nothing like those that were lost, and the people hired for those new positions looked nothing like the people laid off from the old ones," said the 2010 *Help Wanted: Projections of Job and Education Requirements Through 2018* report by Georgetown University's Center on Education and the Workforce. "In the past two recessions, the typical job loser was a high school-educated male in a blue-collar job, such as manufacturing or construction, working in the middle of the country. In the past two recoveries, the typical job gainer was a female with a postsecondary education who lived on either coast and worked in a service occupation—particularly health care, education, or business services."

Rosin's "The End of Men" article emphasized that "women are also starting to dominate middle management" and that the percentage of women in managerial and professional jobs increased from 26.1 percent in 1980 to 51.5 percent in 2009. The article concluded that "the perception of the ideal business leader is starting to shift."

CHANGING MANAGEMENT CHARACTERISTICS FAVOR FEMALE ASCENDENCY

Historically, the overwhelming majority of the world's cultures and civilizations associated leaders with men. Citing five sources, the Wikipedia article "Femininity" lists caring, compassion, deference, empathy, gentleness, nurturance, sensitivity, sweetness, and tolerance as traditionally feminine traits. None of those personal characteristics matched what "The End of Men" called the old model of business leadership: "command and control, with one leader holding all the decision-making power." Leaders, it was believed, needed to be tough, aggressive, and decisive. Those who were unconcerned with being caring, compassionate, empathetic, and so on were believed to be more capable than leaders with those characteristics.

The stereotypes of masculinity and femininity were so accepted that, in a Gallup study covered by *CNBC*, 66 percent of Americans said in 1953 that they preferred a male boss, while only 5 percent preferred a female boss, and the remainder were undecided. The preference for a male boss rather than a female has narrowed over the years: In 1975, 62 percent preferred a male and 7 percent a female boss; in 1982, the numbers were 46 and 12 percent, respectively; in 1993, they were 35 and 16 percent, respectively; and in 2013, they were 35 and 23 percent, respectively.

The declining gap between preference for male and female bosses could be the result of several factors. The most important reason is likely anecdotal—far fewer people knew successful female managers who had a management style that they approved of in 1953 than in 2013. In addition, far more female leaders are in public positions today, including business, politics, and the military (which didn't permit women to supervise men at all until 1971).

As more women have attained leadership positions in the business world, analyses of why businesses succeed and fail have reevaluated assumptions about what personal characteristics leaders should have. Interestingly, University of California, Irvine, professor emerita Dr. Judy Rosener told *USA Today* that brain scans "prove that men and women think differently." The future of men in the business world might depend more on gender diversity in the office and men learning to work with women rather than men trying to become more "feminine" by becoming more sensitive, gentle, and tolerant. Hanna Rosin, in her article, advocated men learning to "behave like a good coach" to motivate their employees, but the data on biological differences means that men perhaps need, instead, to delegate the coaching to female executives. "Rosener says she's concluded that a company with a mix of male and female leaders, with their differing attitudes regarding risk, collaboration, and ambiguity, will outperform a competitor that relies on the leadership of a single sex," wrote *USA Today*'s Del Jones.

Gender diversity in the corporate boardroom is also beneficial, concluded Catalyst, a nonprofit organization that seeks to expand opportunities for women in business. "Companies with three or more women board directors on average outperformed companies with zero women board directors by 84% return on sales, 60% return on invested capital, and 46% return on equity," said Catalyst. The lopsided quantity advantage that men have had in business leadership positions is changing and will likely continue to change in the future.

***

"We couldn't believe our eyes," said Ankur Kumar, former director of MBA admissions at the Wharton School of the University of Pennsylvania. "It was a fantastic moment for us." Kumar was referring to the fact that a record-high 45 percent of the class of 2013 at one of the finest graduate business schools in the United States was women, stated *US News & World Report*. His comment reflects a widespread attitude that exists in academia whenever women make gains in enrollment and graduation at graduate schools as well as in the workplace and boardroom.

Would a graduate school administrator make a similar comment if the percentage of men in a college field of study previously dominated by women was surprisingly high? Let's hope so. Men are resistant to pursuing occupations that have traditionally been considered feminine, but their future opportunities will depend on communicating a positive attitude toward males taking on roles in traditionally female careers.

Although the percentage of female students in business, law, and medical schools continues to rise thanks to aggressive recruitment and other strategies, "The End of Men" noted that nursing and teaching schools have had very little success recruiting male students. "Many professions that started out as the province of men are now filled mostly with women—secretary and teacher come to mind," wrote Rosin. "Yet I'm not aware of any that have gone the opposite way."

The yearning for women to do better in relation to men has spawned many changes at business schools over the years. In its 2008 article "Extra Effort Lures Women MBAs," *BusinessWeek* discussed the endeavors of five business schools—New York University Stern School of Business, Babson College (ranked the number one entrepreneurship MBA program for twenty consecutive years), Cornell

University's Samuel Curtis Johnson Graduate School of Management, Northwestern University's Kellogg School of Management, and the University of Chicago's Booth School of Business—to increase the percentage of women at their schools. The schools' essays with potential female applicants include networking events, mentoring programs, regular coffee chats between prospective students and administrators, summer outreach programs, and a zealous push to have one-on-one conversations.

"If a woman expresses interest in Babson, she will get an expedited phone call back from an admissions officer," the article said. "The school then tries to get her to campus as soon as possible for an admissions event and will often pair her up with a current student involved in the school's Center for Women's Leadership."

The attempts to increase the percentage of women at graduate business schools have paid off. Harvard Business School didn't admit women until 1962. The class of 1975 was 89 percent men. The percentage of students who were men declined to 75 percent in 1985, 72 percent in 1995, 65 percent in 2005, and 59 percent in 2015, according to the school. Most, if not all, universities are trying to attract more women. For example, there's a Wharton Women page but not a Wharton Men page.

Business schools are also making an effort to help students prepare for a world that has become more receptive to the collaborative style of leadership than the authoritative style that existed when virtually every manager was a man. "The End of Men" reported that the Columbia Business School teaches students how to be more sensitive to employees and tries to improve their social intelligence by training them how to interpret body language and facial expressions. "We never explicitly say, 'Develop your feminine side,' but it's clear that's what we're advocating," Jamie Ladge, an associate professor at Columbia, told the *Atlantic*.

A new narrative—one that supports the image of men in historically female roles—needs to be encouraged, supported, and reinforced. A starting point is for colleges to more proactively recruit males into these fields just as they have been aggressive in enrolling females in male-led majors. Similarly, advertising, TV, and film can begin casting males in career roles typically dominated by women.

SHATTERING THE GLASS CEILING?

Historically, there has been a so-called glass ceiling in the United States—and other nations—that has prevented most women and minorities from attaining high-level positions in the business world. It would be an exaggeration to say that that ceiling has been shattered, but many qualified women and culturally diverse executives have attained the C-Suite (senior executive) positions at Fortune 500 companies in recent years. Women have come a long way since 1996, when there was a grand total of half a chief executive officer (CEO) at a Fortune 500 company. Yes, half: Marion Sandler was the co-CEO of Golden West Financial.

Innumerable documents and articles describe the CEOs at Fortune 500 companies. Generally, the number of females increases slightly from year to year, and the articles are often accompanied by accolades about their performance. They, on average, outperform male CEOs in generating shareholder value and profits. The data on companies performing better when they have a mix of male and female executives is, at the least, interesting and, at the most, conclusive.

The Forté Foundation and Catalyst have the best relatively current data on the glass ceiling at Fortune 500 companies. The Forté Foundation reported that women constituted 4 percent (or twenty) of the CEOs at Fortune 500 companies, 14 percent of Fortune 500 senior executives, and about 17 percent of the members of Fortune 500 boards of directors in 2012. "Women have been in mainstream business for over 30 years, but still make up less than 17% of corporate board members in America's 500 largest companies," explained the Forté Foundation in an effort to put the numbers in context.

In an interview with the *Huffington Post*, Bloomberg LIVE editor Stephanie Mehta projected that the percentage of female CEOs will increase, but equality in the "near future" is probably unattainable and shouldn't be the goal.

There are no generic one-size-fits-all conclusions about how women's advances in business will ultimately affect men. There's no evidence that women will reject those management qualities that are more associated with men or that they will universally impose those qualities, such as collaboration, that are more associated with female managers. But it is clear that the historic imbalance between male and female executives will shift in favor of women, and more men will be required to work within women-led hierarchies. The misogynistic work environment, which has been changing as a result of laws and restrictive human resource dictates, will virtually disappear. Young people just entering the workforce have grown up in a female-dominated educational and online culture. The *Mad Men* workplace of the past is foreign to them (and unacceptable).

Women are capturing a growing percentage of entry-level, mid-level, and senior-level management jobs in most major industries, and within the next two decades they will own a majority of these jobs. It's possible that within the career span of today's junior executives, women will gain equality in the boardroom, in the C-Suite, and even on Wall Street, which is perhaps the final bastion of male dominance. Even in politics, the backlash against conservative-led anti–women's rights laws has been a catalyst for the growing politicization of women across America. Globally, women have been at the forefront of the uprisings against radical Muslim repression of women's and girls' rights.

There is no question that Hanna Rosin's insight is correct: "Man has been the dominant sex since, well, the dawn of mankind. But for the first time in human history, that is changing—and with shocking speed." That doesn't mean, however, that the end of men is near.

Men won't be the dominant sex in the future, but they won't be subservient either. The future of men in the business world will be very different from what it has been in the past; we are in the midst of a dramatic transformation. It can be a bright future that will make men healthier and happier if they adapt to society's changes well enough to share workplace and leadership responsibilities without feeling that they have failed and "their end is near." Men in the workplace must adapt to the shifting sands of time and learn to accept that they no longer have a gender-based right to lead.

CHAPTER 3

MEN: CONFUSED, CHALLENGED, CONFLICTED

It's a genetic reality that men are a confused gender. In his book *Adam's Curse: A Future Without Men*, geneticist Bryan Sykes wrote that the Y (male) chromosome "is a mess . . . it is a genetic ruin, a wasteland littered with molecular wreckage." After 281 pages of heavily muscled genetic history going back thousands of years and forecasting the next 125,000 years, Sykes comes to the conclusion that men are on a path toward almost certain doom.

Men are in conflict, suffering from a heavily challenged sense of self. They see the writing on the wall: on one hand, there are "real men," true to their convictions and masters of their domain, holding on for dear life to their traditional place in the world. A real man has dominance over his kingdom; he is not only in control, but exerts physical, financial, and emotional mastery. Many (if not most) of these real men hide their true misogynistic, insecure, cheating, emotionally detached selves from their loved ones, female colleagues, and even themselves. On the other hand, there is the "future man," focused on identifying how to best navigate this new world in which women are gaining power. These men are in touch with their feminine side; are gay or gay-friendly; embrace a woman's role as an equal and often as a superior in executive suites, on the battlefield, and in the family; are comfortable ceding to or sharing financial control with women; and are willing to accept women as emotionally superior.

A man need only to think back to his most recent conversation with other men at a business meeting, party, or sporting event to see into which category he fits. Did he tell or listen to a sexist joke with no sense of impropriety? Would the conversation have been different with one or more women present? A man can think of his last time walking down a street or on public transportation. How did he look at and think about a young, attractive woman in a short skirt? When seeing a beautiful woman walking ahead of him, did he speed up to walk past her and steal a glimpse?

If he is in a supervisory position at work, what are the differences in his behavior with his male and female employees? If he has a female boss, does he respect and respond to her the same as he would a male boss? How would he act differently at a bar or party if his wife or girlfriend were watching? If he has promised sexual and emotional fidelity in his relationship, has he completely abided by that commitment, or has he screwed around and then denied that the affair had any real meaning to him or his partner and was therefore acceptable? How does he perceive the respective roles and responsibilities of his parents, and how are these roles reflected in his own relationships?

The typical answers to these questions all lead to one conclusion: most men today, no matter how enlightened they may believe they are, continue to exhibit and foster the same behavior as men have throughout the ages. Despite the prevalence of the behavior, incontrovertible trends in business, politics, education, entertainment, and virtually every other realm of Western civilization are now revealing these age-old patterns as inappropriate, destructive, and irrelevant.

Whether these behavior patterns are cultural, biological, or psychological, it's becoming increasingly clear that the historical dominance of men is eroding; women are powering up and progressively capturing control and influence in one area after another. Men, as a consequence, are confused, conflicted, and challenged, and while some are embracing this new world, many men and male-dominated organizations are striking back in an undeclared war on women. Still others are avoiding the change and confrontation altogether, remaining passive, emotionally disconnected, detached, and comfortably numb.

CHAPTER 4

THE AGE OF THE DOMINANT MALE HAS PASSED

For those who haven't been paying attention, women in the United States are more influential in the family's decisions than ever before. Women now represent over 80 percent of all consumer spending across almost every category of products and services, according to data from She-conomy. Furthermore, for the next decade and beyond, women will make up 60 percent of students in college and 65 percent in postgraduate classes. Included among these grads are a far greater percentage of black, Hispanic, Asian, LGBT, and other minorities than represented in the general population. This reality covers nearly every college across every region of the country: among our educated elite, straight white males are a declining minority. The political war on women, including battles over congressional districting and voter rights, is a distinctly male challenge to the fundamental and irreversible transformation of society.

One truth lives in the heart of every man whether we realize it or not: our time has passed. The first characteristic we use to define ourselves is gender: it's the core genetic trait we inherit, the first chromosomal separation in our prenatal existence. In *Adam's Curse: A Future*

Without Men, geneticist Bryan Sykes describes mitochondrial (female) DNA as a "model of slimmed down efficiency," while describing the Y chromosome (male) as a "graveyard of rotting genes, whose corpses are nonetheless still sufficiently . . . recognizable, but whose festering remains contain the evidence of their own demise. . . . Without any capacity for repair, the mutations keep on accumulating. Like the face of the moon, still pitted by craters from all the meteors that have ever fallen onto its surface, Y chromosomes cannot heal their own scars."

For all of recorded history, men have been in control. Today's geneticists, however, report that a degeneration of the Y chromosome has been going on for centuries, whereas the X chromosome is strengthening. Men, it seems, are relegated to a future—defined by our genetics—in which we will be dominated by women. (And, lest the cows, sheep, fruit flies, and dandelions laugh smugly at the stupid human male, the same reality confronts all types of animal and plant life. *Scientific American* has documented that among a few species, such as the Japanese Ryukyu spiny rat, the whiptail lizard, and at least seventy species of vertebrates, reproduction occurs without the Y chromosome.)

Society, simultaneously, has been experiencing the same pattern of male decline and female rise. In the past several decades—a shockingly short time—we have witnessed a steady erosion of male dominance that has accelerated past the point of no return. The male chromosome is in a downward genetic spiral and the female chromosome is in an upward climb that is being reflected beyond the womb to everywhere we look in Western society today. Across television, advertising, education, and business, just to start, we're experiencing a shift from a male-dominated to a female-dominated culture. In some political and societal subcultures, the war is intense and the backlash awesome and frightening to behold. From North Carolina to Syria, battles are being fought over many of the same basic issues of men's past power and control versus an inevitable future of female influence.

In other areas of our culture, such as advertising, education, and the arts, the metamorphosis has been more peaceful. Like caterpillars coming of age, women are metaphorically shedding their skins, turning into butterflies, and flying off to explore a new world. Female-dominant characteristics are appearing across all of society and in most cultures and will become increasingly prevalent.

Meanwhile, what men are becoming remains an unknown, and there is no clear vision for a better future. One certain discovery is that men are a confused and schizophrenic group, struggling to adapt in radically different ways. Men fight to retain their traditional roles, holding onto legacy power models that are no longer relevant or sustainable. Men still exhibit all the bravado and hubris of their forefathers, but they are also bewildered and bewitched by a rising tide of empowered females who, by every statistical, logical, and genetic analysis, are moving into positions of strength, dominance, and power.

In *Adam's Curse*, Sykes concludes that "the human Y-chromosome has been decaying for a very long time and will continue to do so." He goes on to say that "there are more active genes in the sixteen and a half thousand bases of mitochondrial DNA than in the sixty million bases of Y-chromosome." The male cells, he explains, have to work harder, producing more toxins with a greater risk of mutation and destruction. It's a deadly cycle for men.

Women can look forward to generations and generations of growing dominance. The age of the dominant male has passed, no matter how aggressively some men may fight to repress females in all areas. Although men and women may agree on many common characteristics and differences (and may accept and retain their traditional roles and relationships), women have won a genetic race that began thousands of years ago. Those mired in the past are genetically doomed to growing frustration, overtaken by women who are embracing the role they've been preparing for since Eve.

The fundamental conflict in men between holding on to and ceding control is playing out in families, companies, schools, governments, and global conflicts. This will continue for the rest of the century, although the balance of power has already swung against men. The future is already written in genetic code, and this reality is everywhere we look. As all-female organizations, clubs, and professional groups gain popularity and relevance, all-male clubs are becoming all but obsolete and those remaining few are populated by men with canes, walkers, and oxygen tubes. Antifemale men's organizations and initiatives are gaining followers, and their misguided diatribes may help soothe men's egos, but they achieve little in addressing men's real needs and issues.

The restructuring of gender norms is a central issue in US politics, as it is for religious groups and societies dedicated to living in a biblical past disconnected from the real world. It's a central issue as women increasingly dominate the workforce and finally move into and take control of C-Suites. One of the great societal challenges of the twenty-first century is how men and women can positively join together and share a common vision for their future relationships.

A new generation of men has been born that is not bound to the same male-imposed rules that have been passed on from generation to generation—rules such as the one lesson every man has been taught: "When confronted by self-destructive behavior and actions, just deny, deny, deny."

CHAPTER 5

DENY, DENY, DENY: MEN'S DESTRUCTIVE INSTINCT TO LIE

Katie Roberts, a thirty-year-old psychology graduate student and military widow from Kansas, shared in an interview that she has high hopes for her three-year-old son. She wants him to grow up to be a stronger man than the "foolish" ones she dates. Katie is not alone in this. While women see their own chances in education improving, many also worry for their sons.

What are we teaching our sons? For generations, men have lived in a state of constant denial. For many, the earliest lesson taught to them by their fathers was that if caught in a compromising situation, the one single rule to live by was to deny, deny, deny. This code permeates society, from "Weinergate" and Chris Christie to Bashar al-Assad's refusal to admit to using chemical weapons and from Bill Clinton's "never had sex with that woman" to the Republican Party's steadfast refusal to admit that the attack on Iraq was misguided.

According to Joe Zychik, author of *The Most Personal Addiction*, dishonesty is the "biggest destroyer of an intimate relationship." Men must fundamentally change their inherent instinct to protect themselves and, by extension, "protect the other person" by lying. Zychik explains that "most people lie to save face. They feel guilty and trapped . . . so they lie. . . . There are some people who lie for malicious reasons. They don't lie only to get themselves out of an uncomfortable situation; they lie to hurt. . . . Other people are so sensitive, they seem to lie almost all the time. They're not malicious and they don't want to hurt you. They're obsessed with not looking bad."

However, Zychik shares, "looking bad from telling the truth is better than looking good through deception."

Despite the truth of Zychik's advice, most men over age thirty have at some point been advised that the best solution, even if caught red-handed, is to deny. The basic model of male repudiation is portrayed in countless films: men are caught in obviously compromising positions (such as in bed with another woman) and immediately refute what is obviously happening. Men have been taught that women want and need to believe the fabrication and are satisfied that their man cares enough about them to lie to protect their feelings. These men are oblivious to the disrespect the pattern implies.

Today, across all aspects of their relationships, more women are now demanding the full truth, every detail, and the ability to decide—based on that—how they will react and what the couple will become. Women are requiring that their relationships be based in honesty, which flies in the face of men's embedded instinct to lie, contradict, and obfuscate the truth.

Ty is an ex-college football player and a rancher. He is also proud to be known as a horse trader. One truism of being a horse trader, Ty shares in an interview, is that if you pull the wool over someone's eyes, you never admit it. "I used to watch my dad trade horses, and whenever he'd sell a green-broke horse to a family looking for a kid's horse or an unreliable horse to someone looking for one that was reliable he would tell me two things, 'That damned sure wasn't the right thing to do,' and, 'But, if we get caught, never confess: "lie till you die."' Ty says this with a big grin on his face and a chuckle.

Ty continues, "You never want to sell bad stock to someone you're likely to be dealing with again in the future, nor friends or family, and you don't want to stick it to someone who is new to the game. But, if some guy has himself convinced that he's a horseman and he doesn't know what he's getting into, I'm not going to be the guy that talks him out of doing something stupid."

Then Ty explains that his father's life philosophy has a flip side. "My mom left him after he got caught cheating for the umpteenth time. His biggest mistake was that he was not honest with her, would never confess, and treated her like a fool. Everyone in town knew he was not only a horse trader but a dirty dog that cheated on his wife, but somehow he had himself convinced that if he 'lied until he died,' she'd eventually believe him. She never did, and he's alone to this day because of it."

Ty's tone changes a little when he begins speaking of his own experience. A little more humbly he starts out, "For some reason I try the same method when I'm in trouble with my wife over this or that. Most of the time it's over something silly that I could simply admit to and that would be the end of it, but for some reason, I fall back into that dishonesty BS and everything goes downhill from there.

"The worst part is that I know she knows I'm lying," he says forthrightly. "So there I am, looking her straight in the eye, knowing that my lying to her probably hurts more than what I actually did. But, now it's just a habit. She's used to it. We almost have an understanding that when I deny something, I more than likely did it, and she doesn't even bother calling BS anymore because she knows I'll just get adamant and swear up and down and rant and rave and cuss as if I'm offended she doesn't believe me." He chuckles humorlessly.

The odds on Ty's marriage surviving are slim, as one untruth leads down a dark corridor of endless others. While the advice to lie and deny may not have been directly imparted, Ty's father and fathers everywhere have shown through words and actions that that is the best option when confronted with a condemning truth. Women have, to some extent, been complicit in this game, rationalizing that the lie is a way of showing affection.

However, the belief that the truth hurts too much to hear is quickly changing. Women are no longer accepting bold-faced lies, and men are struggling to understand and accept these new standards. Most relationships can sustain bad behavior, mistakes, and problems when men admit and address them, but duplicity encourages men to continue the behavior that led to the original falsity. Accountability becomes a "nonissue" as men learn they will not be held responsible for their actions as long as they can lie and get away with it.

Getting away with it, however, is becoming more and more impossible as the Internet and women's aggressive demand for the truth shift the balance of power. It's better for men to control and manage their future by acknowledging their past—both to themselves and to those who are most hurt by their falsehoods, whether those are proactive, by omission, or both.

Yet, most men—in private and public—continue to embrace the fundamental belief that the solution to any problem is to gainsay what happened. It is better to do that than to admit wrongdoing. This advice extends from relationships to the classroom, and from friends even to the law.

In a hypothetical scenario, a teenager cheats on his girlfriend and comes to his father for advice. Since young love is a fickle and fleeting thing, many a dad's instinct would be to advise his son to simply not tell her. Why break her heart when she can just go on living without this burdensome knowledge? And if she does find out, the teenager can simply claim it didn't really happen. For generations, men have learned to deny and in turn tell their sons to as well. Lying and cheating are endemic in sports; Lord protect the young boy who admits he was out at home plate when he's called safe. Truth and honesty have no place in that situation and far too many others—or so men seem to think.

Yes, it's a generalization, but boys are more typically taught to lie their way out of trouble, while girls learn early to tell the truth and use their charm and vulnerability in such cases.

Brad, who asked that his last name not be shared, has worked for the local rural electric association for almost twenty years. He's married, has three kids, and is generally pretty happy with his life. The one "issue" Brad has always had is that he is a womanizer. Brad was a state champion wrestler in high school and had a college scholarship but dropped out of school when his girlfriend got pregnant.

"She was a pretty little thing, still is, but I don't think she was prepared for the likes of me," he says honestly. "Twenty years later, she knows me inside out, but I still manage to do things that she simply can't believe and that hurt her tremendously. She's extremely well liked among the other mothers in our community, so people are far more likely to look out for her best interests than they are to turn a blind eye to my dirty little secrets." Brad says this as if it is a sort of epiphany.

"I had a couple of extramarital affairs, and I swear she knew about them before I ever even made it home. My dad always told me, 'What they don't know can't hurt them.' The problem is," Brad explains with certainty, as if he thinks his father had the right philosophy but that it is merely outdated, "they always know these days. With cell phones and texting and Facebook, news travels faster and farther than a man can in a lifetime.

"The first time I got caught, Jenny was hurt and sad, but she eventually forgave me. The second time, she was furious, and she probably never will forgive me for that one. It never surprised me that she found out; women usually do. What I couldn't believe is that both times she was waiting for me on the porch when I got home. She found out what I had done before I even had time to make the twenty-minute trip from town back home," he says in seeming awe. "I will never have the right to ask how she found out, and I wouldn't bring it up even if I thought she would tell me, but I can tell you one thing, with today's technology, there is no such thing as a secret. There's no such thing as 'what she doesn't know'; it doesn't exist anymore."

Media reflects the realities of life, and vice versa, in this and all things. In Milan Kundera's novel *The Unbearable Lightness of Being* and the television shows *Mad Men* and *Breaking Bad*, artifice is the foundation of the storyline.

In *The Unbearable Lightness of Being*, lead character Tomas loves his wife, but he also loves his hypersexual life as a womanizing bachelor. His wife knows; he barely takes the time to cover his tracks. As the story progresses, she becomes more and more withdrawn until he can no longer get away with a puppy-dog look of shame. He can no longer hide his red hands and he eventually stops his affairs, finding happiness after moving to the countryside with his wife. This novel and the subsequent film were considered progressive when they came out, and just thirty years later, they still capture the realities of many relationships grounded in lying and misogyny.

Don Draper, the lead character in the AMC hit series *Mad Men*, is a slick, sophisticated ad executive whose reality is grounded in lies, deceit, and more lies. Over the course of the show, Draper's falsehoods are progressively exposed, destroying almost every aspect of his life as he continues to focus more on covering up than acknowledging the truth. Although *Mad Men* is one of the most critically acclaimed TV series in history, little was written until the final episodes about the main theme: dishonesty and denial lead inexorably and inevitably to despair and destruction for most involved, with only hope for redemption and a happy ending for some.

In AMC's *Breaking Bad*, chemistry teacher Walter White begins cooking methamphetamine to provide for his family after he is diagnosed with terminal cancer. The series presents a morality tale of a man delving deep into the heart of crime while making horrendous decisions, yet the core of the show is about how his duplicity tears his family apart. After a while, he is no longer lying to save them from the awful truth; he is doing it to avoid facing the reality himself. At the conclusion of the series, veracity is Walter's savior, but he acknowledges he has enjoyed the deception. However, he shifts the need for continued mendacity to his wife, Skyler.

Even though denial is becoming less accepted by women and society, it remains an embedded reality beyond male–female relationships—in business, politics, religion, education, and every part of life. Just as US law does not force someone to testify against themselves, it also does not strictly punish repudiation. While lying under oath is a crime, many alleged criminals have refuted claims and gone unpunished as a result. In 1994, even against evidence and public outcry, O. J. Simpson continually rebutted any accusations, falsifying his way to a "not guilty" verdict in his murder trial. His lawyer's now-enduring motto, "If the glove doesn't fit, you must acquit!" is a lie in and of itself.

In 2012, the Republican Party presidential nominee Mitt Romney came to be known as one of the worst flip-floppers in political history. No matter what he said about his political stance, archival newsclips showed direct contradictions. Romney consistently denied and disavowed. Donald Trump, in his presidential bid, gained popularity simply by embracing and acknowledging his own incongruous statements.

Trump's campaign offers evidence that there's little if any expectation of integrity in politics, but ironically, it may prove to have been the turning point for a society that is becoming intolerant of a lack of honesty.

No matter his accomplishments as president of the United States and after, Bill Clinton's sexual misconduct will always be central to his personal story. While his transgressions in the White House would have gained enough attention, it was his denegation that caused a prolonged, upsetting, and truly memorable affair for the nation, including his impeachment. Clinton commented later in his book *My Life*, "I went on doing my job, and I stonewalled, denying what had happened to everyone: Hillary, Chelsea, my staff and cabinet, my friends in Congress, members of the press, and the American people. What I regret the most, other than my conduct, is having misled all of them." Clinton is the poster boy for deniers everywhere; meanwhile, Hillary Clinton stood by her husband, holding her family together.

Congressman Anthony Weiner was not so fortunate, and his demise was far more rapid; his actions caused him to lose his seat in Congress and his bid to return to politics and public favor. Weiner used social platforms such as Twitter to help unite his fans and spread his views. Unfortunately, under the pseudonym Carlos Danger, he also used Twitter to send a waist-down photo to a twenty-one-year-old woman from Seattle. Although the photo was quickly removed, an anonymous Twitter user called Dan Wolfe intercepted it before it could be entirely erased. This photo was saved and subsequently circulated online and to news media.

In response, Weiner stuck to the age-old tactic of disputing what had happened. While even in 1999 this may have worked, in 2011 Weiner instantly became the subject of global laughter and scorn. People became a part of the story, as they shared and commented on Weinergate. With Twitter, women no longer had to stand on the sidelines and be silent in the face of deception. The Internet turned the scandal into a living thing that grew with each tweet, blog, or Facebook update. The people wanted justice—the truth—and they could get it by keeping the story in the spotlight until their demands were met. No longer confined to newspapers or television tidbits, the Internet made the scandal personal for everyone.

Does Weinergate represent a shift in culture from generations of male denial to future generations of men coming to terms with society's new rules and realities? As more women demand the truth, are men ready to give it to them? Perhaps the deeper question, acknowledging the data emerging from the recent Ashley Madison hack, is whether the threat of exposure combined with women's insistence on truthfulness will result in a shift toward more monogamy or more frank and honest relationships.

With the Internet prompting an openness that society has never before been confronted with, men everywhere have to become more aware of the likelihood that the truth of their actions will be exposed, bringing on inevitable repercussions. Men need to learn that when challenged, it is easier in the long run to tell the truth, no matter how damaging it is in the moment. With a permanent history of their transgressions stored on the Internet, it will become increasingly difficult for men to cling to the old mantra of deny, deny, deny. They may, by circumstance or on purpose, one day reveal the truth to their significant others, colleagues, friends, or bosses—but too late: the relationship will already have been destroyed.

Ashley Madison, Match.com, and AdultFriendFinder profiles; Craigslist ads; visits to stripper bars; affairs; and even assignations with sex workers (those of ex–New York State Governor Eliot Spitzer come to mind) can no longer be assumed to be confidential, no matter what lengths men may go to. Men are moving through a painful period of exposure; all our deepest and darkest secrets are pouring from cyberspace into our living rooms, our bedrooms, and the computers of wives, girlfriends, and journalists.

An emerging generation of young men has grown up with the Internet, and as a result, they have a new relationship with truth and denial. As they learn the inevitability of being caught, their relationships are evolving in a new and more honest way as they learn that secrecy and privacy are fleeting mirages and that there are troublesome consequences to lying. Fabrications are easily exposed; denial is not only unproductive, it is destructive. There is no return path once a lie is told other than digging a deeper and deeper hole—one that gets exponentially more difficult to climb out of.

"Deny, deny, deny" as a male mantra is on a path toward retirement along with so many of the lies and destructive myths that have been learned and passed down by generation after generation. Denial is no longer a viable option. Men need to explain who, when, where, and why, and once that first denial comes in, it's game over. In the age of Twitter, Facebook, Instagram, and Periscope, falsehoods and contradictions are far too easily and quickly discovered. Lying, though, is woven into the male self-image, and although not all men lie (and many women do!), any study of the history of civilization uncovers the reality that men operate on being untruthful. Women, conversely, operate on the truth, and they now have the power to demand the same from their men. In a 2012 blog post published at MariaShriver.com, dating expert and author Ken Solin argued, "Where there's no trust, there's no love. . . . The purpose of men being emotionally honest isn't just to satisfy women, but to live in integrity as men. . . . There's an enormous difference between a man being emotional, and a man being emotionally honest. . . . A woman may not like hearing how her guy feels about her or their relationship, but she'll know his truth, and she can work with that. . . . The walls in relationships can be broken down when both partners trust each other to speak their emotional truths."

A fundamental failure to be emotionally honest is part of the fabric of flawed humanity. What can be changed, and is being changed at an astonishing pace, is the reaction to a lie. No longer will a woman stand idly by; she will demand answers and will rightfully speak out against blatant disrespect and abuse of trust. Mistakes can be forgiven, but the public is less accepting of denials by politicians, instead making fabrications a pulsating living entity forever virally traveling the web. Women and society no longer allow men to get away with deception; in a constantly broadcast world, men must learn to accept this.

As men realize that their former strategies are no longer options, will they learn to own their mistakes? Likely, they will continue to lie, cheat, and deny. But as wives, girlfriends, and the rest of society become less tolerant and more aggressively offended, more and more men will find salvation in simply telling the truth, and as that becomes the norm, male behavior will change. Some men will become more faithful and some relationships will become more open, whereas others will dissolve as the truth makes the status quo untenable.

As we look to the implications for the future, a new generation of men, born in the Internet age, will understand the pitfalls of engaging in actions and infidelity that will inevitably lead to a decision of whether to tell the truth or to refute it. They will witness the exposure and downfall of those who lie and deny and be less inclined to make the mistakes to begin with. Humans will always err, but this new generation will be more conscious of the inevitable consequences of their actions.

CHAPTER 6

MEN AND PERSONAL INTIMACY DISORDER

How will this fundamental shift in society's response to men's denial and the resulting transformation of male behavior affect men's sexual addiction and its impact on their relationships?

While the standard estimate of active sexually addicted men is 3 to 6 percent, this comes from a pre-Internet age. Today, men can go online and engage in an unlimited number of fetishes, fantasies, and emotionally detached sexual activities. A more realistic and honest assessment results when sexual addiction is referred to by its more socially acceptable description: progressive intimacy disorder (PID). In this context, it's likely that between 80 and 90 percent of all men have engaged in some form of sex-related addictive behavior that results in emotional detachment and replaces intimacy. Although their behavior may be in remission, the men remain addicts, and they typically fail to enjoy a committed and intimate relationship that fully satisfies their partner.

PID extends far beyond intercourse and infidelity. It includes all forms of objectification of women, soft- and hardcore porn, strip clubs, contracting with sex workers, multiple affairs and brief serial relationships, cybersex, visiting online dating and chat sites while in a committed relationship, misogynistic behavior, staring at women, repeated patterns of unsafe sex, harassment, following women on the street or in a mall, closeted sexual behavior, rating women based on their "fuckability," compulsive masturbation, voyeurism, exhibitionism, and more.

As a culture, we not only accept but honor, sensationalize, reward, and market images and behavior that are often within the clinical descriptions of sexual addiction and, at the very least, distance men from their female partners. Pornography is perhaps the most accepted online PID among both men and women. Sex work, or prostitution, can prey on the addicted; men expend enormous financial resources and emotional energy outside of their relationships, using the fantasy as an alternative to making real and personal connections. The porn and prostitution industries can at times literally enslave women through drug and financial dependence as well as physical force, making those who fund these businesses guilty participants in a type of slave trafficking.

What few realize is the harm to any relationship that results from just *seeking* outside sexual experiences—even when only online—without regard to the immediate or long-term consequences. While the danger of exposure is obvious and dramatic, the more typical reality is the failure to invest the necessary time and energy in improving the intimacy in an existing relationship: even when a partner does not know, it can still hurt her.

Dr. Robert Weiss of Psych Central explains that

> for active sex addicts, the sexual experience itself can, over time, become less tied to pleasure and more to feelings of relief or escape. . . . Sex addicts abuse sexual fantasy—even in the absence of sexual acts or orgasm—to produce the intense, trance-like feelings that temporarily provide emotional detachment and dissociation from life stressors. . . . Over time, the hidden fantasies, rituals and acts of the sexually addicted person can lead to a double life of lies to self and others, manipulation, rationalization, and denial.

> These defenses allow sex addicts temporarily to escape their core feelings of low self-worth, fears of abandonment, and depression or anxiety, as sexual fantasy and sexual acts are abused in an attempt to fulfill unmet emotional needs.
>
> For the sex addict, sexual acting-out most often takes place in secret, against a background of social isolation, and absent genuine, intimate relatedness. The problem can occur regardless of outward success, intelligence, physical attractiveness, or existing intimate relationship commitments or marriage.

When relationships begin without open acknowledgment of either person's addiction to porn, online chat rooms, sex workers, voyeurism, masturbation, or any other past or present addictive behavior, the relationship begins with a tacit lie. This inevitably leads to the need for more lies and denials that compound the detachment and lack of intimacy so many couples experience, all resulting from the original refusal and inability to be honest with each other.

According to a 2005 testimony before the Senate of the United States on *Pornography's Impact on Marriage and the Family*, 25 percent of all search engine requests are pornography-related, and sex is the number one topic searched on the Internet. Forty-seven percent of families said pornography is a problem in their home. Forty-two percent of surveyed adults indicated that their partner's use of pornography made them feel insecure, 41 percent said it made them feel less attractive, and 30 percent said it made them feel more like a sexual object. So what exactly is so healthy about porn for a couple's sex life—and especially for their romance?

Anne G., in an interview, explained that she learned at an early age from her mother to "never trust a man." Her mom had feared for her life daily at the hands of a raging and violent alcoholic husband. Anne understands where her mother was coming from. Every man in her mother's life—her father, her husband, even the local police force—had failed her. She had every reason to never trust a man.

"I wish she hadn't shared her opinion to never trust a man," says Anne. "I wish she'd said, 'Be careful who you marry.' Or maybe, 'It's okay to trust people until they prove themselves untrustworthy.' To my own daughters, I would say, 'Trust yourself. Trust your instincts, your ideas, your thoughts, your beliefs, and your actions, and then trust the type of man that this practice brings into your life. Live, dance, date, laugh, love, play, dream, and hope, but above all, trust. Trust in yourself, in your higher power, and in your ability to surround yourself with love.'"

In "The Male Role and Heterosexual Behavior," published in the *Journal of Social Issues*, Alan E. Gross examined several characteristics of male role definition. Men continue to define sexual behavior as central to their identity and are far more likely than women to isolate sex from love and strong emotional connections. The most striking conclusion he reached, however, was that the new male description, the "competent lover" as opposed to the "sexual animal" of old, was just as flawed a role definition as its forerunner. He described the modified role of the so-called new male as "equally maladaptive to earlier visions of the male." The sensitive male, as opposed to the aggressive male, is probably not akin to the caged tiger but is nevertheless also not entirely the answer to feminism's need for a more truthful and compliant counterpart.

The early feminist movement challenged male-dominated ideals and institutions. As the women's sexual revolution evolved, female sexuality and influence in relationships moved front and center. *Playboy* both exploited and contributed to the feminist movement by using celebrities and high-profile women to advocate for female control over their own bodies and to champion feminist principles in a sexually charged editorial environment that targeted men by objectifying women and airbrushing them to inhuman perfection.

As objectification of the female body has become epidemic in culture, so has women's sexuality evolved from a subtle to a dominant place in pop culture. Entertainment and advertising are no longer filtered for male needs and interests but have recognized women's emerging power and fully embraced the shift. E. L. James's *Fifty Shades of Grey*, Zane's *The Sex Chronicles*, and other books and films put no-holds-barred female sexuality on full display, serving as entertainment and primers of what women actually want.

Books, music, dancing, movies, television, and fashion all embody how women view their own sexuality. Celebrities such as Angelina Jolie, Scarlett Johansson, Rihanna, and Lady Gaga have acknowledged their sexuality, with Jolie suggesting that being a sex symbol is a good thing. Combine these outward symbols of overt female sexuality with men's inherent tendencies toward female objectification and men's unacknowledged, repressed, and typically private behaviors connected to emotional detachment and disassociation, however, and we have a confused male gender struggling to understand and adapt to a world in which they can no longer rely on tacit and passive acceptance of their sexual addictions.

CHAPTER 7

SEX SELLS AND SO DO MORONIC MEN

Compounding their confusion about sex and their role in relationships is the fact that men are being exposed to more and more advertising that objectifies them or presents them as being incapable of performing even the most basic tasks.

Advertising is designed to sell products and services, to convince consumers to open their wallets and make purchases. However, there is a multifaceted subtext to all of it. Whether it's on TV, in a magazine, or popping up on a computer screen or mobile device, advertising also sells and promotes gender roles, stereotypes, labels, and cultural norms. When a marketing team works to persuade the target demographic to buy a Lexus, Skye vodka, or a bottle of Chanel perfume, the manner in which the company attempts to sell the product or service—that is, the images they use to persuade the viewer to purchase the commodity—reflects the standards and viewpoints of our culture as a whole. Advertising is a mirror that shows where society has been, where it is now, and where it is going. As gender roles shift, so do male and female stereotypes in ads.

The Society of the Spectacle, written in 1967 by the French philosopher and cultural theorist Guy Debord, is a critique and deconstruction of consumer culture. While the text is an analysis and evaluation of life in the early twentieth century, the concepts and theories it presents have not been disproved, discredited, or put out to pasture, as is often the case with philosophical texts over time. On the contrary, the ideas in Debord's critique have only been strengthened and reinforced in the new millennium.

Debord sought to make sense of mass media culture. He was concerned with how images affect how people live and interact. In the age of the iPhone, iPad, and social media—where an infinite catalogue of images is available and branding and advertising are ubiquitous—contemporary society is even more of a *spectacle* now than it was in Debord's day. We live in an era saturated with symbols, pictures, and impressions. Commercials are like movie trailers that never end or ticker tapes that never complete their news loops. Mass media images and commodity fetishisms, Debord argued, have replaced normal human interactions. He wrote, "Just as early industrial capitalism moved the focus of existence from being to having, post-industrial culture has moved that focus from having to appearing." As early as 1967, he understood that "the spectacle is not a collection of images; rather, it is a social relationship between people that is mediated by images." Debord pointed out that advertising and media images are not only a reflection of society and culture but also of how that society and culture perceives itself.

In that context, advertising today reflects a culture obsessed with objectifying both women and men as sexual robots while at the same time celebrating women's intelligence and leadership and denigrating men. In addition to ads that objectify young, virile men, there are more that feature dumb, bumbling, clueless, helpless, childlike men than at any other time in television history. Whether a commercial is about ordering a pizza or buying a new car, TV is rife with incompetent men who cannot even make a decision about which analgesic to take without consulting their wives. Is it possible that men, having lost their earning power, have also lost their role as decision maker in almost every possible purchase decision? Take Pizza Hut, Domino's, AT&T, and Dairy Queen spots—time and again men are represented as jackasses, both literally and metaphorically. Little by little, contemporary advertising is using the shift in gender roles to reshape and rebrand traditional male ideologies.

Looking at marketing messages today tells us male values are more defined by sex and misogyny than by hard work and determination. More than any other creative form, advertising is designed to exist *in the moment*. It not only distinctly mimics the trends in society and culture, it reinforces them. As Debord suggested, it represents "the societal relationship between people that is mediated by images." Change is incremental, including the changing rhythms and dynamics of commercials. Bit by bit, contemporary advertising has been using this shift in gender roles to reshape and rebrand traditional male ideologies.

Through marketing, we can chart a continuum of male attitudes toward women and society's attitudes toward men: Men mostly enjoy the company of other men in bars or on the open range. Men view women as either sexual objects or as wives to whom they are subservient; men are idiots and/or emasculated. Male sensitivity, when used for commercial purposes, is typically either a joke or a tool to appeal to female consumers.

SEXUALITY IN FASHION ADVERTISING

Sex sells. It's a cliché, but it continues to work. Testing the limits of good taste and pushing the envelope with explicit material is the name of the game in the fashion industry. Notable companies such as Calvin Klein and Abercrombie & Fitch have marketed themselves by courting controversy and extremism. The brands are known for sleek, edgy ads featuring barely clothed men and women in suggestive poses. The men and women, notably, are treated equally; both sexes are objectified.

This type of sexual marketing objectifies youth and youth culture more than it exposes gender bias and stereotypes. The gender of the fashion models does not matter as long as the models are young, healthy, smooth skinned, and beautifully proportioned. Sex, it appears, is the ultimate commodity, playing directly to the male flaw of disconnecting sex from love, affection, and emotional connection.

Calvin Klein has been at the forefront of the sexual advertising movement for decades. What can one expect from a designer who, after the company's first attempt at jeans was a failure, revamped the design by, per company quote, "raising the groin to accentuate the crotch, and pulling the seam up between the buttocks to give the rear more shape." Calvin Klein jeans became hypersexualized and needed to be accompanied by an equally sexy ad campaign.

In 1980, Richard Avedon shot a Calvin Klein commercial featuring a young Brooke Shields. This commercial has long been considered the fashion shoot heard around the world. Not only was Shields suggestively posed on all fours, telling the world that "nothing comes between me and my Calvins," she was also only fifteen years old. According to "Sex in Advertising," part of the CBC radio series *Under the Influence* with Terry O' Reilly, despite the fact the Shields's commercial caused a nationwide uproar and was banned from multiple TV networks, "Calvin Klein cried all the way to the bank, because sales of his jeans surged to over two million pairs a month, generating revenues of over $100 million inside 12 months."

Calvin Klein advertisements, however, have never been limited to stereotypes of female sexuality. When Klein first started to design underwear, he chose fashion photographer Bruce Weber to take pictures of Olympic male athletes. All of these advertisements featured buff, muscular men and provocatively emphasized their physical endowments below the waist. One of Calvin Klein's most famous underwear ad campaigns took place in the 1990s and featured then-rapper Marky Mark, better known today as Mark Wahlberg. Ripped, with jailhouse abs and a tough-guy smile, Wahlberg appeared in numerous states of undress in these advertisements, flexing his muscles and looking rebellious, grabbing his crotch, and standing with supermodel Kate Moss draped over him.

Like Calvin Klein, Abercrombie & Fitch is no stranger to courting controversy with images and ad campaigns that feature a hypersexualized view of fashion. The Ohio-based brand continually pushes the envelope of good taste, putting ever more graphic and risqué material in their quarterly catalogues and seven-dollar "magalogs," which were produced until 2003. Over the years, the company has taken the idea of sexual marketing to a new level of provocative and goes so far as positioning buff, half-naked men in the doorways of their city stores.

Fashion is not the only industry to put sex at the forefront of its marketing; advertising has become the leading edge for redefining both the past and the emerging roles of men and women.

THE IDIOT MAN IN ADVERTISING

For examples of the "men as idiots" commercial genre, simply turn on your TV and watch the vast majority of ads for household products, automobiles, financial services, and a host of other items. Men are often characterized as less-than-capable idiots whose abilities can't possibly measure up to a female's competence at even the simplest task.

Some groups are speaking out against the collective advertising world's treatment of men. Glenn Sacks, an attorney who focuses largely on gender rights, has successfully launched campaigns against companies that depict men in a less than positive way. Perhaps most notably, Sacks persuaded Verizon Wireless to pull its 2004 ad about a dad who was overwhelmed trying to help his daughter with a homework assignment. Sacks has also led successful movements against reality television shows that cast men in a bad light and large advertising agencies that he says are responsible for antimale advertising. Other groups like the Masculine Heart (masculineheart.blogspot.com) seek to bring awareness of the way men are portrayed in commercials and the media.

A classic men-as-idiots campaign that blended seamlessly with the "men prefer the company of other men" theme was the "Whassup?" Budweiser commercials at the turn of the millennium. A group of guys talked aimlessly on the phone to one another, saying nothing other than a rapid exchange of the one-word question, "Whassup?" Although the concept may sound dumb to some (and hilarious to others), the commercials were an immediate hit and contributed to an increase of 7.9 percent in the beer's supermarket sales, according to the *Chicago Tribune*. More than a decade later, it's hard to imagine how "Whassup?" captured the male zeitgeist of the time. From kids as young as elementary school to middle-aged adults on the golf course, it was not uncommon to be greeted with a "Whassup?" While some guys may have scoffed at the portrayal of the poor communication skills in those ads, others either welcomed it as a simple way to communicate or merely deflected it with humor. Communication between men has not always been sophisticated, or even fluent, but the Budweiser commercials reflected a general acceptance of men as idiots.

It's always easier to look back and see how different something was. In the case of men a decade ago, all you have to do is watch one of the "Whassup?" commercials and compare it with more recent Budweiser ads. The one that aired during the 2013 Super Bowl depicted the bond between a horse trainer and a young Clydesdale that eventually grew to be one of the official Budweiser horses. This sentimental ad reflects a shift in the openness of men and their willingness to be both rugged and sensitive.

THE SUPER BOWL THAT CARED

The 2015 Super Bowl was notable for its focus on purpose-driven commercial messages and especially on changing gender dynamics. Dove Men+Care, Toyota, Nissan, Always, and other advertisers, including the National Football League itself, clearly communicated a meaningful transformation in American culture and society—or at least a transformation of Super Bowl commercials.

A Victoria's Secret ad that was the norm just a few years ago at the Super Bowl was incredibly out of context and a throwback that proves "men will still be men" and out-of-touch marketers will remain out of touch. Except for Victoria's Secret and an incredibly tasteless CURE Auto Insurance "Don't Touch Your Balls" commercial, 2015 was the least sexist and misogynistic and the most positive message–oriented Super Bowl in history.

Dove Men+Care "Real Strength," which shared emotional moments between fathers and their kids in its Super Bowl spot, recognized the transformation of gender roles and harnessed the opportunity to lead this issue. It's interesting that both Toyota and Nissan concentrated on the changing roles, values, and responsibilities of men. Toyota's "Being a Dad Is More Than Being a Father" commercials commented, "It's a commitment—one that will make a wonderful human being who will make their own choices someday." If you watch it, notice the two soldiers entering the airport along with the daughter—a subtle and sophisticated touch. Nissan's play on Harry Chapin's classic "Cat's in the Cradle" in its "#withdad" commercial is also a relevant and important milestone, although the connection of the messages to brands is tentative at best.

The National Football League's own ad continued a dialogue about sexual abuse that was accelerated by the Ray Rice case; it was too late but not too little and appropriately accompanied NO MORE's "Pledge to Say No More" commercial, which featured athletes, celebrities, and politicians together pledging to end domestic violence and sexual assault. Always Feminine Products took the softer route, asking, "What does it feel like to do something like a girl?" and arguing to "make #likeagirl mean amazing things. Rewrite the rules." This empowering message is all the more relevant because of the environment in which it was communicated—targeting men as well as women, young boys as well as young girls. It may be decades before "throw like a girl" is no longer an insult, but this opened the conversation.

The most fascinating line delivered in any Super Bowl commercial was a statement in a Chrysler commercial made by a one-hundred-plus-year-old man, one of several speaking from the experience and knowledge of old age. His words of wisdom? "You learn not to cheat." Words for men to live by!

The commercial that will probably lay claim to the most culturally prescient and honest comment was T-Mobile's, in which Chelsea Handler and Sarah Silverman debate over who has better Wi-Fi coverage. Sarah, from deep within her underground delivery room (with perfect service) looks down at a newly born baby and sadly says to the mother, "Sorry, it's a boy."

A CULTURE OF EMASCULATION

Advertising for erectile dysfunction has become ubiquitous across the American media landscape, changing the dynamics between men and women, emasculating men, and introducing male sexual dysfunction as a norm to younger generations. It was not all that long ago that Lucy and Ricky Ricardo could not be shown sleeping in the same bed even though they were married. Today, by contrast, Cialis has made a trademark of advertising a man and a woman side by side in two separate bathtubs; the man is always prepared in case the couple might want to climb out of the tub and into bed.

Viagra is the combination of two words: vigorous and Niagara. The naming of the drug is marketing genius, as both words suggest strength, power, and energy. While the drug has been nothing short of a miracle for men who suffer erectile dysfunction, advertisements for the blue, diamond-shaped pill are surprisingly emasculating. They are not male fantasies about being able to transform into an instant stud "for up to four hours." The simple slogan "So you're ready when she's ready" takes the power of sexual initiation away from the man and gives it to the woman. It is the woman, now, who dictates sex: when, where, and how often. These things are no longer in a man's control; his sphere of influence has been diminished. What if a man with erectile dysfunction takes Viagra and his partner is never ready?

It is not only the shift in sexual power that makes these advertisements emasculating, but also the manner in which they are filmed. Although Cialis is targeted to men of all ages, the commercials are distinctly and unmistakably nostalgic. They are softly lit, ethereal, and wispy—filled with sunrises and sunsets, romance, cuddling, and knowing looks and winks. They are like Hallmark Cards representing a healthy, ideal home life like the one Norman Rockwell illustrated in the 1950s. These ads are not selling sex (although *sex* is what the product is designed for) in the manner of Calvin Klein or Abercrombie & Fitch; they are selling family life and a *Good Housekeeping* lifestyle. They are selling a middle-class version of the American Dream.

THE BEER COMMERCIAL: A BAROMETER FOR SEXISM

One reality that hasn't changed much is that women in beer commercials (when they are present at all) are typically sex objects. Just watch any televised sporting event: even the most casual viewer will be all too familiar with the objectification of women in the accompanying beer commercials. We've grown accustomed to the hyperbolic claims and unrealistic expectations: men are manly, women are hot, and everyone at the party has the time of their lives. They're all beautiful, and no one gets stupid-drunk on all the beer being thrown around.

It's hard to top the hyperbole of the Old Milwaukee Beer ads of the 1980s that insist, "It doesn't get any better than this." It comes off almost as a challenge. Really? This is the best it's going to get? Ever? One typical ad from 1984 shows a group of men on a fishing boat in Maine going to a clambake. Another has a group of men (and only men) airboating through the Florida Everglades. They all end with a pristine sunset and one saying to the others, "You know, guys, it doesn't get any better than this." They were handsome commercials shot in idyllic locales with lots of campfires showing a bond of brotherhood cemented by great beer. They were earnest and sincere.

Someone must have realized, though, that there might be a few folks who could disagree with their claims. They may have gotten flack for their boast because their fantasy world didn't include women. In response, Old Milwaukee kept the tagline but stopped taking it seriously. In 1991, the ideal world of bucolic wilderness and male friendship gave way to turbocharged, bizarre, wet-dream male fantasies. The new commercials still had men in a pristine outdoor setting, with someone claiming, "It doesn't get any better than this," but instead of ending the commercial with that tagline, the new campaign starts each commercial with the iconic line, then the voiceover kicks in, and says, "But Doug Patterson was wrong."

Thus was born the infamous Swedish Bikini Team beer commercial format. In one version, a crate of lobsters just falls from the sky (rather than the men catching their own seafood, as they did in the original), to which the voiceover proclaims, "It just got a little better." Then, to oppose the notion that the best life has to offer is a bunch of men hanging out, the Swedish Bikini Team rappels, boats, or para-chutes in, and the day gets "even better." Finally, to top it off, a truck-load of Old Milwaukee shows up. (It seems that the best life has to offer still must include beer!) For fun, watch Will Ferrell's Old Milwaukee commercials on YouTube.

These ads were obviously not meant to be taken seriously, but one must wonder what the writers were overcompensating for when they felt they not only had to include women, but that those women had to be a team of dancing, bikini-clad, platinum-blond, Amazonian-proportioned Swedish women. The Swedish Bikini Team (played by American actresses, for the record) took on a life of its own, making appearances at events, in television shows, films, and even a *Playboy* spread. They were a meme all their own, and they were, of course, offensive. Workers at the brewery filed a harassment lawsuit, and the National Organization for Women protested. One wonders why Sweden didn't complain. The campaign lasted less than a year, but it was incredibly popular. Not only does sex sell but, sadly, male fantasies apparently rarely get any better than blondes and beer.

Beer commercials have often come under fire for being sexist, so much so that it's practically an industry standard rather than a contro-versial statement. It may in fact be that the creators of beer commer-cials are playing to a stereotype that does not exist (and perhaps never did) or that beer commercial creators are attempting to hit a target demographic of sexist male consumers that are purely a figment of an advertiser's imagination.

Heineken's DraughtKeg advertisement was almost universally declared one of the most sexist beer advertisements ever produced. At the same time, the advertisement was panned by almost entirely male critics. Bob Garfield of *Advertising Age* wrote, "It is not out of self-righteousness, but out of genuine astonishment that we castigate, denounce, and generally hold up to ridicule a new ad . . . that is argu-ably the most sexist beer commercial ever produced." The DraughtKeg advertisement implied that the perfect woman would have her essen-tial reproductive organs removed and replaced with a keg. Given the cultural history of men being in control of both a woman's body and her sexual rights, this commercial could hardly be seen as anything but bizarrely sexist.

Indictments similar in tone, if not in content, came from David Groshoff of the *Huffington Post* in regard to a more recent Miller Lite "Man Up" Campaign. Miller Lite released a sequence of commercials showing a man engaged in nonstereotypical male behavior, such as carrying a bag or wearing a scarf. Each commercial would end by ridiculing these men and telling them to "man up" with a Miller Lite. Groshoff noted that although viewers have the ability to choose most types of media they consume, commercials reside in a unique territory—a viewer is forced to watch them. (Yes, times have changed, haven't they?) He believed commercials such as the "Man Up" campaign served to "heighten viewers' insecurities that even the slightest deviations from . . . gender norms merit ridicule."

Meanwhile, Tim Nudd of *Adweek* called Bud Light's "Advertising Executives" sexist and declared it was made by "total pigs." Interestingly, this ad broke the third wall. Nudd wrote that it depicted the perfect idea of a woman, "doing all the chores, leaving her husband free to hang out with his friends, and frequently surprising him with cases of Bud Light." However, once the commercial ostensibly came to a close, it panned out to a room of advertising executives, clearly moved by the contents of the commercial. Is the commercial a metacommentary on how out of touch these older advertising executives truly are? Or is the commercial, as Nudd believes, yearning for a simpler time during which women were merely around to support their men? Unfortunately, the advertisement itself leaves the answer to this question ambiguous.

Another controversial commercial, Miller Lite's "Catfight," angered viewers to such an extent that it was actually pulled from the air. It depicted two young, busty women getting into a tremendous and messy catfight over whether Miller Lite "tastes great" or is "less filling." Again, Bob Garfield of *Advertising Age* noted that male staff members had conflicting reactions to the commercial. "When the AdReview staff . . . encountered 'Catfight,'" he wrote, "we were doubly embarrassed . . . that the sponsor could be so cheap and vulgar, and secondly that we, the entire staff, leered appreciatively at the babes."

This internal conflict and self-awareness is perhaps one key to understanding the path that advertising has taken.

THE SHIFTING DEMOGRAPHIC: WOMEN-FRIENDLY BEER ADS

More than 80 percent of all brand purchases in the United States are made by women, and while brand preferences for beer are heavily defined by the drinker, women remain the primary purchasers. By the 1990s, beer advertisers finally began targeting messages to women, or were at least trying to be friendlier to them. This marketing strategy was featured in the hit AMC series *Mad Men*, which is based around the advertising industry in the 1960s. In one episode, main character Don Draper attempts to create a marketing campaign for beer by targeting it toward women rather than men, on the basis of his knowledge that wives, not husbands, would actually be making the purchase at the store. The client rejected it.

Don's campaign does parallel several that came after the era depicted in *Mad Men*. The 1995 Bud Light "I Love You, Man" commercials presented men as sensitive beings, primarily to appeal to the female beer purchaser and consumer, and represented a major change in how men are portrayed in beer commercials. Three men are sitting on a pier in a lake while fishing. Sentimental music plays as the balding and scruffy thirty-five-ish man in the middle fights back tears and tells the older man on his left that he has something important to say. The man is struggling to express his feelings, but he finally says, "You're my dad, and I love you, man." The father doesn't flinch, doesn't even look at his son after this heartfelt expression of emotion. Instead, he grabs his can of beer. "You're not getting my Bud Light, Johnny," he says. Undeterred, Johnny looks at the man on his right (presumably his younger brother). After the scene shifts briefly to an inside scene of a beer mug, a Bud Light beer can, and a "Make it a Bud Light" promo, the commercial goes back to the pier. Johnny, who was sitting a few inches away from his father and a few feet from his brother, moves toward his brother. "Ray," says Johnny. "Forget it, Johnny," Ray responds.

This commercial lasted thirty seconds, but it was so successful that the unknown actor who played Johnny, Rob Fitzgerald, became a celebrity who appeared on the "Late Show with David Letterman." By the time the "I Love You, Man" campaign ended in 1996, Johnny had begged for a Bud Light in four commercials, but his "I love you, man" line didn't work on his girlfriend or Charlton Heston (playing himself) either. Bud Light was much more successful than Johnny. The *Marketing Campaign Case Studies* blog indicated that Bud Light regained its position as America's bestselling light beer: during the campaign, sales increased 12 percent.

In the 1992 book *Men, Masculinity, and the Media*, Fordham University media studies professor Lance Strate wrote a chapter titled "Beer Commercials: A Manual on Masculinity." Strate said that the characters in beer commercials "exemplify traditional conceptions of the masculine role" and sensitive men are "absent from beer advertising." Strate's conclusion was based on his analysis of dozens of specific ads from the 1960s through the early 1990s. Beer commercials, he wrote, "uphold the myths of masculinity and femininity" and "in the world of beer commercials, masculinity revolves around the theme of challenge."

The 1995 "I Love You, Man" commercials, however, don't conform to Strate's 1992 analysis. Johnny is insincere, but he is aspiring to be sensitive—something that the characters in earlier commercials certainly were not doing.

The "I Love You, Man" commercials might have been a reaction to the changing nature of the beer market, according to the *Marketing Campaign Case Studies* blog. The blog points out that in the mid-1990s, American beer consumption and the number of men who were twenty-one to thirty years old—the "prime beer-drinking years"—were declining, whereas women had been drinking more beer each year for the past decade.

Macho-man commercials were becoming less successful. Many women protested that Bud Light's series of commercials featuring a dog named Spuds MacKenzie partying with scantily clad women was sexist. *Marketing Campaign Case Studies* reported that former Anheuser-Busch executive vice president Bob Lachky told the *Milwaukee Journal*

Sentinel that "treating women as objects is not in tune with today's markets." The "I Love You, Man" commercials appealed to Bud Light's core audience of twenty-one-to-thirty-year-old men by being "entertaining and ironic," but they didn't alienate women because they were humorous and lacked "sexual messaging."

In an essay entitled "Television and the Triumph of Culture," Arthur Kroker, director of the Pacific Centre for Technology and Culture at the University of Victoria, and David Cook wrote that the target audience members of "the fellowship type of beer commercials" such as the "I Love You, Man" series are so-called belongers. "Beer is friendship" in television commercials, they added.

Analyzing the essay in the literary journal *Amaranthus*, Judith Boogaart wrote that the commercials appeal to men who might associate sharing a beer with acceptance and friendship. At the same time, she said, the commercial's portrayal of Johnny's father and brother reinforces "the traditional image of the independent, non-domesticated, outdoor, sports-minded male, whose constant appendage is a can of beer." In the commercial, Boogaart said, Johnny is the loser, the father is the stereotypical tough and independent man, and the neater, better-dressed brother is sophisticated and successful. The father and brother have a "slight revulsion" for Johnny's sensitivity, she added.

The "I Love You, Man" commercials could be regarded as forerunners of later commercials, which portrayed men as losers who depended on their buddies for emotional security rather than as macho athletes and adventurers, according to the article "The Male Consumer as Loser: Beer and Liquor Ads in Mega Sports Media Events." This analysis, written by University of Southern California sociology professors Michael A. Messner and Jeffrey Montez de Oca, concentrated on the beer commercials that ran during the 2002 and 2003 Super Bowls and was published in the academic journal *Signs: Journal of Women in Culture and Society*.

The "I Love You, Man" commercials are part of a continuum that reflects American society's changes. Messner and Montez de Oca's essay details the changes: 1950s and 1960s beer advertisements focused on married couples at home, as beer companies tried to move away from beer as the stereotypical drink of choice for working-class men.

"Beer in these ads symbolically unites the prosperous and happy post-war middle-class couple." In the 1970s and 1980s, these ads changed as society changed: American men were struggling to adjust to women challenging their authority, and beer commercials moved from homes to bars, where women were almost never seen. "Three studies of beer commercials of the 1970s and 1980s found that most ads pitched beer to men as a pleasurable reward for a hard day's work," they wrote, and beer often symbolized freedom from women.

In the twenty-six beer commercials Messner and Montez de Oca studied, men's work worlds, wives, and girlfriends mostly disappeared. The sociologists identified four "dominant gender themes": men as losers who are regularly humiliated publicly, men who need buddies because they're insecure about their masculinity, beautiful women who "sometimes serve to validate men's masculinity," and female "bitches" who threaten men's freedom. These ads reflected changes in American society that "destabilized hegemonic masculinity" and appealed to unsuccessful young men who were angry that they were struggling and had a "desire for revenge against women." Messner and Montez de Oca didn't mention the "I Love You, Man" commercials, but their analysis could lead one to conclude that Johnny symbolized a 1990s man who was having difficulty establishing a long-term relationship with a woman because of his inability to cope with women's growing influence in American society and that he needed the companionship of like-minded men to feel happy and good about himself.

In 1999, an innovative Bud Light campaign titled "Real American Heroes" hit the radio airwaves. Sandwiched between Cher's "Believe" and TLC's "No Scrubs," the ads found instant success by poking fun at the exploits of over-the-top characters such as "Mr. Mail Order Bride Orderer" and "Mr. Miniature Train Modeler."

In 2001, the campaign had a setback. The events of 9/11 put increased attention on actual American heroes and, according to the *Columbus Dispatch*, the ad's "hero" caricatures seemed inappropriate. After a reworking, the commercials made a comeback under a new title, "Real Men of Genius." As it turns out, the timing was perfect, and "Real Men of Genius" was just what the psyche of the American male needed. Marketing-Schools.org reported that consumers don't investigate the quality of beer but rather make purchasing decisions on the basis of identifying with the brand. When the campaign returned to the airwaves in 2002, the country was still reeling from the attacks of 9/11 and starting to feel the crunch of a failing economy. "Real Men of Genius" gave American men a much-needed dose of humor as well as something to identify with. Men who had once been climbing the corporate ladder were now struggling to survive layoffs. Suddenly, "Mr. After-Halloween Costume Shop Salesman" and "Mr. Supermarket Produce Putter Outter" were not only laughable but relatable.

Jim Gorczyca, a former brand manager for Bud Light, told the *Columbus Dispatch* that the company hoped to reach a target audience of twenty-one-to-twenty-seven-year-olds with spots that felt young, fun, and social. By celebrating the pseudoaccomplishments of "Mr. Bumper Sticker Writer," the ads successfully sent the message that pride and humor are not mutually exclusive. By extolling the virtues of "Mr. Parking Attendant Flashlight Waver," they allowed men to be proud of their own accomplishments, despite the fact that they may seem trivial to others.

The *Chicago Tribune* reported that in 2003, the year the "Real Men of Genius" ads made the transition from radio to television, Bud Light commanded over 15 percent of the market, with roughly $1.3 billion in sales. During that year, overall beer sales were flat, as were sales for competitors Coors Light and Miller Lite. Sales for Bud Light, however, were up nearly 7 percent.

The same themes were presented in a far more subtle and sophisticated way in Dos Equis's "Most Interesting Man in the World" advertisements, which featured a suave, debonair gentleman narrating his past adventures. The Most Interesting Man in the World was bold, audacious, and ruggedly handsome; he was a lover and world traveler, a man of sophisticated and refined tastes. "I don't always drink beer, but when I do, I drink Dos Equis," he told us. One assumed that when he was not drinking beer, he was sipping on vintage wine from Bordeaux or swishing single malt Scotch in a tumbler.

At first, the character seemed like the embodiment of traditional male values, those qualities and characteristics that were cherished in previous generations. However, the narration of his youthful adventures was increasingly funny and satirical; the ad campaign has its tongue firmly planted in its cheek. For example, there were lines like these: "He once beat Gary Kasparov at chess, with his left hand," and, "He once traveled to and explored the Virgin Islands. When he left they were just 'the Islands.'" The Dos Equis commercials were not about putting traditional male gender roles on a pedestal; they were about parodying those roles for laughs. The Most Interesting Man in the World might have appeared tough, sexy, and debonair—an Ernest Hemingway type of masculine figure—but he was, in fact, a caricature.

"I Love You, Man," "Real Men of Genius," and "The Most Interesting Man in the World" were commercially successful and shifted the gears from selling beer through sex to selling beer through a caricature of men and the traditional male roles. While beer advertisers such as Coors continue to objectify women in their commercials, the shift to lampooning the "real man" reflects the recognition that men's self-image is changing. But the beer advertisers and their agencies are targeting women, not men, with these messages. It's consistent with the pattern of humorously reflecting back to women the male stereotypes that men themselves may not find all that funny. Because the stereotypes may ring all too true, there's little men can do to defend themselves but laugh along. For generations of younger men, beer commercials and advertising for other products have communicated the image of man as misogynist and man as buffoon.

THE SEXUALIZATION OF MEN

As commercials made fun of men and portrayed sensitive males, they also objectified the sexy male. Old Spice's "The Man Your Man Can Smell Like" campaign, which launched in 2010, has done this more than any other TV commercial in recent history. Before this juggernaut, Old Spice was a fading brand unable to gain any foothold with younger consumers. While it was common in advertising for women to be sex objects, Old Spice turned the tables. Isaiah Mustafa, the spokesman, was always either shirtless or wrapped in a towel, and part of the reason for the ad's success was his sex appeal.

The commercials also offered a broader social commentary: Isaiah Mustafa is black. Turning a black man into a sex object was not common in mainstream advertising. Black men were typically depicted as competitive athletes, showing up in high-octane commercials for Gatorade or Nike. "The Man Your Man Could Smell Like" illustrated the country's more liberal opinions about race and multiculturalism, sexuality, and acceptance.

The first Old Spice commercial featuring Mustafa aired during the 2010 Super Bowl, an event that always brings out the best and most absurd in modern American advertising. It was the Old Spice YouTube channel, however, that turned the commercial into a pop culture phenomenon. A case study of the agency responsible for the campaign, Wieden+Kennedy, by the creative marketing organization D&AD reported that "sales were already on the rise following the launch of the first 'Smell Like a Man, Man' ad. But the Response Campaign grew the brand further, and by the end of July 2010 sales were up 125 percent year on year. By the end of 2010, Old Spice had become the number one selling brand of body wash for men in the United States."

By reshuffling gender stereotypes, using advertising as a vehicle for social commentary, and tapping into viral marketing trends to boost brand awareness, the Old Spice commercial was a game changer. Another game changer that appealed to women in the same context was the iconic 1994 Diet Coke ad "Diet Coke Break." At the time, television commercials that depicted hot, sexy, half-clad female models were cliché, but very few ads objectified men until Diet Coke unveiled this "shocking" campaign. The spot featured a group of office women excitedly whispering, "It's 11:30!" and "Diet Coke break!" to one another and rushing to the window to watch as a hunky construction worker stripped off his shirt, cracked open a Diet Coke, and took a long, sultry swig from the can. This parodied the typical sexist ads of half-naked women lustily drinking some beverage. That was the point. While we reacted to the bikini-wearing female model as "normal," our primary reaction to watching a group of women ogling a man was shock and laughter, because that was *not* the norm.

Jean Kilbourne wrote in *Can't Buy My Love: How Advertising Changes the Way We Think and Feel* that "although these ads are often funny . . . there is a world of difference between the objectification of men and that of women. The most important difference is that there is no danger for most men, whereas objectified women are always at risk. In the Diet Coke ad, for instance, the women are physically separated from the shirtless man. He is the one in control. His body is powerful, not passive. . . . And why is the Diet Coke ad funny? Because we know it doesn't describe any truth."

If sex sells, sex *and* humor must sell even better, since Coke stuck with the Diet Coke hunk for several more commercials. After the initial run in 1994, they unveiled a shirtless window washer in 1998, and in 2007 a hunky lift engineer "rescued" a group of ladies who got themselves (purposefully) stuck in an office elevator. Each of these commercials played Etta James's song, "I Just Want to Make Love to You" in the background (not a very subtle message there). Recently, celebrating the twenty-year anniversary of the campaign, Diet Coke rolled out yet another hunk ad, starring model Andrew Cooper as a gardener being ogled by a group of female picnickers.

However shocking the first ad was, evidently things have calmed down. The reaction to the twenty-year anniversary ad was almost tepid: *Bloomberg Businessweek* called it a "'been there done that' concept." The original ad, they claim, was about empowering women, "which was very clever and well done. Now, so many years later, it seems limited in terms of what it's trying to accomplish."

Does the lackluster reaction to the new shirtless Diet Coke hunk mean that sex roles have evolved or just that we are desensitized to seeing naked bodies? Among Calvin Klein and Dior ads showing nothing but skin, *Game of Thrones* casually tossing off all clothing at the drop of a hat, and anything-goes Internet availability of skin of all stripes and sexes, one man peeling off a shirt seems tame. In fact, the Drum, Europe's largest marketing website, reported one formal complaint to the Advertising Standards Authority in the United Kingdom about the new ad being "irresponsible" and condoning "behavior that could risk health or safety"—but the complaint was because the women in the ad rolled a full can of Diet Coke to the working gardener who was operating a lawn mower at the time! Occupational Safety and Health Administration, where are you?! The Advertising Standards Authority ruled in favor of Diet Coke, saying the ads were "humorous" and a "fantasy"—a rather far cry from the initial furor the original campaign started.

However, scrolling through the viewers' comments, one can still find outraged reactions by men who claim, "If the roles were reversed, you'd hear no end of it from the feminists," which rather ignores the fact that the roles usually *are* reversed. In fact, they're the opposite most of the time, which is why this ad campaign continues to raise eyebrows—because it's *still* not normal.

What has changed is not that sexualization in the media is still rampant, but rather that *everyone* is victimized now. Rather than preventing the objectification of women, our awareness of sexism has simply opened the doors to doing it to men. Congratulations, men, and welcome to the world of societal pressures to conform to body images that are unrealistic and cause you to desperately purchase cosmetics, beauty aids, and diet products because you don't look like that beautiful model in that commercial.

DIVERSITY IN MARKETING

Today, the sexually fueled imagery in advertising is so commonplace that critics have abandoned the argument over what is or is not explicit material and taken up the fight with whether brands are being politically correct or not. Where exactly does a brand draw the line between diversity and targeted demographics? How do brands market to the rapidly evolving male demographic, which does not fit neatly into any of the prescribed baskets they have been comfortably assigned to over the past several decades?

Michael Wilke, the founding executive director of the AdRespect Advertising Educational Program, told the *New York Times* that "as society becomes more diverse, there's more inclusive messaging, which reflects what society actually looks like." This statement may be true, but whether advertising wishes to reflect that diverse society is another question. Today, advertisements that celebrate cultural diversity and acceptance seem normal, especially to younger generations that have grown up with gay, straight, and ethnically diverse friends. Despite this, one cannot help but wonder how older generations or the conservative and religious right who populate America's red states react to seeing a man traveling to his daughter's wedding to another woman (as in an ad by Expedia) or a diverse perfect family in a Cheerios Super Bowl commercial.

The rise of digital marketing empowers more and more microscopic marketing, with greater insights available on advertising effectiveness. Still, marketers invest millions—even billions—in branding and targeting their products and services to the largest and most responsive audiences. As there are more stay-at-home dads and single-male households, and as men become more engaged in purchase decisions, marketers will be confronted with the need to communicate the appeal of their products to both men and women who fail to recognize themselves and their partners in any of the stereotypical ways that have dominated ad campaigns for decades.

Appealing to the newly emerging, more "feminized" male and reflecting relationships that are more culturally accurate is a mountain few marketers and agencies have the skills to scale. The easier route for marketers and their agencies is to direct increasing shares of their ad budgets on targeting female consumers while ignoring men altogether. The trends, however, point to a growing base of male decision makers and to a female consumer who is often ceding the responsibility for many household decisions to her partner or caregivers. With a growing wealth of data available to hone their media selection, it's essential that marketers focus more attention on their creative messaging. If anything is clear from a historical perspective, it's that there's a growing and highly offensive disparity between how men are represented in many ad messages and the positive self-image we hope our young men and boys will adapt. It's more likely that marketers will simply find new and equally offensive ways (to men) of appealing to women by presenting stereotypical male behaviors that no longer reflect a growing population of younger men.

CHAPTER 8

EYES WIDE OPEN: A NEW SEXUAL REVOLUTION

Has the advertising industry's changing image of men and women affected relationships? Most definitely! In contrast to the male-dominated past centuries, today women are defining society's views on sexuality, and they are very adept at personifying—and embracing—the new standards of "sexy," new modes of communication, and new expectations of relationships.

SEXUALLY EMPOWERED WOMEN

Pornography has become ubiquitous, with even hard-core porn available online for free with no age barriers. The generation that has grown up online has also grown up with porn as their primary source of sex education. The pornography and sex toy industries have ballooned in recent decades by catering to their wants and needs, even those of women. In addition, the increased cultural acceptance of LGBT relationships has expanded the market. There are many arguments that porn leads to a decrease in sexual satisfaction, with *Psychology Today* asking, "Is male porn use ruining sex?" Porn rarely reflects any inti-macy, and the ultimate end game of sex is typically the "money shot," displayed all too explicitly.

Has the new revolution given men something to strive for? Absolutely. But porn has created a fantasy image of sex that provides little insight into how they might actually satisfy their partner. Long gone are the days when women did not understand or know that their bodies could have powerful orgasms. Women's magazines and talk shows center on women's pleasure and how to achieve this satisfaction with or without male assistance. Toys on the market now come in a variety of shapes, sizes, and colors, catering to women uninhibited in admitting their desires. Bedroom Kandi, a women's sex toy line, has made millions by developing items that are discreet, in the forms of lipsticks and other objects that can exist in plain sight, yet get the job done.

With so much focus on women achieving physical pleasure, men have been encouraged to become creative in the bedroom, but porn is proving to be a destructive force, giving men an unrealistic sense of how to actually perform and failing to ever communicate the role and value of intimacy. As a result, it's no longer an era in which men are viewed as the bottom line in sexual satisfaction. Now, they are mere participants in a woman-dominated society. If a man is not provid-ing sufficient stimulation, women have no problems being vocal about their needs, to the point where some men may feel emasculated—turning the tables on how men have historically made women feel like objects of male gratification.

Many men are confounded by the seeming inconsistency of women who want a man to be the aggressor, want him to be a sexually satisfying partner, yet also require sensitivity and intimacy, which is what most women truly seek in any relationship that extends beyond a few dates and sexual encounters. If a man wants to connect emotion-ally with a woman, he needs to bring some intimacy into the equation beyond the sexual experience. While porn has its role and its bene-fits, it is hardly an appropriate surrogate for the sex education that is progressively being eliminated from high school curricula. With easy access to porn now available to even the youngest children, a more appropriate solution would be to introduce intimacy and sex education in the early years.

Intimacy has traditionally been a melding of the physical and mental needs of partners. As described by Relationships Australia,

> intimacy is about being emotionally close to your partner, about being able to let your guard down, and let him or her know how you really feel. Intimacy is also about being able to accept and share in your partner's feelings, about being there when he/she wants to let their defenses down.

Although there are numerous programs and resources that teach men how to better fulfill a woman's sexual desires, there are far too few resources that teach men how to introduce intimacy into their partner's life and their own. Jennifer Siebel Newsom, San Francisco–based producer and director of the film *The Mask You Live In*, said that "be a man" and "man up" (as recommended by Miller beer) are among the worst things that boys are told. Boys, she told *ELLE*, "are challenged by hypermasculine norms, and . . . their struggle is in trying to resist: *Why? Why do I need to conform? What's the point? What's the purpose? . . .* It's sort of shoved down their throats that they need to become men really quickly, and that they need to start objectifying women really quickly."

More women today are kicking the door open on their sexuality and power and will not be ignored, regardless of how this revolution affects the male psyche or society as a whole. They are becoming more aware of the dangers of male emotional detachment and intimacy anorexia. They are no longer tolerating the compulsive symptoms of sexual addiction and progressive intimacy disorder by consoling one another that "men will be men" or "men are just fucking idiots."

The standards that once played a huge part in how society's sexual revolution was shaped are now antiquated and no longer acceptable. Sex is now viewed as normal and healthy, alternative sexuality has become openly accepted, and women are demanding intimacy and honesty when a relationship evolves beyond just sex. The new sexual revolution has also pushed women into their own definition of what is acceptable in the home, in the workplace, and on a date. As an alternative to being dominated by men, women of more fluid sexuality—especially college-age women—who are searching for intimacy and honesty are migrating to one another's company, providing satisfying sexual stimulation and emotional connections where men have come up short. Alternative gender definitions are becoming the norm on college campuses, with multiple sexual self-identities beyond LGBT gaining acceptance.

It's no secret that men are feeling the pressure of not being as accepted in the bedroom as they once were, creating a divide between men who are accepting of the women's sexual revolution—the "good ones"—and men who still believe women are intended for men's sexual and social satisfaction—the "bad ones."

In addition to the good and the bad, there is also the ugly. Among the most egregious acts are the organized efforts by federal, state, and local politicians to repress a woman's right to control her own body; the tacit acceptance of rape; the institutionalization of pay inequality; and the imposition of laws that make it more likely that women live in poverty. Governments and courts at all levels may not be quick to correct and overturn these mistakes, but individuals who embrace these archaic and repressive laws must be prepared for future generations to judge them as unevolved bigots and ignorant fools. Governments may successfully pass laws that repress women's rights, but they cannot prevent women from owning their sexuality or demanding intimacy and truth in their relationships.

Can society continue on this path without huge repercussions for the male–female relationship? Women are on the sexual warpath, have forever altered relationships, and have no plans of ever turning back. No longer wrapped in shades of gray, women's effect on society has catapulted the world into a kaleidoscope of sexual color and flipped traditional male/female roles on their head.

MEN, WOMEN, AND COMMUNICATION

An old adage claims that men require sex to feel loved, while women need love to want sex. This might not be true across the board, but there is more than a grain of truth to this. For many women, sex and emotional intimacy are inextricably linked. When the relationship is good, sex is good. However, sex alone doesn't make a strong relationship, nor will it save a crumbling one. This is important for anyone in a relationship to realize, especially if you're the type of man who confuses physical with emotional intimacy.

Author and counselor Gary Chapman, who wrote *The 5 Love Languages*, said that most men identify physical touch as their main "love language." If his partner's primary love language is anything other than physical touch, focusing on sexual intimacy rather than connecting in other ways can lead the partner to feel as though her "love tank" is empty. When a man shows love to his partner in methods appropriate to her love language—through gifts, speaking well of her, acts of service, or verbal affection—her tank will refill and she will feel loved.

Romantic gestures are something that many women desire. Nearly half of all women polled by AskMen in their "Great Male Survey" replied that their partners are never or rarely romantic, although greater than 70 percent of men polled felt that they are consistently romantic. Women are frustrated at not being able to connect with their partners in the way that makes sense to them.

This isn't to say that sex can't be intimate. Many women and men report that the most fulfilling sex is with someone that they love rather than during a casual encounter. A *Scientific American* article, "Sex is Better for Women in Love," explores a study by the University of Geneva in Switzerland and the University of California, Santa Barbara, that examined how amorous feelings improved women's orgasms. If a man naturally views sex as intimate, he might gravitate toward expressing love in ways that turn into sex. However, his partner might feel unloved because his affection always leads to sex and she doesn't feel connected on a deeper level—emotionally, mentally, and even spiritually. Furthermore, resorting to sex as a cure for a disagreement in a relationship might momentarily relieve tension, but it glosses over the underlying issues. Strong communication is essential to a healthy relationship, no matter how significant sexual intimacy is to either partner.

The problem is that men and women don't communicate in the same ways, which can cause turbulence in their relationships. Psychotherapist

Susan Sherwood, in "10 Ways Men and Women Communicate Differently," described communication—or miscommunication—in relationships as a road trip: "It's the middle of the day during a long drive. He is sitting at the wheel, cruising along. She is sitting in the passenger seat, reading, glancing up now and then at the passing scenery. Suddenly, she turns to him and cries, 'Talk to me!' She is not stir crazy; he is not ignoring her. They're just living the classic divide in communication between men and women. She is more discussion-oriented; he is all action."

In the article, Sherwood cited the development of childhood friendships as the starting point to these disparities: girls concentrate on making personal connections in their relationships, through conversations and open dialogue. "Sharing secrets, relating experiences, revealing problems, and discussing options are essential during girls' development. Boys generally take another approach to friendship." Buddy groups tend to be less intimate and more group focused, with conversations centering on activities rather than intimacy.

This dichotomy carries into adulthood. Women continue to communicate through dialogue, emotions, and problem solving, while "men remain action-oriented—the goal of communication is to achieve something." Sherwood noted that these contrasts are, of course, generalizations—some men do want to talk about feelings and some women don't enjoy lengthy discussion—yet there's value in looking at childhood relationships and analyzing "talk versus deeds."

Sherwood stated that "nonverbal communication involves varying levels of body expression, with women usually functioning at high intensity. Faces are animated and hands are in motion, often touching others. Men are more conservative in facial movement and body contact. However, they do tend to be unreserved in sitting styles: sprawling, stretching, and spreading out. The intensity level for women drops for the sitting position—they tend to draw in, keeping arms and legs close to their bodies."

In short, women's body language responds to the interpersonal nature of the relationship and building connections. Men's body language, however, centers on the task at hand. Sherwood noted that men may change their body language to appear in charge, keep calm, or prevent emotional escalation. While these differences are simple in theory, they contribute to a gap in communication that can lead to misunderstanding and detachment.

If men equate sex with love, a sexual rejection can make them doubt the strength of their relationships. However, their partners might not feel amenable to sex because they don't feel that they've been connecting intimately with their partner. When men and women remain mindful of the differences between their intimacy and communication styles, they might find themselves having more frequent and satisfying sex. When they fail, and different intimacy disorders compromise hopes of intimacy, both the man and woman suffer (and often the woman suffers more).

A Tennessee-based sex addiction treatment center, the Ranch, posted the following:

> In a situation few spouses openly address, many women are suffering in silence as their partner lives with sexual addiction or a condition like intimacy anorexia. Both can mean deep physical and emotional deprivation with serious consequences for a spouse.
>
> Stories of spouses whose partners have a sexual addiction often include long periods of emotional detachment and a lack of intimacy, which are recognized as symptoms of the complex disorder. People with sexual addiction may use sex as a way to numb out or avoid creating close emotional bonds, even in a marriage. The results can mean withdrawal from emotional connections and sex that feels almost robotic.

Even without sexual addiction, men and women don't experience intimacy in the same ways, explained psychologist Dr. Kalman Heller in the Psych Central article, "Sexuality and Marital Intimacy." "While these differences get debated in some circles, when it comes to sex, they are real and very clear. Unfortunately, many couples fail to reflect on these differences and integrate them into an understanding of how to be successful partners."

Just because the parties in a couple naturally tend to view intimacy in different ways doesn't mean that the couple is doomed to failure. Being mindful about clear communications can help couples break past this barrier (in addition to jumping over most other hurdles that life might throw at them). The challenge for men is to connect emotionally when they have little understanding of how to actually feel, much less how to show their feelings. Rori Raye, author of *Have the Relationship You Want*, suggests that men should try to let down their guard by being honest about their needs and emotions. That type of emotional vulnerability is the intimate bond most women seek in a relationship. Raye advises men to admit when they feel nervous, unsure, or otherwise out of control. Honesty is often the simple path toward providing women with the equal control they seek in a relationship.

TECHNOLOGY, ONLINE DATING, AND THE DECAY OF INTIMACY

A 2012 study by the American Psychological Association showed that women are more satisfied when their partner is empathetic and understanding toward their needs; however, the study also found that men were more satisfied when they could identify their partner's specific emotion. Before the advent of mobile phones and instant messaging, men and women had to confront their issues in person. As the couple gained a closer understanding of each other, they could progress toward a deeper intimacy as well. Without an empathetic understanding of their partner, men would fail in connecting these two necessary components of intimacy. Unfortunately, rapid developments in technology have depersonalized communication and intimacy. As technology further connects us with larger groups of people, so too does it further isolate us from others. Without a commiserative and deeply personal understanding of their partners, men will fail in becoming truly intimate.

The film *Her*, released in 2014, received both critical acclaim and a diverse range of commentary from international viewers. In the film, a middle-aged man turns his attention to an operating system (OS) while going through a painful divorce. The OS, voiced by the sultry Scarlett Johansson, is able to form complex thoughts and emotions that resemble those of a perfect woman. The system gains a sense of humor along with an insight into the lonely man's life, and together they form a new relationship. She asks nothing from him except for him to be there, and she gives him everything in return. Is it any wonder he neglects the real, complicated, and oftentimes draining physical experiences around him? Although his OS girlfriend may not have a physical body, she doesn't require him to change or face difficult situations.

Women are as conflicted as men in this modern world. Instead of fostering a deep relationship to enhance romance, couples may be more focused on the physical side of intimacy because the emotional side is now mostly dealt with online or by phone. Intimacy is in danger of being reduced to a single-faceted physical phenomenon when, in truth, it is highly complex and involves all of the senses. Avoiding technology is impossible, but for the health of present and future relationships, men and women alike can greatly benefit from concentrating on communicating their individual needs and expectations for more intimate bonds.

ONLINE DATING AND HOOK-UP SITES

Online dating is beginning to lose its stigma and is gaining acceptance as a viable and natural way of courting. The advantages offered by dating sites are obvious and often irresistible: millions of available singles are looking for a meaningful connection and are all located in essentially the same place. Dating sites have rekindled the hope of finding a "soul mate" just when the notion was, arguably, beginning to die out. At the same time, hook-up sites and apps such as Tinder, Ashley Madison, and AdultFriendFinder make it as simple for those already in a relationship to destroy it—or at least find alternatives to it—as it is for singles to find a new partner. It is easier than ever for men especially to seek illicit affairs, explore an online fantasy world of pornography and prurient enticements, and rekindle dormant sexual addictions.

With just a click of a mouse, hundreds of profiles and pictures are instantly available. More than forty million Americans have tried online dating, according to Statistic Brain. With a total of fifty-four million single people in the nation, that's an astonishing number—even allowing for the likelihood of cheaters. Statistic Brain reported that 20 percent of today's committed relationships result from meeting online. The popularity of online dating is actively changing how men and women interact when pursuing a relationship, as well as their roles and expectations.

Although the goal of online dating is to eventually meet in person, the initial dating ritual is vastly different from in the past. Instead of playing off body language, online couples begin by sending messages and viewing each other's profiles. These communications are undoubtedly calculated. When the two meet for a first date, they already have avatars, profile bios, and statistics in mind. While the couple may become closer throughout their relationship, it is often difficult to escape the online persona initially created. What a man writes in his profile may seem true to him, but it is most likely not how others perceive him. Relationships are beginning online, yet even in person they continue to be distorted by social media, texts, and a decreased personal presence. Online dating services may help filter out incompatible potential partners. There are differences among the various dating and hook-up apps, and they certainly offer an alternative to traditional ways to connect. But, for many, they are little more than a virtual fantasy world where they can create false personas and escape the relationship (or lack of) reality in which they live.

Mathematically based matchmaking algorithms helped attract millions by developing the impression that science, much more than instinct, could determine who the perfect significant other is for each individual. The science behind these computer-generated formulas is, at best, dubious. Despite this, most people accept the evidence presented as proof they'll have considerably better luck finding a partner online than they have in the real world. Of course, as is often seen with those who recount their experiences, this can lead to disappointment and frustration when the perfect man or woman doesn't materialize almost immediately.

In addition to using this algorithmic pseudoscience, enterprising web developers realized capitalizing on niche groups, rather than casting a wide net, would appeal to some individuals dismayed by the random selection of singles offered elsewhere. Today, there are dating sites for Christians, Jews, blacks, yoga aficionados, farmers, inmates, redheads, and hipsters, just to start. Whatever the hobby, profession, race, or background, there's an exclusive online dating site catering to it. Some require a monthly fee, some are free, and some are free for basic features but charge for premium. Ultimately, they all connect users with other presumably like-minded people hoping for a stirring connection.

By cultivating the impression that it has all the romantic enchantment of traditional dating at twice the speed and triple the success, online dating has flourished. In reality, the process of contacting, interacting, and dating through online means can be at times (and more often than not) wildly different from that found in the nondigital world. It's certainly possible to enjoy a traditional courtship online, with a man initiating interaction via message, requesting a date offline, paying for the date, and so on. The opportunity to date so many people—thousands, in fact—nurtures a casual attitude toward dating and at the same time is the source of a growing number of affairs and misdirected affection and attention.

An unfortunate example involves Artie N., a freelance graphic designer. After being happily married for four years, Artie opened a Facebook account in 2008. At first, the social networking site served as a means of reconnecting with old friends. It didn't take long, however, for Artie to transition from connecting with old friends to chatting—and then flirting—with old flames.

Artie shared in an interview that, after communicating for quite some time with a recently divorced high school girlfriend, he decided to catch up with her at a local bar while she was in town. He rationalized that it would be far more awkward than the Facebook flirting and that he'd be ready for it to be over as soon as it began. But, fortunately or unfortunately, this was not the case. Artie explains, "My chemistry with Sharon was every bit as amazing as it had been in high school. I made her forget the reason she broke up with me in the first place—unfaithfulness—and we were eager to meet again." Although he lived a two-hour drive from Sharon, Artie soon began making the trek every weekend, inventing excuses about meetings with freelance clients and other professional endeavors.

Artie enjoyed nights and weekends with Sharon for several months, but he couldn't keep his wife in the dark forever. Ultimately, the very tool that had brought this pair of high school lovers together proved to be their undoing. An old mutual friend of Sharon's and Artie's posted a Facebook message about them, which was forwarded to Artie's wife. With the affair out in the open, Artie decided to break it off, but it nearly proved too little, too late. With marriage counseling and a renewed commitment to the relationship, Artie and his wife were able to remain together. However, Artie admits he still struggles with a decided lack of trust on his wife's part, particularly when it comes to the realm of social networking. "My wife searches my iPhone and computer every once in a while. This is a source of tension between us, but I know I screwed up, and I figure it's the least I can do to give her some sort of peace of mind."

He admits that, without the social networking site, he probably still would have found a way to be unfaithful—it just wouldn't have been quite as easy. His story is echoed in those of several other couples who, while initially blaming social media as the cause of their woes, ultimately conclude that it merely facilitated and enabled their existing tendency toward infidelity.

The Internet offers a human buffet of potential dates and hook-ups. Aside from disappointment resulting from unfulfilled expectations and a misguided sense of intimacy, there's another key change happening: women are taking charge even though men still, more often than not, initiate the majority of interactions and offer to pay for drinks and meals. The focus on who pays, who requests dates, and who opens the door, however, is missing the forest for the trees. Women are paying for dates as often as men. Women are sending "winks," "kisses," or messages almost as often as men. The major change isn't who's paying, it's that both men and women are doing the hunting, and it's leveling the dating playing field. The challenge for young men is that there are no clear indications of what game they're playing or what rules they're following. As a result, they may become passive, letting the game unfold without establishing their position.

With online dating profiles showcasing pictures, interests, talents, and careers, everyone is a wild peacock vying for a mate—not just the men—and there are millions of birds flaunting their plumage. The endless parade of potential dates is disturbingly similar to a product wall on the Amazon Marketplace. As Eve, a small business owner in her early thirties, quips, "It's like shopping for humans!" Mae, a commercial property manager also in her early thirties, echoed the sentiment, saying it was akin to "picking someone off a website like a pair of shoes. There's even a return policy." In its brief history, online dating has transformed from the anonymous AOL chat rooms portrayed in the romantic comedy *You've Got Mail* to a social media–based free-for-all.

If people are thought of as goods, especially common goods in high supply, then they'll be treated as such. Women, still ostensibly the choosers, can start ticking boxes on their wish list, a list that grows after each failed date. For some men and women, this materializes as an unwillingness to settle down: there are so many enticing opportunities to pursue, so why commit to a relationship? For others, it manifests as impossible standards. That last date wasn't quite right, but the *perfect* guy or girl is out there somewhere. As Abby G. explains, "When I first started, it was easy to be picky with so many options. Then I found myself getting less picky with the people I'd meet. After my first exciting prospects hadn't panned out, I thought maybe I should try to give more people a chance and that I could be pleasantly surprised by someone I may not have considered. Those didn't pan out either though, and I now have a pretty good idea of what I'm looking for and what doesn't work for me. I'm a bit burned out on planning so many dates, so I feel that I've gone back to being picky and waiting for someone's profile or messages to really impress me and get me excited to meet them."

Connor, a professor in his early forties, notes another dynamic: "Internet dating when you are over thirty is essential because it exposes you to an astronomically larger number of potential dates than the more traditional circumstances of meeting, such as at work, at a bar, or stalking somebody at the Starbucks." Online dating, though, isn't just about the breathtaking number of suitors available, it's also about how easy it is to pick up and discard individuals in this new virtual world of dating. A single text (or a slow fade) can announce the end of a budding relationship now, and it hardly even stings. It's hard to devote time to building a meaningful relationship when a shiny new something is dangling always within reach.

Further heightening this effect is the continued development of mobile apps that allow users to connect, chat, and set up dates in any setting imaginable. Meerkat, Periscope, the Dating Lounge, and an endless array of others contribute to this ease of access, making the online dating world even more competitive and real-life relationships even more easy to ditch.

As the dissonance between online chemistry and real-life chemistry grows, users begin relying heavily on chain dating in a desperate hunt for enthrallment, dismissing anything and anyone who doesn't provide it. Dan Slater, author of *Love in the Time of Algorithms*, points to a new sense of disposability in the dating world, in which participants are less likely to continue in relationships they rate as less than satisfactory. Though Jasmine is now in a committed relationship, she admits to us she has no idea how many dates she went on in the years she spent online dating. Eve claimed fifteen dates in two months, and Abby clocked in at forty-five in just over a year. When asked how many dates they went on that originated offline, it was just two or fewer for the same time period. Sadly, with this date-and-dump technique, there's hardly time to kindle any feeling, but going offline may mean waiting years for a golden opportunity.

Online dating and mating has also transformed lying and misrepresentation from a negative to an accepted—and even expected—behavior. When a relationship begins on the foundation of a lie, such as an inaccurate birth date or outdated photo, that is tacitly or explicitly accepted without accountability, a low bar is set for the relationship. Both partners have embraced deception, and while the chemistry may initially seem strong, the odds for long-term success are diminished.

It seems everyone has a story (or five) about the date with the guy who lied about having kids or the girl who used pictures from high school on her profile despite being in her midthirties. Noah admits in a conversation to spending an inordinate amount of time finding the perfect picture. He recounts, "I took about a hundred selfies before finding the one I wanted as my profile picture. That may not have been a lie but it was certainly disingenuous. I have a rule though, because everyone uses misleading pictures to make themselves seem more desirable. If you're ugly in your profile picture, you must be *really* ugly. Even a '4' can find a picture that makes her appear to be a '7'. But in the upper ranges it's harder. Like a '6' may be able to pull off an '8', but she's never going full '10.'"

Presentation is clearly essential on both sides of the field, and both men and women are keenly aware they need to make an impression. But it raises the questions, What good is lying about something as easily disprovable as appearance? And if we allow lying at the beginning of relationships, are we establishing a threshold of high tolerance for it as the relationship develops? While it may strike many as foolish to lie if getting caught is guaranteed, apparently people are fairly understanding about it. Jasmine confesses, "One person posted a picture from high school, when he was a beanpole. He showed up looking like he could be pregnant with a full-sized me. We had a really high compatibility score, so I thought that even though he lied I might as well see how well we clicked." Eve felt similarly. "People occasionally had misleading pictures or information, which made the date awkward. I would try to be sympathetic to the reasons they might have had for whitewashing certain details." Despite being selective about the characteristics they're seeking, both men and women seem to accept lying, deceit, and misrepresentation.

Ultimately, online dating may prove beneficial, but there are opportunities aplenty for rudeness, dismissive behavior, manipulation, objectification, and acting out. Despite the difficulty inherent in the process, most people remain optimistic. Connor clarifies his experience: "It is a lot of work. You will need to spend a great deal of time and energy before you find a relatively few number of potential candidates. Out of those, only a small percentage will be truly compatible. It's all a numbers game, but when you find the right person, it's worth it." Even those dating offline must now contend with the reality that the object of their affection is likely trawling websites simultaneously. Equally, those in committed relationships need to be constantly tuned in to the possibility that their lover may also be hunting for online affairs, if not on dating sites then through social media.

The future of intimacy is changing. For intimacy to be mutually appreciated, men and women will have to take the time to allow their relationship to grow. This means engaging in meaningful conversation in person, avoiding digital quarrels, and allowing progression at a natural pace. Unfortunately, humankind's natural tendencies are being forced into an unnatural, breakneck pace through technology and the myriad distractions found in the modern world.

According to a study conducted by Western Illinois University's Christopher Carpenter and reported on in the *Guardian* article "Facebook's 'Dark Side,'" the love lives of both singles and couples are heavily influenced by social media, although the result of this influence is fully within the user's control. From breaking up to making up and everything in between, social media is there—and it's not going away. Whether for good or bad, there's no denying that the social media boom has completely transformed the way we interact with one another, both as friends and as lovers. Ultimately, social media must be regarded not as a miracle and not as an evil, but as a complex communication tool. It can positively impact users' lives or tear them apart, but the end result depends completely on the user's intentions.

The future doesn't have to contain only diluted intimacy, and online relationships can be used to connect those who would have otherwise stayed adrift. However, for this to happen, men and women will have to leave their avatars and online behavior behind while in the physical world.

CHAPTER 9

WOMEN TAKE CONTROL IN THE BEDROOM

SHIFTING STANDARDS FOR EXPLICIT MATERIAL

In the 1920s, James Joyce's novel *Ulysses* was deemed pornographic and was banned from publication in the United States due to its frank depictions of bodily functions. In 1933, the novel's ban was put on trial in the now infamous United States v. One Book Entitled Ulysses. The novel won the appeal, and its publication was allowed to proceed without any further interference. Judge John M. Woolsey concluded, "Whilst in many places the effect of *Ulysses* on the reader undoubtedly is somewhat emetic, nowhere does it tend to be an aphrodisiac." No longer was a piece of art banned for being pornographic, or in the case of this trial, obscene. So long as the work contained artistic integrity, it could be sold and reproduced without any legal action against its sexual or possibly depraved content.

The first known incidence of nudity in a movie is from the 1915 silent film *Inspiration*, in which actress Audrey Munson undresses. *Safe in Hell* (1931) provides sexual situations in a rather overt tone (two years before *Ulysses* was unbanned!). In 1953, *Playboy* magazine was released to nationwide success. Featuring a centerfold of Marilyn Monroe, the first copy of the magazine sold out in weeks, and its following issues continued to bring in massive sales. Just twenty years prior, Judge Woolsey's controversial decision had allowed an avant-garde novel to be published in America; now, nude photographs of women were selling in record numbers. In the 1970s, *Playboy* began losing circulation in favor of hard-core magazines such as *Penthouse* and *Club*. Whereas *Playboy* specialized in borderline classy photographs of celebrities, *Penthouse* featured women notorious for their roles in the emerging pornography industry. Even against outcries of pastors, politicians, and feminists, these magazines and films have continued in circulation to this day, culminating in the outlandishly broad spectrum of free, instantly available Internet pornography.

Despite the long history of easily available explicit material (Greek gods and goddesses were classically portrayed in the nude), there are still outcries that society is unraveling due to an increase in sexualization. In October 2015, *Playboy* made the decision to cease publishing fully nude images of women due to the rise of Internet pornography. However, it is debatable whether it can redefine its brand and retain its readership without objectifying women.

The novel *Fifty Shades of Grey* has received criticism, acclaim, and everything in-between due to its controversial portrayal of a BDSM relationship. The novel's female lead learns to enjoy being subjected to various demeaning acts, reflecting the trend toward middle-aged women all over the world shaping their own sexual narratives.

In 1954, the French novel *The Story of O* was an international success. With this came a storm of controversy regarding the novel's degradation of women. Written through the perspective of O, the lead character, the novel presents a scenario in which she is taught various sexual acts that range from "vanilla" to quite shocking. Over the course of the book, she learns to love them and accept her role of submission in the bedroom.

While the novel was apparently written by Pauline Réage, the majority of the public refused to believe that a woman could write such things. The novel derived direct inspiration from the Marquis de Sade, and like his sadistic tales, it inspired both controversy and a feverish following. The confusion, passion, and even anger reached an apex when the author's identity was revealed: Pauline Réage turned out to be the pen name of French author Anne Desclos. The novel was in fact written by a woman, and the public was outraged. These outcries were similar to those against *Fifty Shades of Grey*: a male backlash against the sexual freedom that women have gained and are rightfully enjoying.

Although *The Story of O* may, at first glance, present a degrading view of women, it actually depicts a woman controlling her own sexual narrative. If a woman wants to be submissive, then she can choose to be, be proud of it, and enjoy it fully (and safely). The novel may have shortcomings in terms of plot and characterization, but the one thing that it does explicitly well is provide an offbeat sexual narrative that is entirely for women, and in another rarity, is controlled by women.

A hundred years ago, a woman who expressed sexual desire was believed to suffer from hysteria and require treatment. It was scandalous to speak or write about such things. Now, for one of the first times in history, it is acceptable for women to loudly proclaim their sexual needs. Women are taking the reins and either demanding sexual satisfaction or choosing abstinence as a way of life. Either way, women are in control of their sexuality.

Many narratives are now from women's perspectives, from desiring true romance to being submissive. Women of all sexual persuasions are having their say in the public forum and the bedroom, shaping the sexual narrative like never before. With the expanding female-driven sexual narrative, men are both confused and happy to oblige. Gone are the days when a man can have a frolic in the bedroom with little regard for his female partner's pleasure; now, it's important for men to fully satisfy their partner if they want the relationship to continue.

Sexual guidance books are becoming increasingly popular and widespread among both men and women. For men in particular, there are countless books focusing on pleasing a woman, lasting longer in bed, and providing a romantic experience. Men are flocking to Kama Sutra and tantric sex courses, where they learn to practice the art of slow and healing love to appease their female partner's needs. Viagra and Cialis are not only for sexual dysfunction but are also tools for extending men's erections. Direct marketing of sexual enhancement pills and creams is rampant.

One of the bestselling modern sex-help books is *She Comes First*. The book explicitly details how to orally please a woman. Even featuring this once highly taboo subject, the book soared in popularity and was included on numerous bestseller lists. Women are no longer accepting mediocrity in the bedroom, and as book sales show, some men are making an effort to follow along. There is no longer a single, masculine narrative of relationships or sex; rather, there is a larger narrative growing from the once voiceless women who are no longer confined to accepting what their male partners want. The modern relationship is clearly changing, and once again, women are taking control.

THE EVOLUTION OF CULTURAL GENDER ROLES

What if men and women have been basing their respective sexual roles not on biological imperatives but on cultural expectations and limitations? Furthermore, what if that era has now come to an end? As Allan and Barbara Pease point out in their book *Why Men Don't Listen and Women Can't Read Maps*, "Men and women evolved differently because they had to. Men hunted, women gathered. Men protected, women nurtured. Their brains and bodies developed in very different ways." However, these traditional gender roles have slowly diminished. Men no longer need to be the protective alpha male, and women have more central roles in business and relationships.

The history of Western culture has rightly been labeled as patriarchal, with male dominance as a defining characteristic. This model most probably arose from our species's dim prehistory: the obvious physical differences between the sexes combined with the need for physical strength for survival on a personal and tribal level. Where this male dominance characteristic comes from is fairly clear, but whether it was a learned behavior arising strictly from personal and cultural need or had roots in genetic code over and above the usefulness of physical strength is less certain.

The patriarchy of old had its usefulness. Our species survived largely because of the ability to overcome obstacles and hardships by virtue of physical strength, clearly the forte of the men of our species. Though there are theories that dispute even this, it is fairly clear that being larger and stronger presented a survival advantage in situations of life-or-death struggles. From this early beginning in which "might made right" and strength prevailed, the human species developed into a culture of dominant men and submissive women. As in almost all other species, men engage in competition with one another for women. The ripple effects of this principle of dominance have seeped into almost every aspect of our culture.

There are also hormonal reasons for this characteristic male dominance. Testosterone is a fact of life—an important one without which most species might have died out entirely. Testosterone in many ways defines the male sexual response. It is the primary reason men have greater muscle and bone mass than women. Testosterone is also responsible for male fertility and increased libido, the energy that converts to action in mating.

Although the current gender stereotypes, especially those about women, may have had their roots in our species's prehistory and chemistry, many today reflect beliefs that appeared during the Victorian era. As psychologist Dr. Linda Brannon documented the following in her book, *Gender: Psychological Perspectives*:

> Before the 19th century, most people lived and worked on farms, where men and women worked together. The Industrial Revolution changed the lives of a majority of people in Europe and North America by moving men outside the home to earn money and leaving women at home to manage households and children. This separation forced men and women to adapt to different environments and roles. As men coped with the harsh business and industrial world, women were left in the relatively unvarying and sheltered environments of their homes. These changes produced two beliefs: the Doctrine of Two Spheres and the Cult of True Womanhood.

Brannon clarified that the Doctrine of Two Spheres is the idea that women and men have separate areas of influence. A woman's influence comes from her being the homemaker and caregiver, while the man works outside the home. The home and the outside world barely overlap, and they form opposite ends of a spectrum. This conceptualization of opposition, Brannon continues, forms the basis not only for social views of gender but also for psychology's formulation of the measures of masculinity and femininity.

As Brannon explained further, quoting historian Barbara Welter, the Cult of True Womanhood, arising between 1820 and 1860, claimed that "the attributes of True Womanhood, by which a woman judged herself and was judged by her husband, her neighbors, and society, could be divided into four cardinal virtues: piety, purity, submissiveness, and domesticity. . . . The Cult of True Womanhood held that the combination of these characteristics provided the promise of happiness and power to the Victorian woman and that without these, no woman's life could have real meaning." Although the Cult of True Womanhood was only truly dominant during the nineteenth century, remnants of its beliefs linger in our present-day culture and influence current views of femininity.

For example, the Duggars of TLC's scandal-ridden *19 Kids and Counting* have put the Quiverfull movement on the map, giving it media attention it never had before. Practiced by a small group of Christian fundamentalists, the Quiverfull movement promotes procreation and the idea that children are a blessing from God. Believing that God controls family size and planning, the movement's followers renounce all forms of birth control—the result of which is nineteen Duggar children. Along with that belief, however, is that the woman's role is of the subservient wife, a homemaker subject to her husband's authority. While this movement is only practiced by a small group of Americans, the popularity of the show and scandals surrounding Josh Duggar (including his presence at the Ashley Madison website) have certainly cast it and its antifeminist beliefs into the spotlight.

Starting in roughly the 1960s, the rapid spread of feminism gave rise to a newly perceived equality for women, empowering them in ways that had never before been experienced. The growth of the movement was impressive, and the effects most certainly altered the way many women viewed their intimate relationships with men.

At first, the established "rules of conduct" for polite society as well as intimate relationships held sway, with feminism finding a difficult and sometimes painful path through the obstructions placed in its way by the resistant culture. But the feminist movement continued to grow and over time was highly instrumental in shifting the attitudes of society away from the old model of male dominance.

A glance at the changing roles of women in romance novels is an educational depiction of how the feminist movement has changed our actual relationship patterns. Since this genre is written primarily for women, these role changes might be viewed as a message purely for women; however, this would be a mistake. Men may not represent more than a tiny fraction of romance novel readership, but they are certainly affected by the mindset that emerges from this genre's influence. Women are affected in their conceptualization of gender roles, and their modified views are translated directly into expectations of their mates. Men cannot help but be affected by new perspectives on gender roles when their female partners expect and encourage them to conform. The message and its intensity are only enhanced by controversial novels, such as *Fifty Shades of Grey*, and their Hollywood adaptations.

If feminism was a bitter pill to swallow for traditional male attitudes, the events that have come in the wake of feminism's birth have constituted a painful therapy. Since the 1980s, society has been awakening to other gender inequalities beyond role definitions. Perhaps the most significant of these is the differences in sexual orientation. Today, marriage between same-sex partners is legal across the nation, empowering couples of all gender orientations to have clearly defined marital rights. The redefinition of gender and sexuality to include alternative sexual preferences, including asexuality, has stretched the credibility of the old patriarchal system nearly to a point of no return.

As women continue to earn a higher percentage of high school diplomas and college degrees than men and millennial women outearn their male counterparts, their relationship prospects—finding men on the same playing field—begin to look pretty bleak.

Jane F., a forty-year-old single attorney in Key Biscayne, Florida, shares in a conversation that "most men you meet are jerks. They still have the 'me Tarzan, you Jane' attitude when dealing with marriage, dating, or commitment. It seems they are still living in the Stone Age. Jane should have wrapped the vine around Tarzan's neck, pushed him and Cheetah out of the tree house, and told him to get a job and not come back until he did. Men just really need to listen to a woman and let her tell him what she needs, not what he believes that women in general need."

Betsy F., a thirty-five-year-old divorcée with three young children, says in an interview, "Men in today's society really need to learn what women want in their relationships. We are not the same women as we were in the Victorian Age. We have progressed and still are progressing, and the future is ours to take."

With their traditional dominant, moneymaking position eroding, where does that leave men? Roles will only continue to shift as women gain influence and power. Men will need to rethink old-fashioned ideals ingrained from childhood or else face losing their romantic relationships.

Evolutionarily at least, the male-dominated system worked. But if it worked so well, why are we changing? That question undoubtedly has been asked by many a man who considered the status quo to be just fine. But as the Greek philosopher Heraclitus pointed out, the only thing that is permanent is change itself. Our species, just like everything else, is growing and changing in many ways. The inevitability of change does not guarantee its success, nor does it ensure good effects or even clarity about whether the changes we're experiencing are positive or negative, necessary or frivolous, wise or unwise.

There can be little doubt that substantial changes have taken place and are continuing to take place in the gender roles found in today's culture. There is wide disagreement, however, on many points regarding the nature of these changes, their causes, the degree to which they are culturally imposed, and the justifications for their continuing influence. Various changing societal norms are usually thought to be responsible for what are seen as new gender roles. But other factors are at work as well and are instrumental in producing changes in the role of men—and women—in romantic, professional, and family relationships. These additional factors include personal, generational, and maturational issues that have resulted in what we see today as the role of a man in intimate relations.

One study goes so far as to question whether the changes being witnessed are actual changes in the perceived role of a man or are merely "surface alterations." In "The Male Role and Heterosexual Behavior," Alan Gross makes a case for these new male characteristics being no better than what they replaced. These "new sensitive men" have their own problems, which stem from the very same maladapted learning processes that gave us the man's man: the macho lover, the stereotypical sexual animal that now seems to have become passé.

Whether skin deep or profound, changes are happening. The patriarchal male role has become less commonplace and less acceptable as the norm. How gender roles are being newly interpreted, particularly in the intimacy of romantic or sexual relations, is perhaps the most important element of these changes. With reproduction at stake, it could turn out to be important for the survival of our species.

WHAT WOMEN WANT: SEX AND EXPECTATIONS

Kelly S., a twenty-one-year-old college student at the University of Michigan, asks in an interview, "What is wrong with men today? You are in a social setting or a party, you give him the eye to let him know that you are interested in getting to know him, and what does he do? The idiot turns around to see who you are looking at and then goes right back to his drink. Is he brain dead or just stupid? He is at a party solo, and I assume he is looking to meet someone new, and his attitude turns me off. Why do I always get the frogs and not the prince?"

Jackson M., a forty-plus-year-old divorcé, explains in a conversation that he has a differing point of view on what he calls the Disney fixation. "We also watched *Cinderella*, *Sleeping Beauty*, and *Snow White*. But when I date a woman and we seem to click, I feel like she's wondering if I'm her Prince Charming come to sweep her off her feet. It sets a very high standard that few men can live up to."

Cheryl G., a Minneapolis shipping agent, admits in an interview to her quest for a prince, explaining that she's realistic about her relationship with her husband, "But [I'm] unwilling to let him think that because there's a ring on my finger it gives him license to sit on a couch with a beer or go out with his buddies while I do 90 percent of the housework and child care. I'm bringing home as much money as he is." She adds, "We never see what Prince Charming does after he sweeps Cinderella off her feet, or what he did before that either."

Fairy tales, it seems, need to be written with a new narrative that builds on the qualities beyond charm and good looks that translate into a successful marriage and positive parenting. Most of the stories in the discussions about men and marriage today warn women to beware and suggest they should not expect men to live up to the storybook standard.

It's tough for a man to live up to modern notions of the perfect mate, the perfect gentleman, and the perfect provider. In reality, Prince Charming and Cinderella now have three sons and two daughters, a mortgage, two car payments, and college tuitions, and his mother-in-law just came to live with them; or they're divorced.

It is not just married women who feel let down; single women feel the same and find themselves increasingly unhappy about the choices available to them among single men. Suzie A., award-winning blogger of *Suzie the Single Dating Diva*, wrote on her blog, "How many men these days will actually stand up for their woman or any woman in general? Many men these days are either brutes . . . selfish and only after their happiness and pleasure . . . or the other extreme, whiny wimps."

Cyndi C., a single forty-four-year-old psychology professor at the University of California and a "self-proclaimed dyed-in-the-wool feminist" poses in an interview a rhetorical but increasingly voiced question, "Are men necessary?" Answering her own question, she exclaims, "Are you crazy? The only thing men are good for is to procreate, and then it's all over. It's like the praying mantis or the black widow spider— have sex, procreate, and eat them. Less mess and all-around trouble."

Instead of waiting to be saved, women are saving themselves. Research studies show that many women today are marrying men who make less money and have fewer years of education than they do.

Psychologists and sociologists call this phenomenon "marrying down," but women just call it "living in the twenty-first century." An AskMen article, "Things Women Want," tells all: "Men are pretty simple creatures, really. If a woman is attractive, we want to meet her. If she turns out to be interesting, intelligent, and/or funny, we want to get to know her better. Women, by contrast, are a little more complicated. The things women want are often like grocery lists of prioritized criteria they use to determine whether or not a man is dateable. And female criteria are significantly more nuanced than the monosyllabic qualities men tend to look for: 'nice,' 'hot,' and 'smart.'"

On the other hand, the article goes on, women are a bit more demanding; they want an independent, financially stable, funny, and caring partner, who is also competent in bed. They also value men they can freely talk to and who will actually listen.

Sometimes, all a woman needs is for a man to listen. This is more challenging than it sounds—men are very action oriented. A man needs to show a woman he has the capacity to pay attention to her and to connect both physically and emotionally.

Research into men's and women's hormonal levels, spearheaded by sex expert Alfred Kinsey in the 1950s, has long shown that men reach their sexual peak at age eighteen and women reach theirs in their thirties and older. Nora M., a divorced fifty-year-old real estate broker in New York City, says in a conversation, "How damn unfair is that? A woman reaches her peak when the man in her life is a couch potato who thinks he's Brad Pitt. I love sex, but the men I find to date and have sex with, especially the younger ones, tend to perform in the bedroom like they think they're in a porn movie. They don't know the first thing about intimacy, emotions, or communicating . . . or oral for that matter." She sighs.

Sharlette C., a thirty-nine-year-old computer programmer for the government in Washington, DC, explains to an interviewer, "They say that Washington, DC, is the land of the movers and the shakers. Well, it sure has to be on Capitol Hill because it sure is not when you get into the bedroom. I am at the prime of my life, and all I can find are momma's boys or divorced men who want a mother to take care of them. If

I date a younger man who is virile and hot to trot, other women look at me like I've robbed the cradle. Rob the cradle or no sex . . . go figure."

An AskMen article that asked, "What do women consider good sex?" quoted Dr. Emily Nagoski's *Good in Bed Guide to Female Orgasms*: "Men are like driving standard transmission—if you move through the gears in the right order, you will get where you want to go. Women are like baking a soufflé—the outcome depends on the ingredients and the chef, sure, but it also depends on the reliability of the oven, the altitude, the humidity of the day . . . more variables, more variability."

Our perception of the roles assigned to us in sex and romance is changing. How we respond to the expectations of others and in the process define our expectations of ourselves is similarly shifting. As awareness grows surrounding society's influences on gender role identification, the stereotypical male-dominated picture of a romantic relationship recedes.

CHAPTER 10

SISTERS GOING THEIR OWN WAY

Actress Cynthia Nixon caused an uproar when she described her same-sex relationship and lesbian identity as a choice. People who believe sexual preference is innate said that she was giving ammunition to antigay bigots who decried homosexuality as a sinful choice. Others took it as another sign that women were "giving up" on men.

Sexual orientation is a highly personal—and sometimes fluid—matter. The question is, Are more women choosing relationships with other women because of a lack of suitable men? Is the current male identity struggle harming men's chances of having relationships, marriage, and a family?

In his historic study of human sexuality, Alfred Kinsey discovered that many people are not strictly straight or gay but experience desire along a spectrum. Further research by psychologist Meredith Chivers, discussed in *ELLE*, revealed that women respond to a wider range of sexual stimuli than men do. It's quite possible that even women who consider themselves straight are likely to find another woman sexually attractive. If the men around them are presenting unenticing options, it only makes sense that women would open the field to consider one another as suitable partners.

The 2013 National Survey of Sexual Attitudes and Lifestyles revealed that the number of women who have had a same-sex partner has increased from 1.8 percent to 7.9 percent over the past twenty years. While much of this can be attributed to an increased acceptance of same-sex relationships, it also stands to reason that dissatisfaction with the men in the dating scene plays a role as well. A 2015 study, authored by Elizabeth Aura McClintock, suggested that a woman's sexual orientation may be influenced by her romantic options. Live Science wrote that the more attractive the woman was rated in the study—and presumably her ability to attract men—the more likely she was to identify as completely straight. In addition, women were three times more likely than men to experience a change in their sexual orientation during the course of the study. With the high number of women expressing discontent with the status quo, something obviously has to change. Men who crave relationships may have to examine their place in the changing social climate.

Women who have tired of searching for a "good" man are often concluding that even the good ones are bad. As Evergreen State College history and family studies professor Stephanie Coontz told *ELLE,* "Women tend to get more dissatisfied with marriage over time than men do. Women spend a lot more time doing the emotional work in marriage, and that's tiring."

Furthermore, although women are nearly as likely as men to have a career outside the home, men haven't quite caught up with the responsibilities of maintaining a household. Sociologist Arlie Russell Hochschild first described the so-called second shift in 1989: women would work a full day at a paying job and then come home to deal with housecleaning, caring for children, and cooking meals. Twenty-five years later, the situation has changed, but not much. According to a 2014 international study by the Organisation for Economic Co-operation and Development, women put in eleven more hours each week on routine housework than men do.

Men seem to be held back from full participation in the home based on now-outmoded ideas of what is considered men's work and what is considered women's work. It only makes sense that this would lead to resentment over time and harm relationships. Coontz told

ELLE, "We're socialized to want to marry, but then once we get there, we're like, Huh, why am I doing so much housework?" When women are resentful of inequity in the relationship and just plain tired from too much work, intimacy can be difficult.

The most obvious solution is for men to be more conscious of work that needs to be done around the home and establish a pattern in which partners divide the different household responsibilities or trade off nights handling them. He cooks dinner Tuesdays, Thursdays, and Sundays while she does dishes; they alternate weeks doing laundry, vacuuming, and cleaning the bathrooms. However, this has a few drawbacks. Most men are willing to pull their own weight, but chances are they are not as aware of what work goes into a household since they (likely) weren't brought up doing the same amount of housework as their sisters were. Furthermore, many women are hesitant to delegate. No one wants to be a nag. To complicate matters further, if she has a specific way she likes a chore to be done, his methods might not meet her approval. And though men argue that they contribute far more time and physical effort into outdoor housework, women tend to be more active gardeners, and in many neighborhoods you can see more women on the tractor mower than men. All of these challenges can leave couples as dissatisfied and alienated from each other as they were when he wasn't even trying to help.

There is one thing that the traditional breadwinner/homemaker split has going for it: simplicity. Everyone knows what they are supposed to do, so no one inadvertently skirts duties. The man brings in a paycheck, and the woman tends to the home. The alternative, being more often explored now, is to reverse the roles and have the man in the homemaker role. A small but growing number of families have found that this is a far more workable and satisfying arrangement. If she's in a growing field and he's having trouble finding work, it only makes sense for her to go out in the workplace while he tends the home. Although these men are often criticized for being "unmanly," many say that the perception doesn't bother them. UT News reported that in a study of two hundred stay-at-home dads in Austin, Texas, several dads agreed that one of the benefits of being homemakers was showing their children that they don't have to adhere to strict gender roles. They also say they are happier for it!

"When my boss told me that I had to make a choice between work and my family, it was an easy decision," one Austin dad told the University of Texas researchers. "My wife made more money and had good insurance, and I could do freelance writing, so I began to stay at home with my son. My in-laws probably had some serious doubts about my staying home, but, really, most everyone has been very accepting of our situation because I think they can see how happy we are."

Women now earn over 60 percent of all college degrees, according to the Bureau of Labor Statistics. The recent recession was dubbed the "mancession" due to the large number of men who lost jobs. (At one brief moment in the recession, women actually had a higher level of workplace participation than men.) Additionally, male-dominated fields that required little advanced education, such as manufacturing, have been ailing for years. As a result, men have felt a decaying of their stature in society. This has led to a crisis: men are trying to find out where they belong if not at the top. Predictably, it has also had an effect on their relationships with women.

Beginning a relationship is tough for men. Although men and women use online dating sites in roughly similar numbers, women have far more options than men do. A 2013 Business Insider analysis of user activity on the dating site AYI (Are You Interested?) notes that a man has to send eighteen messages to a woman his own age to be even 50 percent sure of getting a response; a woman need only send five for the same certainty. Because of this dynamic, many men wind up approaching dating online as a numbers game. It commoditizes the experience and can make it harder to feel a connection. Because women receive so many more messages, they can afford to be choosier, leading to a different emotional engagement.

A small but significant minority of men have concluded that feminism has ruined everything. The Men Going Their Own Way movement (often abbreviated as MGTOW) advocates a complete disengagement with women: no marriage, no relationships, no male–female friendships, and usually no sexual contact either. In fact, when women visit the MGTOW website, and are identified as female, they're immediately redirected to a screen full of kitten photos.

The Reddit forum "The Red Pill" is another of the more extreme destinations for men who feel disenfranchised by the new normal. The predominant strategy advocated by this forum is to avoid marriage at all costs. Relationships are regarded with suspicion; members instead advocate maintaining hook-up relationships with a large number of women for as long as is convenient. While some men who have "swallowed the pill" say that they'd like a relationship, a sizable percentage of men seem to believe that path is for chumps.

This misogynistic disdain for women displays itself in language, as well. A guy who is weak is a "pussy." The athletically untalented male "throws like a girl." When two guys argue, a third might sneer, "Girls, girls!" to insinuate their behavior is unbecoming in some way that is somehow disgustingly female. Women, on the other hand, are unduly praised for doing things that seem manly. Consider the last decade's cigar trend and the number of photos of women smoking thick stogies or the admiration for a woman who takes her whiskey straight. In the popular Comedy Central video "The Last F*ckable Day" featuring Amy Schumer, Julia Louis-Dreyfus, Tina Fey, and Patricia Arquette, Julia celebrates her last f*ckable day (in the eyes of Hollywood) by lighting up a cigar. The truth is, there is nothing inherently female about arguing or not excelling at sports nor anything particularly masculine about liking a strong drink or smoking a giant cigar. These are not behaviors that are based on sexual biology.

During the recession, gender roles in many homes shifted, with more men taking on chores such as cooking and cleaning. Marketers hopped right on board with that trend, pushing products at men in often hilarious ways. For example, Powerful Yogurt's high-protein yogurts were marketed as "Brogurt." Granola bars emphasized their protein content to draw men, whose body image issues are more likely to involve seeming strong and muscular over being thin.

Those who studied buying trends (instead of hopping on bandwagons!) had a few surprising revelations, however. Julie Murphy of Midan Marketing told *Quartz*, "Men are from Mars and women are from Venus, right? We thought [differences in shopping habits] were going to be earth-shattering, and there would be so many differences between genders. But we found they're very alike." It turns out that, when buying food, men and women are more similar than not, no matter how items are marketed to them. Could it be that we're overthinking gender differences?

Maybe not. In his self-help book *Gunn's Golden Rules: Little Lessons for Making It Work*, fashion consultant Tim Gunn said, "I have heard women complain about men holding doors for them, as if it is inherently offensive and implies that they are weak." He's far from the first to trot out this familiar antifeminist observation; on the contrary, it's one of the most common criticisms made of feminists. Does it have any grounding in actual human interactions, though?

The Miller-McCune Center for Research, Media and Public Policy covered a 2014 study by psychologists Megan McCarty and Janice Kelly, researchers at Purdue University, who decided to see what effect, if any, a held-open door had on the recipient of the act of courtesy. In the experiment, they positioned a male research assistant near a bank of doors. He timed his approach to the building to match that of students, both male and female. In some cases, he would open the door for another student; in others, he would allow them to reach the door first or enter the building through an adjacent door. Once inside, another researcher asked the student questions about how he or she was feeling that day, self-esteem-wise. They quizzed 196 students in all.

The researchers discovered that women's self-esteem was unaffected by having a door held for them. Men, on the other hand, felt feminized, inferior, and dependent when the same courtesy was extended to them. Could it be that men tell the stories of feminists being offended by held-open doors because it's a projection of how they would feel in the same place?

Men need to overcome ideas that being the recipient of assistance or courtesy is a comment on our own personal abilities—and, even if it is, so what? Until we, as a society, divorce negative perceptions from femininity, we'll never be able to get past the common male fear of being perceived, in any way, of being like a woman. Men need to develop the strength not to fear weakness.

In addition to perceptions of femininity, other real-world factors can be feeding men's fears of intimacy. In the *Psychology Today* article "Fear of Intimacy in Men," psychologist Seth Meyers described male patients who want relationships but are terrified of being hurt if they allow themselves to be vulnerable. Many of these men are afraid because of their own parents' histories of divorce.

Divorce rates are one of the mixed blessings of the 1960s women's movement. In past eras, women had little choice but to stay in unhappy or even abusive relationships. As divorce laws were liberalized and women gained a foothold in the workplace, divorce became more common. Marriages didn't magically become less stable—wives and husbands became more able to free themselves from the ones that weren't working.

This freedom, however, came at a steep price. As divorce rates grew, more children saw their parents split, often acrimoniously, from each other. Mothers, the most common custodial parents, would remarry, bringing a whole new set of potential problems. As a result, fewer adult men have successful parental relationships to model their own romantic partnerships on. Dr. Meyers told *Psychology Today*, "Men who, as children, had an absent parent, a parent they lost, or a parent who abused them in any way are going to have an awfully difficult time seeking out and maintaining a healthy relationship. The wake of trauma can make romantic relationships almost unbearable and undoable if the man has not processed the trauma and worked through all the associated thoughts and feelings."

The same dynamics that made it easier for women to divorce made it easier for men not to marry. A woman pursuing an education and a career is not holding out for marriage before agreeing to a sexual relationship. Economic and reproductive freedom means that men can have nearly all of the benefits that were previously only available in marriage.

Despite societal changes, women still, whether through socialization or some other force, ultimately crave marriage. The boyfriend of a decade who doesn't want to tie the knot becomes less attractive over time. Additionally, women now tend to be more purposeful, while many men appear, without the driving forces of family that would have moved them in the past, stuck in a permanent adolescence.

CHAPTER 11

HETEROSEXUAL WOMEN AND GAY MEN: THE NEW RELATIONSHIP

As women become progressively more disenchanted by the pool of available straight men, they are turning not only to female relationships but also to stronger friendships with gay men. A gay man and a straight woman exchanging love advice has become a media institution in the United States: *Will & Grace*, *Sex and the City*, and the reality program *Girls Who Like Boys Who Like Boys* have all explored the topic.

Researchers have found quantitative data and a theoretical evolutionary reason behind the alliance. According to Texas Christian University's Eric Russell and colleagues, the trend may be rooted in the lack of mating competition between gay men and straight women, making them natural allies. Russell explains that they are not vying for the same sexual partners and therefore trust each other more to give objective relationship advice.

Russell found during his research that when a group of gay male research volunteers thought that a person giving them advice was a straight woman, they valued it more than similar advice from a perceived gay or straight man or a lesbian. The same was true when a straight female thought the advice giver was a gay male: she trusted his advice more than that coming from a perceived straight man or a straight or lesbian woman.

The study also found that although men and women tend to value each other's advice equally, straight women tend to limit it to talking, whereas gay men were more likely to seek the help of straight women in finding a mate. The difference may relate to the comparatively minimal dating pool each side has available to them: only 3.5 percent of the US population self-identifies as gay, lesbian, or transgender, per a 2013 Gallup poll. It makes sense for a gay man to enlist matchmaking help from a heterosexual woman, who may have befriended other gay men.

In response to the topic's popularity, Russell began a website, Gay-Straight Relationships, posting past and current psychological research about gay male–straight female relationships. Studies included on the site have found that a friendship with a gay man gives a heterosexual woman a feeling of security and a positive, sexually desirable self-image. Women who prefer the company of gay men observe that often a heterosexual man will focus on her physical appearance rather than her personality and internal qualities, making any relationship inherently superficial and insecure. A gay man is more likely to focus on her more enduring qualities, such as her sense of humor or personal interests, since he has no instinct to date or establish a romantic relationship.

In Russell's study, gay men said that "their friendships with straight women tend to be 'meaningful' and 'deep,' whereas their platonic relationships with other gay men were described as 'shallow' and 'superficial.'" The trust that develops due to the natural lack of competitiveness allows them to more comfortably discuss a wide range of topics, from clothes, weight loss, decorating, and hairstyles, to more serious topics, such as finances and friendships. Gay men and straight women are not only aligned because of the inherent absence of sexual competition; they also benefit from their mutual experience of dating men. They can relate to the shared physical attraction to men and the frustration in handling the male psyche, helping them develop a friendship based in empathy and mutual understanding. The less complicated relationship that gay men and heterosexual women enjoy allows them to form a deeper and more trusting relationship.

No studies yet have examined lesbian–straight male relationships, but Russell and colleagues hypothesized that the relationship advice between the two groups would not be as objective or beneficial. A heterosexual man tends to have a higher sexual drive, and even in a friendship with a lesbian may be motivated by physical attraction despite her being interested only in dating women.

The complications that arise in straight female–male friendships involve a similar issue. A straight man may misinterpret a friendly social engagement, embrace, or other gesture of affection as sexual interest, even in an established platonic relationship. A heterosexual man may be hardwired to value his evolutionary drive over the professed boundaries of others. The study also found that gay men have similar concerns maintaining a nonphysical friendship with other gay men: an underlying sexual tension prevents a genuine bond from forming, and as a result the men tend to focus on discussing superficial topics. Consequently, gay men reported valuing a personal bond with a heterosexual woman more than one with another gay man.

Russell's study responded to the dearth of academic literature explaining the prevalence of gay male–straight female close friendships such as those he has noticed in his own social group. In addition to the study's modern cultural relevance, Russell's conclusions may have societal usefulness as "a bridge between the gay and straight communities." Furthermore, access to good advice is a significant factor in a person's happiness as well as an important influence in romantic partner decision making. Finding a trusted companion to whom you can dish about love can have repercussions that go beyond gossip, impacting long-term personal life outcomes.

The study has hit a nerve in the US public, which has been using the term *fag hag* to describe these women for decades. The bond between a gay man and a straight woman is unique and may reflect a social tendency to avoid risk, insecurity, and conflict. Now that research has discovered support for the behavioral pattern, it may spark a wider conversation about the gay and straight dynamic and modern problems in finding romance.

These issues are particularly relevant today, with marriages declining in success compared with years past. As the divorce rate continues to remain at about 45 percent, as reported by the *New York Times*, and the cultural acceptance of LGBT rights continues to grow, these relationships offer a window into the changing romantic climate of the United States.

TV AND MEDIA: REFLECTING CHANGE, LEADING CHANGE

CHAPTER 12

WILL & GRACE: THE TV SERIES THAT CHANGED AMERICA

Art, in its best form, allows you to experience life and ultimately changes the way you view the world. *Will & Grace* was one of those rare television shows to do just that. It was entertaining, but it did more than just amuse its viewers: it was one of the first public explorations of gay male–straight female relationships, presenting America with a completely fresh perspective.

In September of 1998, following the failure of ABC's *Ellen*, *Will & Grace* launched on NBC, the first prime-time television program to have an openly gay male lead character. The show defied expectations, running from 1998 through 2006, and was the highest-rated sitcom in America among viewers ages eighteen to forty from 2001 to 2005, according to Christopher Castiglia and Christopher Reed's book *If Memory Serves*. It opened doors and prepared America for future shows based on homosexuality, possibly because, contrary to popular belief, it wasn't about homosexuality. Instead, the show was about understanding and being able to value and appreciate one of life's greatest gifts: friendship.

While the show's premise is about two best friends—Will and Grace—one who happens to be heterosexual and one who does not, the plot continues a formulaic sitcom standard: will the odd-couple pairing eventually be consummated romantically?

Granted, the setup of Grace having her life revolve around finding the perfect man doesn't exactly flatter women. The show focused on her relationships and sexual encounters, and rarely crossed the "comfort line" people may have had in terms of delving into Will's relationships and sex life. Viewers at the time were okay with a woman having a "gay best friend," as long as they didn't have to hear too much about his personal (or sex) life. It was especially palatable if he was upper class, white, uptight, and not acting in an overtly "gay" manner that made people uncomfortable. Grace had several lovers on the show, portrayed by actors such as Harry Connick Jr., Edward Burns, and Woody Harrelson. Will had an occasional one-episode fling but was never shown in a long-term relationship, though it was mentioned in the first season that he'd previously had a seven-year relationship.

The center of comic relief was usually Jack, Will's close friend. Jack was out and proud but was so over the top that he was also fairly nonthreatening. Everything about his one-dimensional character was designed to set up the laughs. Like gay character Oscar Martinez in *The Office*, Jack is witty and sarcastic; unlike Oscar, he is a caricature, written to be the campy butt of jokes. (Oscar, on the other hand, is intelligent and a bit of a dork—and he is also a white-collar Latino.)

Jack's flamboyant, theater-loving, loudmouthed personality served another purpose by contrasting with Will's "pass-for-straight" demeanor. Will became a safer, easier-to-digest approximation of a gay man. This was in line with the new asexual but "masculine" image of gays presented in the media—an image that didn't challenge mainstream society's heteronormativity. Will has restraint and a brain; Jack is promiscuous and flighty. The dichotomy asked gay viewers, "Are you a 'Will' or a 'Jack' type of gay?"

Whether *Will & Grace* taught the uneducated public much of anything about real LGBT issues (or about nonstereotypical thought) is debatable, but one thing can't be argued: there are more gay characters on television now. *Will & Grace* earned a place in cultural history as the vehicle that brought homosexuality out of television's closet. The question now remains, Is the sheer quantity of gay characters on television somehow more important than the quality of those representations?

Joe Biden was quoted on *Meet the Press* saying that his personal belief was that *Will & Grace* had done more to advance the cause of the gay population of America than anything else. Biden's opinion aside, critics were initially dismissive of the show, some calling it a "gay *Seinfeld*" and others doubting that a program devoid of romantic chemistry between the female and male leads could possibly last. As we have seen, these critics were incorrect: *Will & Grace* went on to run a total of eight seasons and receive eighty-three Emmy nominations and sixteen Emmy Awards.

Part of the show's success was the fact that it was, in part, simply a "gay *Seinfeld*." Being gay, however, was not the central theme of the show. Although the two main characters were a gay man and his straight female friend, the show was not focused on issues related to homosexuality. Instead, it followed a standard sitcom formula while happening to have gay characters among its cast. This lack of emphasis on being gay made homosexuality less of a loaded issue and pushed it toward the background, paving the way for later shows that would introduce LGBT issues.

Many of the central conflicts in *Will & Grace* dealt with standard problems such as finding work, romance, fighting with friends, and having children. In this way, *Will & Grace* demonstrated to audiences that a show did not have to be about the homosexual community if it was to include a homosexual main character. It also showed that the concerns of the gay community—friends and family—were the same as the concerns of the straight community.

WILL & GRACE: BEFORE AND AFTER

Prior to *Will & Grace*, there were few popular gay-themed shows. The same year that *Will & Grace* launched, Ellen DeGeneres had already stirred controversy with the show *Ellen*, in which the title character (and the actress who played her) had come out as gay. Ellen's "coming out" episode garnered a huge amount of response from viewers, but the show was cancelled soon after. When Ellen Morgan first came out on the show, criticism was so intense that DeGeneres reported being followed in her car by strange men, and the show's executives had to screen calls from angry viewers.

Today, it has become far more acceptable to have gay characters on television and to avoid making homosexuality the emphasis of the show itself. Even when homosexuality is prominently featured, a program is free to cover other topics. *Six Feet Under, Glee, The New Normal, Modern Family, White Collar, Warehouse 13*, and *Orange Is the New Black* all have one or several gay main characters, but this is rarely explored as a theme of the shows. Having lead characters who are gay without their sexuality being the focus sends the message that being gay is as normal as any other random character trait, such as red hair or being left-handed.

Modern Family is a direct spiritual successor to *Will & Grace*. The show gets a lot of mileage out of humor involving the gay couple in the show but at the same time has been welcomed by viewers and has consistently achieved high ratings. As with *Will & Grace*, being gay is not the emphasis, but it does play a major part. The program has been criticized at times for not indicating any physical chemistry between the two gay leads, but it has also won many awards and seventeen Emmy nominations.

Will & Grace has also been credited with the development of *Queer as Folk, Queer Eye for the Straight Guy*, and *Boy Meets Boy*. All three of these shows gained widespread acceptance and achieved commercial success.

Queer Eye for the Straight Guy was an excellent example of a show that presented a point of view of the gay community that had previously been unexplored by the straight community. In the program, gay men completely made over a straight (and typically macho) man. While it was not a perfect representation, it still went a long way in communicating the fact that the gay community is not a threat, nor ever would be a threat, to the lifestyles of the straight community. The program garnered some criticism due to being rooted in stereotypes, but it was nevertheless extremely popular.

Six Feet Under was a unique series in that two of the characters were gay and their relationship was heavily featured despite central themes that dealt with other topics. The gay relationship was given no more or less weight than any others in the show and was framed in much the same way as them. *Six Feet Under* proved to be a crowd favorite and was not crippled or held back by the homosexual content. The show humanized its gay characters and gay relationships in a way that was extremely relatable (as well as critically acclaimed).

Another series that introduced gay themes was the legendary TV series *Thirtysomething*. In an episode in season three, artist Russell meets ad executive Peter. The two men, with a bit of prodding from mutual friends, are introduced and arrange a business meeting over dinner. Peter gives some excellent professional advice about Russell's upcoming art exhibit and shows his keen ability to read Russell through his artistic expressions. The two hit it off, and they spend the night together.

From the very beginning, Russell is trying to talk himself out of being attracted to Peter. It's not that Russell is not gay—both men are somewhat guarded yet openly homosexual. The late eighties and early nineties was the height of the HIV/AIDS epidemic, and very little was known about the disease. Everyone in the gay community knew someone who either had the AIDS virus or who had already died from it. This common thread is brought up very casually when Russell and Peter are in bed together for the first time. The casualness of their tone speaks volumes. The epidemic was a very large, very real part of their lives, and checking the obituaries for familiar names is something only two gay men could speak about in the same context as checking the sports page or the daily crossword puzzle.

Even though Russell's relationship with Peter had the dynamic of being gay—foreign to most heterosexual viewers—their relationship otherwise was very relatable. Russell's hesitance to approach Peter, for example, even with Melissa's encouragement and full support, was the same found in any new relationship. People watching could not only relate to his fear of commitment but could see a little more into the gay world because of it. His vulnerability allowed viewers to imagine what it must have been like to avoid attachment for the fear of losing yet another close friend.

Peter, in this episode, was even more apprehensive than Russell. He allowed Russell to make all the first moves, and even though he accepted each advance, it was with cautious reserve. While he admitted he was open with most people about his sexuality, which was particularly brave for that period in time, he shared Russell's fear of attachment. Seeing the two of them attracted to each other but at the same time so afraid lent an element of sadness to the storyline. Both characters were very likable, attractive, and successful people—viewers automatically wanted there to be a happy ending, such as seeing two people who should get together actually be together. The opportunity to relate to two gay men was a gift from the writers of the show to viewers that had never been given before.

As Harvey Milk, America's first openly gay politician (who was later, tragically, assassinated), said, "Every gay person must come out. As difficult as it is, you must tell your immediate family. You must tell your relatives. You must tell your friends, if indeed they are your friends. You must tell the people you work with. You must tell the people in the stores you shop in. Once they realize that we are indeed their children, that we are indeed everywhere, every myth, every lie, every innuendo will be destroyed once and for all."

Before *Will & Grace*, TV programs approached gay themes extremely cautiously. In *Three's Company*, the main character Jack has to pretend to be gay in front of their landlord in order to be allowed to live with two women. After *Will & Grace*, shows such as *Thirtysomething* brought a completely new mindset, breaking stereotypes that needed to be obliterated. Being gay was no longer going to be anyone's punch line. It was part of life, a reality that was finally coming to light after being the elephant in the room for so long. *Thirtysomething* writers did more than create gay characters for their show: they gave them a voice and made them visible. It was controversial at the time, yes, but very much appreciated by gays and straights alike who could no longer stand the injustice of homosexuals being seen as unequal.

As acceptance for homosexuality grows, it is very likely that shows will keep including gay characters more often, both in supporting and leading roles. Shows may de-emphasize the topic of homosexuality, instead focusing on the characters' personalities. Being gay will no longer have to dominate; characters will be well-rounded, complex individuals who also happen to be gay.

As gays gain more visibility and prominence in society and in media, the cultural image of the "real man" will change with it, and as a bonus, objectification of women will become less prominent. It may be political correctness or it may be a reflection of how studios perceive reality, but today, gay male characters are portrayed as more sensitive, creative, enlightened, intelligent, honest, intimate, and emotionally tuned in than straight male characters. It's ironic and controversial that the image of the ideal man currently emerging in society and in media has gay qualities. Young straight men exposed to role models of gay men who are successful with women both on TV and in life will be more likely to emulate their behavior than the less respected and less successful behaviors of the traditional misogynistic, objectifying he-man who has dominated media and society since the beginning of time.

CHAPTER 13

THE MEDIUM IS THE MAN

One thing on which we all have to agree is that the media—whether movies and film, television, radio, newspapers, magazines, the Internet, or advertising—not only wields an enormous influence on how we visualize ourselves but also on what we think about and how this applies to our gender and our lives. It is through the media that we learn about the latest political developments, economic forecasts, or medical breakthroughs. Like it or not, the media has helped shape our viewpoints on what is normal, what is probable, and what is desirable.

Mass media does not just entertain and inform people, it also communicates the stereotypes, beliefs, and values of society. Stereotypes are particularly commonplace in the media because they are easy to create and audiences respond to them. Stereotypes create assumptions and help crystallize and shape public perceptions. If Hollywood's depiction of men's roles through films and TV is any indication, men have been exposed to conflicting values and views of how society sees them from decade to decade.

Along with our superheroes and antiheroes on screen, a new version of male gender roles has emerged. These men are seen as more human and more real than characters of the past, having openly and publicly embraced their emotional sides. These male role models are very different from the male standards of the middle half of the past century. Take Tom Cruise, Brad Pitt, George Clooney, Orlando Bloom, Jude Law, Tom Hanks, Leonardo DiCaprio, and Matt Damon—not one (except perhaps Clooney) would have been accepted in the old John Wayne school of rugged leading men. Hollywood is leaning toward a "softer" side of masculinity, one that affirms sensitivity and sensuality over power, brawn, and bravado.

The final fourteen-episode arc of the legendary series *Mad Men* is destined to become a landmark season, continuing the saga depicting the progressive downfall of men (as personified by the realities outlined in this book). From father to son, there is a genetic bond among men—the DNA of detached, disconnected, self-centered behavior. The true storytelling of *Mad Men* is its brilliant portrayal of the real man of the 1960s and 1970s. Social scientists and therapists will be studying *Mad Men* for generations, and it will increasingly be recognized as one of the first of a new wave of honest storytelling about men's destructive role in relationships, told with the females' perspective at the forefront. Don Draper's second wife, Megan, rejects him and his behavior upon realizing Don's pattern of infidelity, reflecting the truths of women who have experienced male dishonesty and detachment—and every women has.

TV in the 1950s portrayed an idealized version of reality, displaying thin, beautiful women and charming, well-trimmed men. Sitcoms such as *Leave It to Beaver, The Adventures of Ozzie and Harriet,* and *Father Knows Best* were popular because male roles presented the man as "king of his castle." Until the first half of the twentieth century, we still assumed that men and women both had marriage and family on their minds as their ultimate goal. A married couple was considered the fundamental societal unit: the breadwinner and the happy homemaker, the provider and the nurturer.

Men who refused to get married were romanticized as mysterious strangers or threatening Casanovas. Women who did not marry were considered spinsters or old maids. These concepts implied that marriage would somehow limit a man, whereas it completed a woman.

Television in the 1950s defended men's leadership role in the household and the family unit. As we were watching these shows, the father, the provider, the man of the house arrived at home each evening from work, took off his suit jacket, put on that old comfortable sweater, grabbed his pipe, and dealt with the everyday problems of his growing family. The wife was delicate, soft, fully coiffed, and beautiful and went about her daily household chores in a dress and pump heels with a string of pearls around her neck. The Anderson family living in Springfield (*Father Knows Best*) and the Nelsons of Sycamore Road in Hillsdale (*The Adventures of Ozzie and Harriet*) presented the ideals of education, marriage, and family as the foundation of a productive and happy life.

In *The Honeymooners*, both Ralph Kramden and Ed Norton were laughable, lovable buffoons of husbands who had a crisis during each episode, argued with their wives, and by the end of the program had to apologize and admit that their wives were right.

The beloved sitcom *I Love Lucy* centered on the endearing characters of Lucy Ricardo and her husband, Ricky. Lucy was a naive and ambitious housewife who wanted to share the spotlight with her show-biz husband (a Cuban singer and bandleader), often dragging them both into trouble. While Ricky is often annoyed by Lucy's schemes and stubbornness, he eventually supports her. Most important, Lucy aspired to a role beyond that of loving wife, mother, and housekeeper.

Marge Simpson (*The Simpsons*) is perhaps the most iconic TV mom of the nineties and the first decade of the twenty-first century, ironically contrasting the supportive, nurturing archetype with the chaos of a moronic husband and a hell-raising son. Marge is a glimpse into what bubbles under the surface when you appear to be June Cleaver to the casual observer. June Cleaver of *Leave It to Beaver* was charming, warm, and often funny in her own right beyond playing the straight woman to her mischievous children, but as with most television mothers at the time, her primary role was to serve as a source of stability and a figure of parental authority alongside husband Ward. All the same, she would be the prototypical mother for hundreds of sitcoms to come, and the icon against which all TV mothers are compared. Though seemingly patient and tolerant without end, Marge Simpson reaches a breaking point that the TV moms of June Cleaver's day would never be allowed to reach. Whenever she has gone a little too long without all of her hard work being validated or acknowledged, Marge makes sure she is heard. A pivotal episode for Marge, and future TV moms for that matter, would be "Homer Alone," when the stress of motherhood finally sends her into an anxious breakdown on the highway, resulting in an extended stay at Rancho Relaxo.

Bewitched was perhaps the first sitcom to acknowledge just how much work goes into being a mother and how much power the matriarch of a given household really holds. That *Bewitched* was written by a staff of male writers is actually a testament to the American mother in that the best explanation they could come up with for how much a mom gets done in a day was "magic." Elizabeth Montgomery carried the show with a knowing smile and the personal strength and confidence that comes with being a several-hundred-year-old master of the dark arts.

The changes in society began to be reflected in the changing roles of men on television in the late 1960s and early 1970s. Episodic sitcom shows in the early 1960s began to pioneer the male role model as a widowed father raising children on his own. Most of these fathers had additional support from family members or hired help. The most popular show of this era, *The Andy Griffith Show*, depicted Andy Taylor as the sheriff of the small town of Mayberry, North Carolina. He has the added responsibility of raising his son, Opie, with the help of Aunt Bee, who resides in the same household. Other outstanding shows depicting the widower/father were *My Three Sons*, *Make Room for Daddy* (later renamed *The Danny Thomas Show*), *Flipper*, and *The Courtship of Eddie's Father*. *The Andy Griffith Show* was an anchor for Ted Turner when he converted his sleepy Atlanta TV station into TBS Superstation, and the series remained the network's ratings leader for years.

In the *Forbes* article "The Changing Roles of TV Dads," Dwight DeWerth-Pallmeyer, director of communications studies at Widener University in Pennsylvania, said, "We really began to see the splintered dad in the late 1960s and the 1970s." The article explains further that "after the Vietnam War and Watergate scandal, American idealism was breaking down and so were our male and father figures. Archie Bunker of *All in the Family*, as an example, was flawed and harbored bitter prejudices." According to DeWerth-Pallmeyer, these sitcoms, and the issues they addressed, presented "a very different image of the father and a greater societal disenchantment."

Valerie Reimers's article "American TV Sitcoms: The Early Years to the Present" further analyzed the character of Archie Bunker: "Unlike the cultured fathers of the earlier decades, Archie represents blue collar rather than white-collar workers. The supposed 'perfect' family of sitcoms following the upsurge of television sets in America during the 1950s and 1960s was being replaced by colorful language and outrageousness of another 'typical' family."

Encyclopaedia Britannica's Steve Allen described television in the 1990s as a "loss of shared experience." He continued, "Traditional family comedies such as *The Cosby Show, Family Ties*, and *Growing Pains* (ABC, 1985–92) remained on the air into the 1990s, while at the same time more 'realistic' shows featuring lower-middle-class families such as *Roseanne, The Simpsons* (Fox, begun 1989), *Married . . . with Children* (Fox, 1987–97), and *Grace Under Fire* (ABC, 1993–98) introduced a completely different vision of the American family." What characterizes these shows is that they feature a nuclear family but are not necessarily centered on the man of the house. The conflict in the household is resolved most often by the man learning some positive life lesson from his wife.

Pew Research Center data revealed that in 1960, close to 90 percent of all children in America lived in a two-parent household. In 2013, according to the US Census Bureau, 43 percent of US children lived in a fatherless home. In the beginning, television reflected an idealized version of how most of the population saw itself. The best living situation was a single family in a home with two parents and two or three children. Everyone was middle class, everyone was white, and everyone was certainly straight. The first hint of breaking through this shell may have been when single fathers first appeared on TV. Although shows still followed a social formula, they were different enough to break the mold and create a new character type: the single dad.

The first era of television dads in the early 1960s through the 1970s followed a similar formula. The men were family men or widowers, had solid, middle-class careers, and all found motherlike figures to care for their children so they could go out and be the traditional provider. Single dads, while groundbreaking, still had to fit in with the network norm. By the 1970s, some dads had jobs that barely paid the rent, and some weren't technically even dads at all. These scenarios were front line for television but were actually only beginning to reflect what fatherhood looked like in real life.

The 1980s and 1990s ushered in the era of the pseudodad. Network producers felt confident that middle America was loosening up its views enough to accept unconventional relationships—to an extent. There were still plenty of widowed fathers, but there were also uncles and family friends who became instant fathers through the deaths of relatives or childhood friends. These shows were almost always comedies and ushered in the era of the bumbling father with the intelligent kids.

In this television epoch, dads were seen as men without a clue, as if they'd never paid any attention to children until the day they were suddenly forced to take care of some full-time. They gave bad advice, got into tangled situations, and generally relied on the wise counsel of their small-fry relatives to save the day. They, of course, took the credit for this wisdom more often than not. The era of these TV sitcoms expresses the beginnings of the end of the age of dominant males. This period also began the time of the fantasy TV dad, both in science fiction shows and kids' cartoons. While science fiction is, by nature, cutting edge, the cartoons were groundbreaking in that single fathers were seen as a normal part of life for the first time in shows aimed at children.

Map out a broad timeline of the American sitcom dad and you go from Ozzie Nelson of *The Adventures of Ozzie and Harriet* to Peter Griffin of *Family Guy*. At a glance, that looks like a fall from grace. Comparing the image of a "real" man through pop culture is the surest way to track where we've been, where we are today, and where we are going.

Once the proud patriarch, the king of the castle, and the tent pole that sustained the entire family unit, the modern TV dad is more frequently a punching bag. Just track the devolution of today's most iconic TV dad, Homer Simpson: you have a character who began life as a lovable oaf but who has slowly become a clothesline on which the writers hang broad "dumb fat guy" jokes that could be used with a dozen other fathers on TV right now. Certainly, most Homer jokes would work for Peter Griffin, and vice versa. *The Simpsons* and *Family Guy* writers have been caught swiping gags from one another from time to time, and there was even a *Family Guy* / *The Simpsons* cross-over episode in 2014, aptly titled "The Simpsons Guy."

The issue is not so much that fathers are portrayed as big-bellied lunkheads but that throughout the history of television the portrayal of the father has generally been pretty one-note. Ozzie Nelson (*The Adventures of Ozzie and Harriet*), Ward Cleaver (*Leave It to Beaver*), and Jim Anderson (*Father Knows Best*) could have traded places with one another and the casual observer would scarcely notice the cast change. The loving-yet-stern, strict-yet-warm patriarch was nearly the only portrayal you'd see of TV dads between the 1950s and early 1960s.

Examining the individual males that make up the long family tree of men on television, it's clear that the change is a little more nuanced than a simple devolution from Andy Griffith to Peter Griffin. Like almost every father in pop culture in the 1950s and early 1960s, the wise and understanding father on the classic show *Leave It to Beaver*, Ward Cleaver, left the day-to-day running of the household to his wife, June. When it came to the important decisions about life and behavior though, Ward was always there to guide his sons Wally and Beaver. He indulged his sons' antics, understood the challenges they faced getting through their problems, and always had the correct advice to get either of them out of trouble.

Ward Cleaver is perhaps more iconic than Ozzie Nelson simply because *Leave It to Beaver* has had a longer shelf life, airing on television for generations who grew up well after the final episode had premiered. However, without Ozzie Nelson, there would likely have been no Ward Cleaver. Ozzie Nelson was essentially a broad, archetypal, perfect father. The image was so iconic, so neatly trimmed, that even the real life Ozzie Nelson couldn't live up to the standards set by his television alter ego. The warm, understanding Ozzie Nelson of TV and radio was in contrast to the strict and domineering off-screen Ozzie Nelson, who prevented his children from going to college in order to keep his television series running.

Some portrayals essentially paint the real-life Nelson as a dictator. In reality, he was simply a more complex person than the simplistic, two-dimensional dad he played in entertainment. For instance, much of the motivation behind bringing up his children, David and Ricky Nelson, in show business came from Ozzie's wanting to spend more time with his family. Both the idealized Ozzie and the vilified real-life Ozzie that some biographies have portrayed are simply made up. In any event, the fictional version reflected the father that many dads hoped to be, the father that many children wanted, and the father that simply couldn't exist in real life. Although TV dads have been through the wringer in recent years, it's a lot easier to live up to the example set by Homer Simpson than to the one set by Ozzie Nelson.

In *Father Knows Best*, Jim Anderson was perhaps the most idealized father ever seen on television. This classic 1950s businessman worked against type and actually enjoyed spending more time with his family than he did advancing his career. His sense of humor was evident, and he indulged his children in ways that even frustrated his wife at times. Anderson was the good example that all children need, taken to extreme heights. He gives up an important Chamber of Commerce meeting to go see his daughter's school program, he takes his wife on a second honeymoon and can't enjoy himself because he's worried about his kids, and he even delivers newspapers in the rain to spare his son. Jim Anderson is the dad everyone wanted and that every television father is held up against.

There may have been single fathers on television before *The Andy Griffith Show*, but as far as the genre goes, they may as well not have bothered. Andy was an überfather, wise and kind and never losing his temper. The show was all formula, all the time, giving us a comfortable tale each week while never much upsetting the social norms. Andy Taylor was the sheriff of Mayberry and a widower with one son, Opie, played by Ron Howard. The stand-in mom for Opie was Andy's matronly sister-in-law, Aunt Bee. In each episode, Andy gives Opie a piece of wise advice about life, Opie gets into trouble using his interpretation of the advice, and Andy calmly sits down with his son and has a heart-to-heart talk about doing the right thing. This gentle show was hardly groundbreaking, but it was a comfortable way to spend some time with the family. Andy Taylor reflected a lot of what society at the time thought of as great fatherly characteristics. Men weren't generally expected to raise children on their own, then. When they were forced into being single parents, they inevitably relied on mother figures to help with the children and to give a softer side to their naturally gruff exteriors. TV fathers in the 1960s gave knowing advice and guided their children onto the correct path in life, but they left the hands-on loving to their female counterpart, except maybe for one manly hug at the end of the show.

Throughout the history of the television sitcom, the stereotypical dumb man has been a staple. On *The Honeymooners*, Ed Norton is the original dimwit, playing against the blustering Ralph Kramden. Although best of friends most of the time, Ed often angers Ralph with his goofy antics and ends up getting thrown out of the apartment. When the two come up with unlikely schemes, it always seems to be Ed who messes up with comedic results. Beloved by most of the television-watching public in his day, Ed Norton is universally viewed as one of the best comedic sidekicks of all time.

Of all the brainless comedies in the 1960s (and there were many of them), the best example featuring an airheaded male character may be *Gilligan's Island*. Gilligan is the idiotic man-child who ruins every attempt to escape from the deserted island through bad choices, misguided attempts to help, or out-and-out clumsiness. Gilligan doesn't have a mean bone in his body, but it's guaranteed that everything he touches will end badly. At the same time, fans of the show argue that he's the bond that holds the castaways together.

Archie Bunker (*All in the Family*) shifted the dumb guy narrative from slapstick to mean spirited while staying in the sitcom genre. Rude, racist, sexist, insecure, and ignorant, Bunker was the bigot we somehow managed to love. At the same time as he lampooned their obstinate attitudes on feminism, civil rights, and progressivism, Bunker gave a voice to many embittered, undereducated members of the working class who often felt they were being devalued and left behind by a quickly changing culture. During times of change, such as the 1960s and 1970s, it becomes very easy to vilify and dehumanize those who disagree with the progressive movement on a political level. *All in the Family* helped humanize a group of people that young Americans had come to regard as "the bad guy," while at the same time ridiculing their basic inhumanity and destructive bigotry.

The imbecile character evolved a bit further when *Married ... with Children* came along, in which Al Bundy (played by Ed O'Neill, who would later star in *Modern Family*) added a sense of anger and irony to the hopeless situations he found himself in. All he wanted from his life was to watch television, drink beer, and not be bothered by his wife and children. He didn't particularly like any of them, but he showed his love in the end. In the meantime, his life choices left him as a shoe salesman with no chance of advancement and two out-of-control teenaged children. The series gained a reputation for the then-fledgling Fox TV network for its willingness to tackle controversial and nontraditional topics. Although Bundy was frequently portrayed as wrong in his ignorant, insecure leadership of his family of disrespectful children and a lazy wife, American fathers at the time found something real and relatable in the character. In the progressive early 1990s, many men felt that it had become unfashionable to be a hardworking, straight, white male, and though he spoofed their insecurity, Bundy nevertheless became something of an icon for a demographic that was starting to feel as marginalized as others have been made to feel by American television for a long time.

Although Danny Tanner may have been the official dad of *Full House*, this home of little girls was packed with inept and bumbling male adult role models. Uncle Jesse with his rocker personality and sportscaster Uncle Joey added to the mayhem caused by having a preteen, a tween, and a toddler running around, all looking for a stable adult in their world. This was very much a formula comedy, and Tanner was a throwback to an earlier time. He tried to be the wise father figure, but often his intelligent children got into situations that stymied him. The other two men in the house were no better, often causing more trouble than what they were trying to prevent. Danny Tanner was a somewhat gentler return to classic-television-era fathers, an Ozzie Nelson for a jaded world. For obvious and not so obvious reasons, *Full House* earned as much scorn as praise from viewers who were split on whether to enjoy the simple escapism of the show's sweet, inviting world or to laugh it off as unrealistic and hopelessly naive. Played by foul-mouthed comedian Bob Saget, father Danny Tanner was unbelievably sweet and understanding, perhaps even by *Ozzie and Harriet* standards. Even the lyrics of the theme song underline the show's nostalgic outlook on the golden age of the sitcom: "Whatever happened to predictability? The milkman, the paperboy, evening TV."

The most iconic TV father in recent memory—and perhaps the defining TV character of the 1990s—Homer Simpson (*The Simpsons*), has changed as a character from season to season. The crudely drawn father of *The Tracey Ullman Show* shorts in the late 1980s was essentially a loud, brutish bully who represented little more than childhood fear of one's father. When the half hour series debuted on Fox, we saw a remarkably nuanced and loving portrait of the American father.

Americans who did not watch *The Tracey Ullman Show* first met the Simpson clan by way of a Christmas special in 1989, wherein Bart gets a botched tattoo at the shopping mall, forcing Marge to use all of the Christmas gift money to have the tattoo removed. Although the show could focus a little heavily on Bart's antics in early seasons, this first episode dealt with some surprisingly adult material, with Homer desperate not to let his family down for the holidays.

This version of Homer bears little resemblance to the Homer of the 2010s. Season one Homer Simpson didn't hesitate to take a humiliating job as a mall Santa to buy his family gifts. He thought nothing of sneaking onto a farm and stealing a Christmas tree when he couldn't afford one (he explained away the birdhouse, with a real bird in it, as an ornament). This Homer Simpson was oafish, slovenly, and not that bright, but he never thought twice about making the sacrifices necessary to provide for his family. Ironically, he may have been TV's most human and real portrayal of the American father, struggling to support his loved ones with his limited skill set. Eventually, Homer would become, well, a cartoon character. Is he still funny? Sure. But Homer J.

Simpson is no longer a source of inspiration for the modern father, and he hasn't reflected the heroism that goes into parenting for a long time.

At first glance, Peter Griffin is a terrible father. In truth, *Family Guy* is such a surreal show as to border on the abstract. Peter is not so much a bad father as he is a Salvador Dali-esque portrait of a father who appeals most to a generation where nearly half of all children grew up in a fatherless household. Nobody's taking Peter seriously as a role model or as a father figure. This is, in part, what makes him so fascinating and lets us know exactly where we stand in regard to the portrayal of the father in popular media right now. There still aren't a lot of shows in which the father simply isn't there. If TV were a true reflection of American society, 43 percent of sitcoms would take place in a fatherless household. However, once you throw out the father, you throw out many sitcom tropes, and *Family Guy* is built on parodying such clichés. So, the next best thing to an absentee dad is one who is so absurd and otherworldly in his behavior that he may as well be absentee because everything he does is too wacky to take seriously.

The counterpoint to TV's dumb guy is the womanizer. As in advertising, in which the idiot or the misogynist dominates, TV series seem to gravitate naturally to similar male characteristics. *Family Guy* may be a cartoon, but it's definitely one that's aimed at the adult population. Griffin's neighbor and friend Quagmire is the over-the-top version of every womanizer television has to offer. He has a job that jets him around the world (airline pilot), and his life revolves around only one thing: sex. Every statement out of his mouth is a double entendre, almost as if he never got past the age of thirteen. His living room turns into a love nest at the touch of a button, and he has no morals to guide who he will or will not try to sleep with. He's slept with his neighbor's wife and even tried to bed Peter's daughter, Meg, once she turned eighteen and legal. As long as the person is female, Quagmire will try to add her to his long list of conquests.

In AMC's *Mad Men*, Don Draper is the quintessential womanizer. He's slick, he's well-off, he has few morals, and he's charming when trying to attract a woman. In early seasons, the ad executive spends seemingly half his life sneaking away from his suburban family to have one of his many affairs. He's slept with clients, his daughter's elementary school teacher, pot-smoking hippies, random businesswomen, and models he's come across during his business dealings. In later seasons, he beds his neighbor's wife and struggles when she breaks it off with him, as he progressively confronts his pattern of lies and denial and his destructive lifestyle. Don is a multilayered character, but every layer just reveals more secrets. His infidelity leads to two divorces, the disillusionment of his teenaged daughter, and ultimate self-awareness. Perhaps no series in history has so accurately captured the rise and fall of the American male from heroic role model to last-of-a-breed loser.

To a young man growing up today, fatherhood as presented on TV appears to be a thankless job. Tony Soprano of *The Sopranos* and Walter White of *Breaking Bad* are contrasted with wives who only want what's best for their families, just as Marge Simpson and Lois Griffin provide stability to counterbalance their husbands' chaotic personalities. An argument could be made that television simply isn't making an effort to commend men's devotion to their families because it's less commercial and more difficult to generate ratings with flawed yet devoted family men. Ray Donovan (of the show of the same name) and Frank Gallagher (*Shameless*) on Showtime are more compelling than most of the male TV characters who have been introduced in a plethora of recent failed sitcoms and dramas about men taking back their manhood.

Bob Belcher of *Bob's Burgers* is a father who shares family leadership with his wife and allows his children to be as strange as they please, but as far as being influential goes, it remains to be seen whether or not other producers will take the baton and run with it. *Modern Family*, too, offers an admirable patriarch in Ed O'Neill's Jay Pritchett, who is both a grandfather and a father to an infant at the time of the show's first episode and the polar opposite of O'Neill's former character Al Bundy. Unique in showing a father who has more than twenty years of parenting behind him from the very start, again, time will tell if *Modern Family* marks a trend away from negative, unflattering portrayals of father figures on television along with its landmark portrayal of a gay married couple.

CHAPTER 14

NERDS AND GEEKS: THE NEW "REAL MEN"

The TV male was once an admired man-about-town, smooth and suave with a James Bond–type of mystery, using women as decorative objects and discounting their emotions and worth. Today, all too many TV males are either defined by their traditional "macho" qualities or are looked down on by audiences because they are portrayed as being unsympathetic or villains instead of heroes.

An alternative male role model that has emerged on the TV landscape recently is the more appealing, sensitive, and modern nerd who has ironically evolved into the image of a twenty-first century "real man." It's become cool to be a geek. Society and popular culture have long portrayed thin, shy, and intelligent men as dorks and made them the object of ridicule and scorn. Movies and TV have done a lot in reinforcing the archetypes of the Mad Scientist, the Weak Coward, the Guy Who Will Never Get a Girl, and the Clumsy Guy. They're often played as comic relief and make good sidekicks, but they're never the hero. Clark Kent and Peter Parker are heroes camouflaged as nerds, but now nerds are coming out of hiding and becoming the symbols of the new real man.

Suddenly, men who used to be objects of contempt are the heroes, not only in pop culture but in real life as well. The media holds a mirror up to society, and when the old-style geeks started emerging as successful men, they began to be represented that way on the big and small screens, too. Nerds of all types are enjoying a renaissance today, armed with the knowledge that they can solve problems that brute strength can't. Society has changed, and the problems we face have, too. When it comes to intelligence, innovation, and coming up with solutions out of the box, geeks and nerds rule, hands down. Once shown as weak, ineffective, and never attractive to women, they may now come closest to actually portraying a real man with whom women can relate and connect not only emotionally but romantically.

The TV series that has done the most to catapult nerds into pop culture's mainstream is CBS's *The Big Bang Theory*. What's different about the four main characters from leads in other shows is that they've all turned what made them outcasts in high school into advanced degrees and university jobs as cutting-edge scientists. They are well respected in their fields, but at the same time their essential nerdiness has never gone away. The men have a hard time talking to women, they collect super hero action figures and science fiction merchandise, and they spend their time playing obscure card games. Every self-professed geek can probably relate to at least one of these characters, from the immigrant to the socially awkward beanpole with Asperger's, and they fill every major nerd archetype known today.

The brainiac has done a complete turn-around on television in the past fifty years, reflecting their role reversal in general society. The impact of technology, and especially the computer revolution, has shown the value of intelligent men and their contributions. Today's nerd may be socially awkward, but he's also a highly esteemed member of society, functioning at his job and often making much more money than the average person. We recognize his odd quirks, but they're more often seen as charming instead of laughable. There are more of these men on television now than ever before, and they're played as regular people and not just for comedic effect.

Gamers were once looked down on as antisocial geeks who only interacted with others like themselves in basements and back rooms.

The popular conception of one is of a person who spends his life reading about dragons, rolling oddly shaped dice, and arguing cryptic rules about elves and dwarves. They are seen as a bit obsessive compulsive, interested only in their games to the exclusion of every other subject. These same men came into their own once the computer age began. With online gaming gaining acceptance with a widespread audience, the people who wrote these games became celebrities, sought after at conventions and on talk shows.

The first and best known of the game geniuses, Gary Gygax, wrote intricate war games in the 1960s and early 1970s. In 1973, he and a partner created Tactical Studies Rules (now TSR, Inc.), the role-playing game company. Gygax introduced Dungeons & Dragons at a science fiction convention later that year, and it was an instant underground hit. TSR manufactured games, dice, and module packs, setting off a worldwide craze for tabletop role-playing games. Gygax's Advanced Dungeons & Dragons set the standard for the gaming industry. The concept of Dungeons & Dragons is the basis for popular games today such as World of Warcraft, for characters like Lara Croft, and for the multibillion-dollar online gaming industry. This pioneer of simple cardboard games set the stage for numerous inventors to become wealthy and admired in today's society.

Few men embody the classic view of the late-twentieth-century nerd like the computer geek. Often ridiculed as weird and different, the truth is that most of them really didn't care. They were too busy creating an entirely new way to change the world and find stardom. Bill Gates not only founded Microsoft but also funds charitable organizations that are making a difference. Mark Zuckerberg was a Harvard undergrad who created a revolutionary website that eventually morphed into Facebook. His savvy knowledge of Internet workings and willingness to use hacking methods to benefit his site have made him a global powerhouse who has changed the way people communicate and connect.

Society has changed, and perceptions of what constitutes a real man have changed along with it. Popular culture has followed, highlighting more men with brains and fewer with simple brawn. With the three dominant TV role models (dumb, womanizing, and nerdy) surrounded by the likes of the lying and cheating Tony Soprano, the überviolent Jack Bauer of *24*, and the guidos of *Jersey Shore*, what's a woman to do? The time is right for more positive, progressive portrayals of the American man. There's simply no way of knowing yet whether Bob Belcher of *Bob's Burgers* and Jay Pritchett of *Modern Family* mark a new trend or if they are merely speed bumps on the way toward a television landscape with very few admirable male role models.

CHAPTER 15

NEWS ANCHORS REFLECTING SOCIETAL SHIFTS

Probably the most reliable male role models on TV over the past several decades have been newsmen, with Jon Stewart best embodying the legacy of Edward R. Murrow and Walter Cronkite, as a man both men and women can trust and respect. In contrast to the stoicism of yesterday's newsmen, *The Daily Show*'s former host Stewart ushered in a new era of self-aware, comedic, and internationally minded newscasters. Whereas Murrow commanded the audience through facts, authority, and the chain-smoking masculinity of his times, Stewart attracted viewers through sharp wit, biting satire, absurdity, and compassion. As a self-described "fake news program," *The Daily Show* thrives in controversy. Stewart represented the liberal uprising of modern American males who laugh at themselves, admit their mistakes, and are not compelled to lie in order to avoid confrontation.

Comparing Stewart with Murrow shows a striking contrast between the two prominent newscasters. Murrow's authoritative, deliberate, and penetrating commentary was a means of education, reaffirmation, and sometimes even hope in very troubled times. Rising against the perils of McCarthyism (i.e., opposing subversion through widespread, baseless accusations), Murrow had to fight for truth, freedom of the press, and in many ways, even his own livelihood. Stewart, however, used the nation's problems as fodder for comedy. More men today, especially younger men, want to laugh at the world even as they understand there are problems, that life is tough, and that more often than not the odds are stacked against them.

Former *NBC Nightly News* anchor Brian Williams's career demise after being caught in a blatant lie about his coverage in hostile territory personifies the new reality being faced not only by men but by everyone. There is no privacy; deceit and denials will be uncovered, and there will be repercussions. Whether the lies are about fidelity, cheating, or facts on a resume, veracity is the surest path to successful relationships—whether they be at home, in romance, or in a career. News commentators especially are expected to be society's bastions of the truth, and should be held to a high standard. Stewart's brand of cynical and comedic journalism is empowering a new generation of commentators on the state of the world and those in it, but integrity remains a fundamental tenet of the craft.

Equally important as a role model, MSNBC news anchor Rachel Maddow also personifies a new type of cultural icon: the strong and opinionated woman. With an overtly direct demeanor founded on intelligence and an articulate, aggressive, and sweetly confrontational style, Maddow challenges traditional news standards. As the United States moved through a period of declining resistance to gay marriage, Maddow was openly out and a vocal advocate. She challenged her guests and refused to conform to expected norms of reporting style or political point of view. In that context, she is a role model not only for women but for men as well in an increasingly accepting world in which the very notion of masculinity is expanding and becoming more complex.

While the mass media play a huge role in defining and archiving past and present culture, they also create role models and characters who offer a prism through whom we can envision the future. For most of us who have grown up in the Western world, our whole lives have been defined by media. Through it—especially in television—we can look back at decades of male and female role models and society's perception of relationships. In TV and film, we see that traditional "real men" are an endangered species, with declining relevance, whereas women, always the stabilizing force, are wearing the mantle of leadership and dominance.

CHAPTER 16

TV FEMINISTS: LEADING OR FOLLOWING SOCIETY?

Television responded to the feminist movement that grew through the mid-1960s with series such as *That Girl*, an old-fashioned show about a single woman living and working in the big city with the help of her boyfriend and her father, and *The Mary Tyler Moore Show*, a new kind of sitcom about a single woman making it on her own. The famous opening title sequence for the show closes with a shot of Mary walking in her new neighborhood and cheerfully flinging her tam-o'-shanter into the air, depicting freedom from her past and a new beginning. *Entertainment Weekly* ranked the scene as the second greatest moment of 1970s television. The theme song lyrics inspired a generation of women:

> How will you make it on your own?
> This world is awfully big, girl this time you're all alone
> But it's time you started living
> It's time you let someone else do some giving

While Mary Tyler Moore and Marlo Thomas (*That Girl*) introduced working women on TV as positive, independent characters, possibly the most influential lead female character in TV history was Maude Findlay, played by Bea Arthur, who appeared as Edith Bunker's cousin on *All in the Family*. Before leading her own series (*Maude*, also created by Norman Lear), Maude was already breaking ground as an outspoken forward-thinker whose assertive approach to spreading feminist and liberal values could get her into trouble. In many ways, Maude was a sort of bizarre mirror image of Archie Bunker: an aggressive, domineering, uncompromising voice of the future rather than the past. Upper-middle-class rather than a working stiff, progressive rather than regressive, feminist rather than sexist, Maude shared with Archie an overbearing, opinionated presence and little else. For many working men, Maude was something of a refreshing admission that the left had its Archie Bunkers, too, and that some women could be as overbearing as some men.

An invigorating and groundbreaking character in more ways than one, Maude may not have been the first outspoken progressive woman to headline a TV sitcom, but where many female TV characters had merely talked about women's rights, Norman Lear's Maude stepped up the game. In one controversial storyline, Maude found herself with an unwanted pregnancy at age forty-seven, a couple months before Roe v. Wade, and underwent an abortion. Daring for 1972; daring for today.

Another breakthrough female character was the opinionated, brash, and unyielding matriarch of the Conner clan, Roseanne, played by comedian Roseanne Barr. Barr insisted on honestly portraying the life of a mom with three kids in a family that's just making ends meet in a television landscape of upper-middle-class women who managed to have three kids without losing their figures, their perfect hairdos, or their tempers. Her hands-on approach to producing the series, overseeing every script and storyline herself, was the deciding factor behind the show's brutal honesty about life for working-class families in the 1990s. *Roseanne* was also pioneering in its willingness to show us a household with a strong-willed feminist matriarch, and yet this did not take away from the strength of John Goodman's father character, Dan Conner. Dan loved, respected, and feared his wife, and earned love and respect in return from his wife and children alike. Here, in contrast to Al Bundy's feminist-phobia, we saw that feminism could mean partnership rather than subversion and that a nuclear family could be just as strong a support system whether it was a man or woman at the head of the household and whether or not the family had a lot of money to throw around.

In the more recent TV landscape, the mom who may have most closely reflected the standards set by Roseanne is Carmela Soprano (*The Sopranos*), who was the cornerstone of that family unit and offered a glimpse of what life is like for a mother whose marriage is a source of both unbelievable frustration and incredible power. Carmela is seen using her mob wife status on more than one occasion to intimidate others, and of course, she reaps the privileges of having a highly successful criminal for a husband. More than strictly a mob wife with no agency of her own, Carmela truly shines when striking out to become a real estate investor in later seasons. We see her striving for an independent financial future for herself and her children that comes with no strings attached, something that many women can relate to when seeking self-reliance after years spent in a one-sided marriage.

Actress Edie Falco shifted roles from HBO's *The Sopranos* to Showtime's *Nurse Jackie*, another TV first—a pill-popping, drug-addicted, highly competent nurse who struggles with her own infidelity, lies, cheating, and denial. Yet she remains connected and committed to her family, her work, and herself even as her addiction ultimately drowns her. *Nurse Jackie* and Falco may be considered in the sitcom category for Emmy Awards, but she reflects the tragic realities of too many men and women.

American television has, at times, been progressive, changing the culture that it represents. More often than not, as we've seen in earlier chapters, television is more reflective than avant-garde, and sometimes normalizes certain aspects of American life. We watch *The Simpsons* and say, "Maybe it's okay that my family's a little crazy." We watch *All in the Family* and find a new understanding of that uncle who's always saying offensive things. We may not approve of what he says, but Archie Bunker validated that a prejudiced human being has feelings, can be as sensitive as he is offensive, and can also be appropriately demonized for his bigotry. *The Simpsons* became the longest-running series on television, and arguably the most successful, because of the show's sense of validation: you can watch it and feel that your own rough-around-the-edges family is actually normal. The Belchers of *Bob's Burgers* reflect what many families look like today: eccentric, plucky, and just scraping by.

The de-emphasis on positive male role models and fathers in American culture has arguably been a major factor in the growing rate of fatherless households. More children are growing up in fatherless homes than ever before, parents are working longer hours, and the public schools are in dire need of a change that responds to this and embraces technology and the Internet as teaching tools. We've seen these trends reflected to an extent on *Bob's Burgers*, and it's clear that a very different type of real man is resonating with people growing up today. Television and media both lead and reflect those shifts and will continue to be a dominant influence in society and culture.

GENDER CONVERGENCE AND WOMEN'S STRUGGLES

CHAPTER 17

GENDER CONVERGENCE

Four in ten American households with children under age eighteen now include a mother who is either the sole or primary earner for her family, according to a 2013 Pew Research Center analysis of census and polling data reported in the *New York Times*. This share has quadrupled since 1960. Almost 75 percent of breadwinning women are single. Of married couples, 24 percent include a wife who earns more than her husband, versus 6 percent in 1960, states the analysis. Economic columnist David Leonhardt wrote in his chapter "Pulling Back from the Crisis" in *The Global Economic Crisis and Potential Implications for Foreign Policy and National Security* that women's average weekly pay has jumped 26 percent since 1980; during the same period, men's pay has increased just 1 percent (adjusted for inflation). Today, women in their twenties (traditional childbearing years) earn more than men of the same age in many American cities, including New York, Chicago, Boston, and Minneapolis. Citing US Census Bureau data, Saraya Roberts said in a *Daily Beast* article that "20 percent of fathers with working wives regularly care for their children (by comparison, 23 percent of marriages were found to have stay-at-home moms [in 2011], a surprisingly equivalent statistic."

In many respects, men and women traveled different roads through the twentieth century. By the end of the century, however, women were catching up economically, socially, and politically; the roads were on the inevitable verge of intersection. In a 2007 research study documented in Jeremy Adam Smith's *The Daddy Shift*, sociologists Dr. Monahan Lang and Barbara Risman conclude, "The evidence overwhelmingly shows an ongoing shift toward 'gender convergence,' that is, an increasing similarity in how men and women live and what they want from their lives."

At the beginning of the twentieth century, only one in five workers in the United States was a woman, according to data in the book *Labor's Home Front*. The Bureau of Labor Statistics reported that by 1950, women accounted for nearly one-third of workers and by the year 2000 more than 46 percent of the US workforce was made up of women. Today, the most recent Bureau of Labor Statistics data showed that more than 55 percent of US workers are female and that percentage is growing.

Women benefited from, and responded to, the quickly shifting social and economic landscape during the two world wars and the years that followed. Female workers also took advantage of the transition to the postindustrial world and a growing service economy, taking on newly emerging jobs that did not require the physical strength or present the risk associated with industrial work. Regulatory changes have led to an increase in the number of women in traditionally male strongholds, with female employees often required in federally funded projects, including construction. Most of us have noticed women in hard hats working on road crews as we pass by, and it's no longer surprising for your cable TV or telephone installer to be female.

The first wave of feminism arose during the late nineteenth century and early twentieth century and focused mainly on women's voting rights (see more in Chapter 20). Second-wave feminism came on the scene in the early 1960s. Spearheaded by Betty Freidan and her best-selling book *The Feminine Mystique*, feminists began to call for workplace equality and put issues such as birth control, abortion, sexuality, and female roles in marriage into public discussion for the first time. Friedan once famously told a New York crowd, "If divorce has increased by one thousand percent, don't blame the women's movement. Blame the obsolete sex roles on which our marriages were based," as cited in *The Ultimate Guide for Men & Women to Understand Each Other.*

Although second-wave feminism gained some momentum through the 1970s, women were still maintaining responsibility for most of the housework and child care. Men, reluctant to forego the "head of household" stature, embraced the added income their wives provided but were slow to reciprocate by contributing equally to the household upkeep.

HOLLYWOOD'S STAY-AT-HOME DADS

By the 1990s, it was not uncommon to have families that differed from the two-parent model. Today, more mothers are at work, divorce rates are higher, and multiracial couples, stepfamilies, and openly gay parents are much more prevalent. Pew Research Center data from 2013 indicated that fewer than half of all children (46 percent) live in a traditional family structure of two married heterosexual parents in their first marriage. These rapid changes have led to a restructuring of gender roles, including fathers taking on more responsibility at home and an increase in the number of stay-at-home dads.

The iconic 1983 film *Mr. Mom* put a stay-at-home dad on screen for the first time, making a man the primary homemaker and caretaker. Although it was a comedy, the movie presented the possibility for a switch in gender norms. It mimicked real life in its story about a recently laid-off man who takes over housework and child care duties while his wife returns to work. This comedy made millions laugh as actor Michael Keaton's character, Jack, struggled to take care of the house and kids, but the core of the film showed that men were serious about sharing responsibility with their wives. Although Jack was resistant and, at first, incompetent as his wife grew increasingly successful and highly skilled at her job, the film underscored the ability of men of the 1980s to build new identities as homemakers and stay-at-home dads when economic calamity struck. Rather than a traditional narrative that would ultimately return the man to his "rightful" place as the primary wage-earner and head of household and the wife to her more traditional role as stay-at-home mom, *Mr. Mom* deconstructed the expected Hollywood storyline and made the case that a modern dad could stay at home and have the opportunity to share child care and domestic duties by choice, even in good economic times.

In the 1980s and earlier, it was extremely rare for a film or TV dad to be in a primary caregiving role and equally unusual for women to be portrayed as primary wage earners. Times have changed. A *Daily Beast* article from 2012 stated that

> the Geena Davis Institute on Gender in Media released a report titled *Gender Roles & Occupations: A Look at Character Attributes and Job-Related Aspirations in Film and Television*. It found that, on film, women are almost 12 percent more likely to be depicted as caregivers, legal guardians, or parents than men. Meanwhile, 21 percent more men are depicted with jobs than women and, even when they are employed, women don't tend to be depicted in the "upper echelons of power." TV was found to be slightly less "lopsided," with only 10 percent more men depicted with jobs than women (who were also more present in "higher clout" positions than they were on the big screen). . . . [B]oth genders were equally likely to be caregivers on the small screen.

Although the study was positioned in a negative context, arguing that both TV and films are biased toward traditional male/female roles, the stats also tell a story of dramatic, and positive, changes in how gender responsibilities are portrayed today compared with in the past.

Since *Mr. Mom*, there have been many film and TV depictions of stay-at-home dads, the *Daily Beast* article continues, but most are uncomplimentary and out of touch with reality. Dr. Elwood Watson, coauthor of the 2011 book *Performing American Masculinities: The 21st-Century Man in Popular Culture*, is quoted in the article saying that most on-screen househusbands are presented as dysfunctional. "They tend to be people who lack motivation or they are emasculated or they're not the smartest men." This typical Hollywood narrative, which diminishes the value of child care and housework when men provide it but values it when done by a stay-at-home mom, needs to change if movies and TV shows are to accurately reflect societal trends.

MILLENNIAL WOMEN: DOING IT ALL

As men suddenly find their economic options limited, they have also been enjoying their first taste of "the men's movement" or "male liberation" as a sort of extension of the women's movement. Men are giving themselves permission to become more actively involved in their family lives than ever before and, to their surprise, are beginning to have society's approval for their new roles. Just as this shift allows men to explore their nurturing side, more and more women are entering the workplace and the universities—not just in the traditionally female roles of teacher or nurse, but as lawyers, doctors, scientists, executives, and almost anything else they want to be.

Millennial women grew up being told they could be strong, independent women. They were taught that they could have any professional career they set their minds to and that the glass ceiling had essentially been broken. They were told that they could have it all: a job, a family, and a social life. What many of them weren't told, however, was that there were some things they could opt out of.

When women began developing professional careers, something very interesting happened: they didn't drop their other responsibilities. Today's millennial woman is still embracing being a wife and a mother—even if she is the primary earner. Even as their male partners accept more responsibility in the home, many working wives still take on the majority of the housework and child care. *NBC News* reported that psychologists believe women assume these responsibilities even when their spouses are willing to share them due to deep-rooted notions about traditional gender roles.

As a result, women consistently report higher levels of stress in these relationships than men, according to the 2015 Stress in America survey conducted by the American Psychological Association. The segregation of duties has led to them feeling as though their work is never done. Women are finding themselves putting in eight-to-ten-hour days at their jobs and then coming home to more chores. The survey states that "the gap between men's and women's stress levels has grown, and women are not feeling any better when it comes to stress management."

It's not surprising that countries that have higher levels of gender equality claim a more equal division of household labor. In Nordic countries, the division of labor is fairly equal; in Asian countries, where gender issues have been notoriously neglected, the division of labor is worse. The 2014 Organisation for Economic Co-operation and Development employment survey relays that Asian men, particularly Korean men, are the least likely to engage in any household work. On average, Asian women do about ten times as much housework as the men—even when both parties work full-time jobs. This is leading to many women rejecting marriage entirely, choosing instead to live on their own.

Part of the problem inherent in the system is that men tend to avoid doing anything perceived as being feminine, whereas women do not avoid doing things that seem masculine. Women have picked up careers, but some men still shy away from the presumably feminine work of child-rearing, cooking, and cleaning.

A 2013 Pew Research Center analysis of the American Time Use Survey indicated that men have over forty more minutes of leisure time during their day than women, even when both are working full-time. "Most of the gap is found in front of the television set. Fathers spend 2.8 hours more each week than mothers watching TV or using other media. Fathers also spend more time playing sports or exercising than do mothers," Wendy Wang from Pew Research said.

The document suggests that the cultural norm needs to be shifted by teaching the millennial generation to have a more equitable and fair distribution of labor and to be more conscientious about cultural patterns that lead men to want more leisure time. Women, who are concerned they are already emasculating their men, take on a dis-proportionate amount of the housework and child care. The report adds that mothers are more focused on taking care of their children, enabling men to have more time on their own while the mother takes on the brunt of the child-rearing. This holds true even when the father and the mother spend similar amounts of time at work.

RISE OF THE COOKING DAD

Conversely, a new wave of men has emerged: dubbed "gastrosexuals," they are twenty-five to forty-four years old, well read, well traveled, and enjoy cooking. Although traditional factors of a man's attractiveness— physical health, personality, salary—have not diminished, a man's ability to wield a chef's knife now makes him a more suitable partner for many women. Fifty percent of women questioned in a PurAsia food survey assert that a man who can cook is more attractive; one-quarter of men surveyed replied that they use their skills with sauces and chef's knives in order to meet and impress women, reported the *Daily Mail*. The article goes on to say that one in five women under the age of thirty-five stated that their male partner makes better meals than they do. The 2015 Bureau of Labor Statistics "American Time Use Survey Summary" revealed that from 2003 to 2014, the share of men doing food preparation (and cleanup) on an average day increased from 35 percent to 43 percent.

The source of these men's inspiration? Television, according to several studies, including one by Total Greek Yoghurt. The younger generation grew up with Food Network stars and Iron Chefs. While their moms and dads were spending more time at work and less time in the kitchen, TV cooking and celebrity chefs demonstrated that cooking skills can be a masculine trait. Gordon Ramsay, Emeril Lagasse, and Bobby Flay are "manly" men who can create meals that make our mouths water (although Flay's marital travails have diminished his popularity and his brand). Shows like *Iron Chef* are male-dominated, with articulate and (usually) attractive men serving up dishes to (usually) attractive women for comments and criticism. NBCUniversal's Esquire Network has a cooking competition called *Knife Fight* in which chefs compete not only with their dishes but with words as a crowd of diners (most of them female) cheer, jeer, and egg them on.

Food Network and the Cooking Channel reported 65 percent female viewership in 2013, said *Broadcasting & Cable* magazine, matching the breakdown of which gender is now responsible for putting a meal on the table. The *Guardian* ran an article in which Nigella Lawson, food writer extraordinaire, claimed that she would be happier about men doing the cooking if it meant that they would clean up the kitchen once they had finished getting the food on the dining room table.

COPARENTING

While some economically displaced dads stay home and raise their kids as a stop-gap measure, desperately hoping to go back to work as soon as possible, other dads discover that they enjoy parenting and became adept at ignoring society's ambivalence toward this new gender role reversal. Most dads find themselves somewhere in between: enjoying the experience of bonding on a deeper level with their children but also wishing that it had been a conscious decision rather than an economic and circumstantial necessity.

This loosening of traditional gender roles not only gives both men and women newfound freedom to explore aspects of their personal and professional lives that had historically been unavailable to them, but also prepares the way for the concept of coparenting. Coparenting—defined as parents sharing substantially, although not necessarily equally, in decision making and responsibility for the physical and emotional care of their children—is now a primary expectation among engaged and newly married couples.

This newly perceived freedom to redefine gender roles, combined with an increased expectation that both parents be fully involved in their children's lives, allows couples to rewrite, if not literally reverse, the rules for mothers and fathers. Although the movement is just beginning to reach critical mass and popular acceptance, a "typical" role-rewritten couple has begun to emerge.

COUNTERINTUITIVE TRENDS

Marriages and relationships have been shaped by economic changes in society since the economic downturn at the end of the twentieth century and through the first years of the twenty-first. Men have faced increasing insecurity over lost wages, while women have gone to school, advanced in their careers, and earned more money. What began as an economically based shift in traditional career roles for men and women as individuals has evolved into a new family dynamic for couples.

Even with these new dynamics, many mothers work fewer hours and earn less than women without children. Men are not likely to give up their roles as provider either, as technology and home-based businesses allow many stay-at-home dads to continue earning income while taking care of the children.

A 2013 study, "Gender Equality and Relative Incomes Within Households," by economists at the University of Chicago Booth School of Business and the National University of Singapore analyzed the possible trends in gender identity and relative household income. In that paper, as quoted in the *New York Times*, the researchers wrote, "In looking at the distribution of married couples by income of husband versus wife, there is a sharp drop-off in the number of couples in which the wife earns more than half of the household income. This suggests that the random woman and random man are much less likely to pair off if her income exceeds his."

The study, as described in the *New York Times* article, also uncovered that "wives with a better education and stronger earning potential than their husbands were less likely to work," meaning if they had the potential to make more than their husbands, they were more likely to avoid working altogether. The *Times* revealed other striking—and seemingly counterintuitive—trends from the research:

- "Couples in which the wife earns more report less satisfaction with their marriage and higher rates of divorce."
- "When the wife brings in more money, couples often revert to more stereotypical gender roles."

- "Gender identity considerations may lead a woman who seems threatening to her husband because she earns more than he does to engage in a larger share of home production activities, particularly household chores."

THE CORPORATE IMPERATIVE

As highly educated young women move into the workforce, delay marriage, and are motivated by educational debt to succeed financially in their careers, both men and women will need to overcome societally imposed norms that threaten men and cause women to revert to a stereotypical role. The evolving realities of relationships make it impossible (or at least very difficult) to maintain the traditional male-dominant position of fiscal control. The age of the financially dominant man has passed; we are entering a new period in which women are increasingly responsible for their family's monetary well-being. Just as we are raising boys to become competent dads, girls must be prepared for the growing possibility that they will one day take financial responsibility for their partners and children.

The cultural shift toward gender equality in caregiving and breadwinning roles affects the modern workplace, which must continually adapt to accept child care as an essential and normal part of the human worker experience. This shift requires that society and businesses encourage the growth and health of families in which fathers are more prominent in their role as child caregivers. "Male professionals in part-time roles say they have few role models—and even fewer in senior leadership at their firms," reported the 2015 *Wall Street Journal* article "Dealing with the 'Daddy Track.'" The article quotes Josh Levs, author of *All In*, a book about improving father-friendly workplace policies, who points out that "the vast majority of men say they prioritize their families over work, but the workplace is itself caught in a vicious cycle. The men who do not prioritize their family are often in charge of the company." Dads need male role models who are willing to speak positively about their experiences and support child care and parenting. Community support groups and networks need to reinforce the importance of paternal leave to care for newborns and support for stay-at-home dads.

Although many couples will cling to the traditional roles of parenthood, most parents will begin sharing caregiving and money-earning responsibilities and behaviors. The number of stay-at-home dads will continue to grow, as will the number of hours that men spend taking care of their children. Economic opportunities for women are certain to grow as more women go to college, work full-time, and increase their earning power. These factors will propel momentum toward greater gender equality at home and at the workplace, even though some measure of income inequality will probably linger for years to come.

CHAPTER 18

WOMEN'S STRUGGLE FOR ASCENDANCE

Women's power is ascendant, but there are disparate perspectives on the implications of women becoming more powerful in education, the workplace, politics, society, and their own relationships. Some men and women question the increasing role of women in these fields and, as a result, some women are waiting for the other shoe to drop—for men to snatch the power back.

This colors the way some women approach interactions with men, the way they see women's issues in the political sphere, their response to sexual harassment in the workplace, their innate fear of sexual violence from strange men, and their own marriages. Women are agitated that men do not see things from a woman's point of view—and for the most part, they refuse to tolerate it anymore. They remain hopeful, however, that with their own work and dedication, they will have fulfilling relationships with men and raise sons who will mitigate the failures of previous generations.

STRUGGLES IN THE WORKPLACE

Gains in women's educational attainment often lead to significant improvement in women's experiences in the workplace, but the current dynamic between women and their employers is complicated. In a world in which women are the working majority and are equally likely to be the family provider, women expect their employers to take their needs into consideration. Unfortunately, women do not think their employers are listening. They still fear sexual harassment and its repercussions. They are angry when they find the glass ceiling is still there. On top of all this, some are pushed to the brink of fury over continued expectations that they shoulder the major burden at home as well.

Enter Sheryl Sandberg, the chief operating officer of Facebook, whose bestselling book urged women to "lean in" during the crucial early years of their careers. Sandberg argues that women should convince themselves that they can "have it all," meaning a fulfilling career, marriage, and an active family life. She puts the onus on women to make up for the failings of men—at home and in the workplace.

Many women find this expectation to be unrealistic. Anne-Marie Slaughter left a prominent career serving under Hillary Clinton in the US Department of State. When she told others of her plan to cut back, they strongly discouraged her from writing about it. In an article she wrote for the *Atlantic* in 2012, she said that many women chastised her for her perspective that women may not be able to "manage to rise up the ladder as fast as men and also have a family and an active home life (and be thin and beautiful to boot)." Women who support Sandberg's vision believe Slaughter should not have relayed how difficult it is to maintain this balance.

Finding work/life balance is incredibly difficult for both men and women who are dedicated to performing well in both spheres. A Women You Should Know feature on the Fourth Annual Women's Entrepreneurs Festival quotes Geraldine Laybourne, founder of Oxygen Media, telling a crowd, "I lived a perfectly joyous life of imbalance. And the only profession that needs balance is yoga instructor." Several mothers of young children feel that it is impossible to be a good parent and a good employee. Emma Taylor, a thirty-one-year-old science professional in Maryland, said in an interview that she believes that the changes to workplace discrimination laws are superficial, especially for mothers. She argues that businesses remain old-fashioned. "Companies still frown on the need to go to doctor's appointments or simply take breaks to express breast milk," she says.

Elizabeth Larson, a thirty-seven-year-old writer from California, agrees. "I don't see how just sucking it up is going to make a difference," she shares in an interview. "Most of the time in the workplace, women deal with older men with different attitudes. They take me seriously if it suits them."

Although 75 percent of women of the millennial generation (born from about 1980 to 2000) think there should be changes made in the workplace to achieve gender equality, only 15 percent have said that they personally faced gender discrimination in their own careers, according to a 2013 Pew Research report. Elizabeth Snyder, a twenty-six-year-old social research specialist from North Carolina, shares with us her belief that "issues tend to be less related to a person's sex, and more based on educational level." Perhaps in some circles, the threat of women taking over has led some men to pay attention.

Of course, not everyone has been listening. Sexism is still present in the twenty-first century, albeit in far more subtle forms. Women no longer need to fear losing their jobs due to pregnancy, for example, and they may be hired on their merits. Unfortunately, they continue to face types of sexism similar to those endured by their mothers and grandmothers. While sexism and sexual harassment is no longer overtly tolerated, women are still expected to accept a certain degree of unfair treatment due to their gender.

Women believe that calling attention to men's sexist behavior will have negative repercussions. They understand that they can rise to greater heights in the company than ever before, and they are afraid to jeopardize that. When Taylor encounters sexual harassment, her first instinct is to brush it off. "My response, however, is always to chuckle and make a comment back at him," she says. She, like most of her peers, is afraid to challenge those higher up on the ladder. She does not think she will get fired for speaking out, as the law has many protections now that even her mother would not have had. She fears instead that if she is not seen as a team player, she will risk future promotions and make her coworkers feel unfriendly toward her.

While some women, like Taylor, admit that they try not to make waves, others call it as they see it. Lyn White, a forty-five-year-old counselor from Virginia, claims in an interview, "I usually open my big, fat mouth and do my best to drag the ugly into the light of day." She feels that making people see where they have gone wrong sets a tone of what she is willing to accept from her colleagues. Katie Roberts, the psychology graduate student and military widow, says that women have to stop bowing down and listening to sexist comments; they must instead start presenting themselves in such a way that men will be afraid to challenge them.

MEN'S ROLE IN WOMEN'S SUCCESS

At the grassroots level, women say that progress happens through men, not women. They want men to step up and shoulder the burden of making a better work environment for everyone. Erin Moore, a thirty-six-year-old project manager from Florida, sees inclusion and exclusion happening at the same time. At her workplace, as in many others, she noticed that the business administration has made an effort to add women to higher-level positions all over the company—all except one, that is. Moore is on the board of the women's networking group that focuses on supporting women's development within the organization. "There are absolutely no men in the group," she tells us. "It seems no men want to be a part of developing women." This makes Moore angry: her company forces equality in many arenas, but men still do not show an interest in what she sees as basic human dignity. Moore claims that men's apparent inability to see women as equal makes them lesser in her eyes.

Elizabeth Larson argues in an interview that, for once in their lives, men need to follow women and be brave about challenging patriarchal norms. She says, "Real, permanent change will not happen until men recognize that they are every bit as screwed by the patriarchy as women."

In the media business, many women have quickly risen to the top, with women in senior management positions at several multibillion-dollar agencies and media companies. In most instances, men have been active advocates for advancing these women's careers. Although these dynamics may not be apparent in other industries, women are rising through the ranks in almost all leading growth industries as the glass ceiling is being shattered.

RAPE, IDIOT POLITICIANS, AND THE WAR ON WOMEN

During the divisive 2012 national election, many women, prompted by the Democratic Party, started to think of the behavior coming from their employers and politicians as a cultural war on women. The war described a number of statements and policy measures from state and federal politicians, alongside other prominent right-leaning people, that threatened women's ability to make their own decisions. The term "war on women" put Republicans on the immediate defensive.

Over time, women lost interest as the concept became almost exclusively identified with reproductive ideology and freedom. Women still feel that their views are not fully represented and that politicians do not have their best interests at heart. It has been clear that at the state and federal level, legislative bodies have made the abolishment of abortion a priority, with hundreds of new laws being voted on and many being enacted.

The way women see the war on women is largely influenced by their relationship to the issues. Rachel Pruitt, a thirty-five-year-old attorney from Florida, shares in an interview that she has a hard time taking the campaign seriously because she feels it does not apply to her. "It seems mostly about reproductive rights," she says, "and since I can't even reproduce, it means not much, honestly." This inability to reach women applies especially to the upcoming generation of women, who tend to see political issues in less abstract terms. Katrina Cook, a sixteen-year-old high school sophomore from Utah, admits in an interview that worrying about reproductive issues does not rank as a high priority for her.

The Democratic Party has cut back significantly on its use of the phrase "war on women," though the primary issues remain a concern for party leaders. The ongoing discussion regarding abortion rights and contraception, especially relating to the Supreme Court decision in favor of Hobby Lobby, continues to make women angry. They worry that the Democratic Party does not have the guts to make men (and conservative women) see these laws for what they are: a return to a time when women had no control over their lives. They believe that the only way to silence stupidity is to vote idiots out of office.

Lyn White sees these decisions setting a terrible precedent for the future. "I have been highly frustrated by the simultaneous actions of conservatives to restrict access to birth control and [their] efforts to reduce funding for welfare programs that feed and aid the poor," she says. "They bitch about welfare queens and the lazy poor who want to keep having children so they can collect more taxpayer money, but at the same time remove their ability to limit how many children they may have."

Elizabeth Larson found the Hobby Lobby decision, as well as political trends making abortion illegal, absolutely infuriating. "These acts make me want to spit nails," Larson says. "It is not enough that the Republican Party simply must nominate every moronic Tom, Dick, and Harry who has an opinion about rape. No, they have to take away every right women have to protect themselves." She hopes that these politicians will be punished for their insensitivity and intransigence (even saying she would not mind if former Congressman Todd Akin were roasted over a spit for his stupidity!).

SEX, VIOLENCE, AND DOMINANCE

Even with a rise in prominence and power in many arenas, women still feel more vulnerable. They risk attacks from friends, relatives, and strangers ranging from harassment to murder. Elliot Rodger, filled with impotent rage about his inability to induce subservience in the young women he encountered, went on a shooting spree in the community of

Isla Vista near the University of California, Santa Barbara. Seven were left dead, including Rodger, and thirteen were injured.

In the aftermath, many men sought to demonstrate that Rodger was an outlier. This angered women, who wanted men to understand that men who kill women simply because they are women do not deserve any kind of justification for their behavior. They emphasized that violence against women will not stop until men are forced to recognize their complicity in a culture that subtly condones it.

Some women perceived that Rodger, grown into a withdrawn man, sought to make a name for himself in a much bigger way. Emma Taylor, the thirty-one-year-old Maryland science professional interviewed above, expressed a perspective shared by some researchers that this was Rodger's way to find glory, saying, "I really think that society in a way glorifies the whole murder-suicide thing."

Many people, to the aggravation of women everywhere, looked for ways to blame the victims. Karen Jackson, a sixty-five-year-old retired IT professional from Utah, conveys in a conversation her traditional assessment of the attack. "I am envisioning a man who isn't very confident, asking women out of his league," she says. "Maybe they laugh after he leaves. He feels shunned." Her thinking is consistent with those who believe it's unlikely that his attack was unprovoked, and that his victims must share some portion of the blame. That attitude shows the battle that women face against men, as well as against women with more conservative viewpoints. Jackson's reasoning echoes the arguments of those who contend that a woman must somehow be responsible for being raped or molested.

These days, important national events prompt big social media campaigns, and the killing in Isla Vista is no different. Shortly after the attack, people adopted a campaign on Twitter using the hashtag #NotAllMen. The campaign hoped to gain awareness and traction for the idea that most men are not violent toward women, even as cases like Rodger's take over the national spotlight. Instead, all it did was send a message that protecting women from violence is nowhere near as important as establishing that men are not to blame for cultural misogyny.

Unsurprisingly, #NotAllMen inspired almost immediate back-lash, in the form of #YesAllWomen. This response reminded men that although most men are not responsible for attacks against women, all women have reason to fear men. Within just a few days, #YesAllWomen had over one million tweets, reported *CNN*. Each one told a story of a woman's fear of potential or actual violence from the men around her. It demonstrated women's determination to set men straight. No, women would not accept men's attempts to make it seem like mass killings by young, disturbed men are just anomalies that may be freely ignored.

Sasha Weiss, a story editor for the *New Yorker*, wrote that the campaign was absolutely necessary for men to begin to understand where women are coming from. Although Rodger's writing indicated that he had long past lost grip on reality, the argument is familiar. When women are treated as prizes to be won, men engage in violence against women, whether the women targeted are physically injured or not. As long as this behavior pattern persists, women will continue to mistrust men.

RAPE CULTURE AND SCHOOL COVER-UPS

For decades, activists have decried a culture that makes rape an apparent inevitability, filling the media with sexual violence, punishing women for behavior that inspires sexual excitement in men, giving tacit approval to men to be forceful, and discouraging rape victims from coming forward. These behaviors are the very definition of a rape culture. Young men are raised to believe that it is a woman's fault if they rape her, and they are encouraged to act out violent fantasies with a mashup of sex and violence in print media, films, video games, and everyday interactions.

The problem is reaching a fever pitch in high schools and colleges, a hotbed of adolescent and young adult sexual activity. It seems that when a school encounters illegal behavior, the administration's first goal is to keep it out of the press. The problem is all over the country, in secondary schools, colleges, and universities.

Rape is apparently so mainstream that high school faculty, administration, and students simply overlook it even as they watch it happen. The case of the Steubenville High School student who was raped by two football players and then subjected to a public smear campaign because she had the audacity to report it was bad enough. Unfortunately, in a world where adolescent boys command girls to perform oral sex on them in the nooks and crannies of the school under threat of bullying, worse things are bound to happen. *USA Today* ran an article describing an event in Salisbury, Maryland, in which a fifteen-year-old student was raped in a high school hallway while class was in session. Parents were enraged at the neglect the school showed in creating an environment where this sort of violence can happen, and many pulled their students from the school as a result.

Women now fight back with the hope that these institutions will penalize the offenders instead of their victims. In Los Angeles, rape victims sued Occidental College, a private liberal arts school, charging that the school imposed minimal punishment for a serious crime and implied that the women who filed complaints were smearing the college.

Harvard University, Swarthmore College, and Bob Jones University have faced similar charges. At Bob Jones, counselors reportedly told rape victims that they owed forgiveness to their attackers, who were not penalized. These women believe that unless the schools themselves are brought to justice for these cover-ups, they perpetuate rape culture.

HUMAN TRAFFICKING AND SEX WORK

Sexual assaults in schools are just the tip of the iceberg for young women. Commercial sex trafficking is yet another risk many girls and women face simply for being female. Prostitution, whether from commercial trafficking or not, is usually forced and always hurts women.

As people have become aware of the horrible inequalities women and children in the sex trade face, many women have worked tirelessly to change the fates of these victims. The United States has several laws against human trafficking, covering forced prostitution and forced

labor for individuals of all ages. Martina Vandenberg, the president
and founder of the Human Trafficking Pro Bono Legal Center, explains
that, unfortunately, it is extremely difficult to bring criminals to justice
because their victims are fearful of pressing charges. In an interview
with Diane Rehm of NPR, Vandenberg noted that the most disgusting
cases often involve high-ranking officials. Diplomats and their families, she said, have immunity from prosecution—and they use that
allowance to its full extent, forcing workers from their own countries
into sexual slavery.

Vandenberg's organization trains lawyers to represent clients who
are victims of trafficking and refers those victims to qualified representation. Sadly, without hope that they can win the case, most victims
choose not to file charges. In fact, only 149 cases have been filed in the
last ten years, largely because of victims' fear that publicity will lead
their captors to them or result in further suffering, reported the organization's website. Vandenberg and her group hope to dramatically
increase that number, aided by groups such as the Polaris Project and
the National Human Trafficking Hotline that discover cases of human
trafficking and free the victims.

Although many see trafficking and sex work as two different concerns, they are closely intertwined. When it comes to engaging sex
workers, some women believe that it is just something that men do
because they can. Most women no longer accept the "boys will be boys"
mentality that allowed men in the past to frequent sex workers with
impunity. Mary Williams, a forty-three-year-old mother of three who
lives in Virginia, holds no sympathy for "johns." She says in an interview,
"Anyone who picks [sex workers] up is basically committing paid rape."

Emma Taylor agrees, declaring, "The men who solicit these women
are taking advantage of people in a horrible situation." Furthermore, if
the man frequenting the sex worker is married, many women agree
that he deserves no mercy. In Sweden, the laws have been reversed,
through the legalization of prostitution but the criminalization of hiring a prostitute. The results have been stunning, with the virtual elim-
ination of prostitution and the freeing up of a court system that was
overloaded with prostitution cases. Similar role reversal laws are being
considered in several countries following Sweden's lead.

RELATIONSHIPS, FIDELITY, AND HONESTY

Mercy within the context of relationships is an enigmatic concept. Most women in happy marriages feel they must create a delicate balance between intimacy and freedom—between allowing their spouses to be who they are and cracking down on blatant disrespect. Wives expect that their husbands will be honest with them and are frustrated when they are not. Women abhor infidelity, and most believe that men who cheat deserve to be alone, if not strung up for it. Other women, though, think that relationships can transcend such transgressions; they hope to build loving relationships that will be fulfilling for the couple and provide a good model for their children.

While some women understand the function of so-called "white" lies, they almost uniformly agree that lying about an extramarital relationship is a big problem. Erin Moore says, "I think anyone who cheats is an awful person." Some are more vehement. Mary Williams believes that men who cheat "should be tied to a tree, wearing honey-coated pajamas, in a forest filled with hungry bears."

Young women generally have a black-and-white view of marital infidelity. Susan Black, a twenty-year-old restaurant server from Idaho, believes that men who are unfaithful should not be given an opportunity to explain. "I think once a cheater, always a cheater," she says in an interview. "If he is willing to go and cheat on you behind your back and then come home and sleep in the same bed as you, then he is just using you." When a woman finds herself in that situation, Black argues, she should gather all the evidence to her side, and "hit him with all of it." In her view, promiscuous men show themselves to be lesser than the woman, and the woman should make that loud and clear. "Once he has cheated," she says, "guess who wears the pants in this relationship."

As women marry and their marriages develop, however, they often take a more pragmatic approach. Emma Taylor, the Maryland science worker, says, "My gut reaction is to say all men who lie and cheat are horrible people, but I know this not to be the case."

Women who have grown up with the knowledge of cheating fathers or other male relatives live with the constant awareness that their partners could stray. "It's a fear that will never leave me," Elizabeth Snyder says, "that I will be the wife who is cheated on." Women nurture anger at unfaithful fathers long into adulthood, even as they attempt to foster good relationships with their sexual partners.

HOPES AND EXPECTATIONS IN RELATIONSHIPS

Women base a great deal of their expectations for their marriages on their relationships with their fathers, especially if that relationship was difficult. They feel honor-bound to fix potential problems in their own relationships to avoid becoming like their mothers. "They always say that girls marry their fathers," Moore says. "In this case, I married someone just like my stepfather, and that's a good thing."

Ultimately, women hope that the future of their relationships will have a strong basis in honesty. Black says the ideal partnership would involve a man who is not afraid to let her go out with her friends and who will not cheat on her. Snyder echoes the sentiment, saying, "I hope to continue having an honest relationship with my husband, in which I continue to trust him implicitly." Katie Roberts, too, believes that one day, she will find a man who will be as trustworthy, dedicated, and hardworking as her late husband.

Women also expect that their hard work will reap benefits for the next generation. "I feel like I have done a good job of navigating my own way through this man's world and done my part to make it a little more equal world," Lyn White says. "Now, it is more about what I can do to raise my sons up to be good men."

WOMEN ASCENDANT

There is no doubt that women's power is increasing. As they receive better education, assert themselves in the workplace and politics, protect themselves from sexual violence, and nurture their interpersonal relationships, women build networks that make their efforts more effective than men's. Even if they cannot see it, women shape their world today in ways that are unique and transcend tradition. Men must recognize it now, or risk being left behind.

MEN, WOMEN, AND POWER: THE NEW REALITY

CHAPTER 19

MEN ARE NOW THE UNDEREDUCATED GENDER

The one area where women can claim unparalleled gains is education. Women have made up the majority of college students since the 1970s. Decades of outnumbering men in the classroom made women smarter and more adaptable than their male counterparts. Unfortunately, not all women see this as a win for feminism, instead doubting that this trend will make men take them seriously in the workplace. Some women also worry that, years from now, ill-educated boys will become ignorant men who make the same mistakes as previous generations.

In 2012, the National Center for Education Statistics noted that women made up nearly 57 percent of fall enrollment in degree-granting postsecondary institutions. This statistic holds through graduation, as well: In the 2010–2011 school year, women obtained 57 percent of all bachelor degrees awarded. In 2016, this percentage is forecast to surpass 60 percent.

As a whole, women hail these numbers as a reflection of a positive change in education and the workplace. Lyn White, a counselor living in Virginia, sees good reason to be cautiously optimistic. She worries that women are not making gains in the science, technology, engineering, and mathematics (STEM) fields, which are in higher demand and feature better pay and job security; the vast majority of those jobs still go to men. White sees payback coming, however, for men's underperformance in higher education, saying, "It seems like it won't be too long now before more women will simply be more employable than many men."

Others see this trend as just another hurdle women have had to cross to get men to listen. Erin Moore, the project manager in Florida, believes that women still face an uphill battle when it comes to applying their degrees to their career goals. "To me, it demonstrates that women feel they need to work harder than men to make it."

Some women find this expectation exhausting. Elizabeth Larson, the writer from California, obtained a master's degree when she felt that her bachelor's was not enough to compete with men. "I'm tired of feeling like I need to use my initials so that the hiring manager cannot tell I'm a woman," she says. "I got a master's just so I wouldn't get edged out by men half as smart as I am."

Women's established dominion of college enrollment raises some alarm bells for education experts and parents alike. Educational psychologist Lori Day wrote in the *Huffington Post* that the state of boys' education in the United States has reached crisis levels. Boys create 90 percent of schools' discipline problems, are three times as likely to be medicated for attention deficit hyperactivity disorder (ADHD), and represent 80 percent of all high-school dropouts. Day notes that the educational environment is set up to reward stereotypically feminine behaviors and to punish boys for not demonstrating the same attitudes. As a result, she reasons, it is no surprise that young men are languishing in college. After all, the schools demand sensibility and focus, and boys are not rising to the challenge.

In a column entitled "Why Males Don't Go to College," gender issues expert Glenn Sacks wrote, "As the percentage of males on our college campuses continues to decline, many observers are finally beginning to ask questions. Much of the discussion has focused on the fact that boys at all levels K–12 have fallen seriously behind their female counterparts, and how our schools are not meeting boys' needs. This discussion of males' educational problems—particularly the problems of low-income and minority males—is long overdue, and boys' sagging educational performance is the main reason for the increasing disappearance of male students from our college campuses."

In 2003, in response to the growing problem of men becoming an undereducated gender, Michael Gurian of the *Washington Post* wrote, "Where men once dominated, they now make up no more than 43 percent of students at American institutions of higher learning . . . and this downward trend shows every sign of continuing unabated. If we do not reverse it soon, we will gradually diminish the male identity, and thus the productivity and the mission of the next generation of young men, and all the ones that follow."

Ten years later, the *Post's* forecast has come true. What is the new reality, and what are the implications of the trend toward men becoming the undereducated gender?

In 1960, 65.8 percent of college students were male, said the US Census Bureau's 2012 *Statistical Abstract of the United States*. Since then, the percentage of male college students has decreased; by the early 1980s, women outnumbered men in American colleges. In 1980, men represented 51.1 percent of college students. This percentage declined to 49.3 percent in 1985, 46.6 percent in 1990, 44.9 percent in 1995, and 42.6 percent in 2000. In 2009 (the last year covered by the Census Bureau's 2012 report), 41.3 percent of American graduates were male, and 58.7 percent were female. The National Center for Education Statistics forecasts that by 2020, men will represent 41.1 percent of college enrollees. Considering current trends and realities, this may be an unrealistically optimistic outlook.

Although the percentage of American men graduating college is slightly higher than it was twenty years ago, the percentage of women graduating college has exploded. The *Chronicle of Higher Education's* "Men's Share of College Enrollments" indicates that the number of women earning doctoral degrees increased 68 percent between the 1997–1998 and 2007–2008 academic years, and the number of women earning master's and professional school degrees increased 54 percent and 35 percent, respectively.

"The boys are about where they were 30 years ago, but the girls are just on a tear, doing much, much better," Tom Mortenson of the Pell

Institute for the Study of Opportunity in Higher Education told the
New York Times in its "At Colleges, Women Are Leaving Men in the
Dust" article.

The 2012 Census Bureau report also revealed the following:

- About 916,000 women and 685,000 men earned bachelor's
  degrees in 2009.
- Women have consistently surpassed men in master's degrees
  since 1986, earning about 397,000 to men's 260,000 in 2009.
- Women surpassed men in doctoral degrees earned between
  2005 and 2009, earning about 35,000 to men's 32,000 in 2009.
  (As a point of reference, men had a 2:1 advantage in 1985.)
- Men's edge in professional school degrees was 33,000 to 2,000
  in 1970; in 2009, it was 47,000 to 45,000.

In 2009–2010, women were awarded roughly 50 percent more
master's degrees than men (417,828 vs. 275,197 degrees) according to
the 2013 publication, "Gender Disparities in Educational Attainment
in the New Century," sponsored by Brown University. The numbers
were reflected among minority groups as well: 17 percent Hispanic
women versus 12 percent Hispanic men, 62 percent Asian women versus 58 percent Asian men, and for 14 percent Native American women
versus 11 percent Native American men, said the report.

"Women's growth in professional and doctoral degrees has been
slower than that for bachelor's or master's degrees, only recently
reaching parity with men. In 1970, men completed sixteen times
more professional degrees (such as medical, dentistry, or law degrees)
than women," wrote the Russell Sage Foundation in their "The Rise of
Women" article. "Since 1982, the number of professional degrees completed by men has declined slightly (from 40,229 in 1982 to 34,661 in
2010), while women's professional degree completion has increased
almost twentyfold—from 1,534 professional degrees in 1970 to 30,289
in 2010," stated the report.

The pattern for doctoral degrees is similar, according to Brown's
"Gender Disparities" study: "Men completed almost eight times as
many doctoral degrees as women in 1969–70 (58,137 doctoral degrees
to men versus 6,861 to women). By 2009–10, women received more
doctoral degrees (81,953 versus 76,605)." CCAP (the Center for College

Affordability) wrote in *Forbes* that "the female domination of higher education prevails across all types of schools." If these trends continue, the gender gap in professional and doctoral degrees may soon resemble the female-favoring gender gap in bachelor's and master's degrees.

The Organisation for Economic Co-operation and Development (OECD) stated in the 2012 Better Life Index that "on average across OECD countries, 35% of women aged 25–64 attain a tertiary education compared with 31% of men." Another OECD Better Life Index chart ("New Entrants by Sex and Age") showed the following:

- The United States had 1,695,242 female and 1,461,707 male college students in 2011.
- Twenty-two of the twenty-seven other nations had more female than male college students.
- Germany, Mexico, and Turkey had fewer than 10,000 more men than women in college.
- Korea was coming much closer to parity, while Japan remained an outlier.

The National Bureau of Economic Research report "Why Do Women Outnumber Men in College" said the percentage of college students who are male has declined in every OECD nation, concluding that "women now outnumber men in college in almost all rich nations."

The highlights of the 250-page 2012 OECD document include the following findings:

- Boys are more likely to drop out of high school than girls, "particularly in the high-income countries."
- Girls are one full year ahead of boys in reading skills by the end of high school and boys are "far less likely to spend time reading for pleasure."
- Boys are ahead of girls in math skills, but the math gap is "small" compared with the reading gap.
- Teenaged boys in rich countries are 50 percent more likely than girls to fail all three basic subjects in school: math, reading, and science.

THE MYTH OF HIGHER PAY FOR THE EDUCATED

There are many reasons why men are no longer going to college, but it appears that one of the most compelling may be that those who do are not finding themselves with significantly improved income opportunities. It has been well documented that the newest generation has crippling amounts of student debt from earning degrees that may or may not have transitioned directly into dollars earned. Women may be going to college to decrease the gender pay gap; however, postsecondary education may not be as economically beneficial for men as it is for women. The Center for American Progress, in a comprehensive report on the topic entitled "The College Conundrum," came to the conclusion that for a significant subset of the male population, a college education simply isn't worth the investment.

A study in 2009 showed that one in five men who obtain a college degree do no better than someone who obtained only a high school degree. These numbers are alarming—20 percent of men who do go through the trouble of obtaining a college degree are actually doing worse than their less-educated peers because they have also accrued student loan debt. One in seven women who obtained a college degree fell into a similar category, implying that men who get a college degree run a higher risk of not gaining anything for the value.

Evidence from a paper entitled "Gender, Debt, and Dropping Out of College" in the journal *Gender & Society* indicates that male students are far more unwilling than their female peers to take on huge amounts of student loan debt in order to graduate from college. This confirms what colleges and universities throughout the United States are discovering for themselves: it isn't just that more women than men are enrolling, more women are also continuing in school until graduation.

The *Wall Street Journal* in "Why Men Are More Likely to Drop Out" explains that men will leave school before going deep into debt because there are more and better employment opportunities for men without a college education than there are for women who don't have degrees. Men who don't have a college education may find jobs in manufacturing or construction; women who lack advanced education, on the other hand, have few opportunities beyond notoriously low-paying jobs in service industries. This is countered by the *Economist*, which declared in its 2015 cover article "The Weaker Sex" that "pay for men with only a high-school certificate fell by 21% in real terms between 1979 and 2013; for women with similar qualifications it rose by 3%."

An article that appeared in the June 28, 2013, edition of the *Los Angeles Times* explained that prospective first-time home buyers with student loan debt are discovering that their debt is preventing them from qualifying for mortgages. The total amount of unpaid student loan debt is currently in excess of $1.1 trillion. On average, recent college graduates owe $27,000 in student loan debt, but rough estimates indicate that 13 percent of students who have unpaid debt owe between $54,000 and $100,000.

The 2014 rate of default on student loans is 13.7 percent. Those who default experience a devastating blow to their credit rating, which can affect every aspect of life, including employment opportunities and the ability to rent a house or apartment. Purchasing a home will be impossible for those who default.

The One Wisconsin Institute ran a survey in 2013 and found that the average length of time it takes for a bachelor's degree holder to pay off their student loan debt is twenty-one years. For those who went to college but didn't graduate, the estimated amount of time it will take to pay it off is seventeen years; for those who received graduate degrees, the time extends to twenty-three years.

However, none of this addresses why female college graduates appear to be doing better than male grads. A *New York Times* article suggested that female graduates of college may be doing better than men simply because they are more driven to succeed. In 2006, before male college attendance became as large of an issue as it is now, the *New York Times* found that women were taking their college studies far more seriously than men. They were found to have higher grade point averages than men, and men were found to take advantage of the social aspects of the college campus in greater numbers. Professors noted that though they had good male and female students, the quality of the women was more evenly dispersed than that of the men. Female students tended to range across a spectrum of very good students to very bad students, whereas male students tended to cluster either at very high or very low on the charts with very little in-between.

Women may see greater value in a college education because of the role it plays in determining their standard of living and preventing them (and their families) from living in poverty, reported the Center for American Progress. As more lucrative job opportunities become available to women (as they have in recent decades) higher salaries that come from degree-requiring jobs not only provide women with a justifiable incentive but also motivate women to complete college. The simple reality is that women are faced with a choice between going to college and being able to get better-paying jobs or being stuck forever in lower-paying jobs that don't require an advanced education.

WOMEN: THE NEW EDUCATED GENDER

There are now one million more female than male college graduates nationwide. As recently as 2000, those numbers were reversed, according to *Advertising Age*'s coverage of the US Census Bureau's American Community Survey. This trend is likely to continue for several reasons:

- **Laws:** The United States legal system has made strides in passing laws that ensure fair treatment of women in education and in the workplace. These laws have permitted women to pursue additional career and educational options previously unavailable to them.
- **Changing the stigma:** Career options for women have expanded from what was traditionally available. Women are now leading Fortune 500 companies and serving in key executive and management roles. In addition, home and family responsibilities are becoming more equally distributed among male and female partners, leveling the playing field when it comes to balancing work and home life.
- **Acceptance:** Women are seen in a different light in society than in previous generations. Society has cultivated a greater acceptance of business-minded women and made it permissible for women to seek and succeed in a career.

- **Title IX:** The educational playing field changed forever with one piece of legislation. When the US Congress passed Title IX as part of the Educational Amendments of 1972, it opened the door for women to gain unprecedented access to higher education. The amendment prohibited universities and colleges from allowing gender-based discrimination, including sexual harassment, failure to provide equal opportunity in athletics, and discrimination based on pregnancy, in any academic or athletic program receiving federal financial assistance. Applying Title IX to higher education produced a steady stream of changes throughout the remainder of the twentieth century. Many universities and colleges worked feverishly to become compliant with these new standards to avoid the risk of losing federal funding. Title IX has made a profound impact in both academics and athletics in the decades since it was first passed. Colleges and universities could no longer refuse to admit female students or expel them if they became pregnant. Additionally, they could no longer restrict female students to courses and degrees that corresponded with traditional female occupations.

CHAPTER 20

POLITICS AND THE SLOWLY SHIFTING SANDS OF TIME

We are coming down from our pedestal and up from the laundry room. We want an equal share in government and we mean to get it.

A woman's place is in the House—the House of Representatives.

—Bella Abzug

"Battling Bella" Abzug, the speaker of the words above, was a lawyer, a social activist, and one of the first women to serve in the US House of Representatives. When Abzug was elected in 1970 as a representative from New York City, she joined a very exclusive club: just two other women were in the House, and one woman was serving in the Senate. Low as those numbers were, they were record-breaking at the time.

You might believe that things have changed for the better. After all, in the 2000s alone, we've seen a woman serve as majority and minority leader in the House, as a vice-presidential candidate, as a viable presidential candidate, as secretary of state, and we may even see one as president of the United States. (As this book is being written, Hillary Clinton leads all polls in her campaign.) Despite these advances, Bella's battle rages on today. There may be a record number of women serving in the Congress, but women are still woefully underrepresented in all branches of state and federal government.

Though women constitute a majority of the population—50.8 percent women to 49.2 percent men according to 2010 census data—you certainly wouldn't know it when looking at the past and present state of US politics. Until the late 1970s, women were almost completely excluded from major elected seats across the branches of US government; even today, men still hold more than 81 percent of the seats in Congress.

That's not even the full picture. Add a healthy dose of sexism, misogyny, bias, and disinformation into the mix, and you have the US political system. From "legitimate rape" to "preordained rape" and from furor over hairstyles to slut-shaming, all you have to do is turn on the TV or go online to witness evidence of the war on women. Whether it's political marginalization through exclusion from leadership, media coverage that focuses on female politicians' fashion choices instead of their platforms, political pundits who propagate sexist—or even downright misogynist—paradigms, or politicians who spout unscientific nonsense in an attempt to control women's reproductive choices, women's involvement in US politics has been characterized by marginalization, opposition . . . and tenacity.

Given that the American political system is, theoretically speaking, a representational democracy, why are women so underrepresented in the US political arena? The answers, as always, lie in the past.

For many years, women's involvement in the US political arena was limited to behind-the-scenes support of a husband or other family member. The first president, George Washington, was greatly helped in his political career by the family wealth and connections of his wife, Martha.

A century later, the fight for women's right to vote officially began at the Seneca Falls Convention of 1848, where early suffragettes such as

Elizabeth Cady Stanton, Susan B. Anthony, and Lucretia Mott helped draft the *Declaration of Sentiments and Resolutions*, a list of resolutions that included the following:

- That all laws which prevent woman from occupying such a station in society as her conscience shall dictate, or which place her in a position inferior to that of man, are contrary to the great precept of nature, and therefore of no force or authority.
- That it is the duty of the women of this country to secure to themselves their sacred right to the elective franchise.
- That, being invested by the Creator with the same capabilities, and the same consciousness of responsibility for their exercise, it is demonstrably the right and duty of woman, equally with man, to promote every righteous cause, by every righteous means; and especially in regard to the great subjects of morals and religion, it is self-evidently her right to participate with her brother in teaching them, both in private and in public, by writing and by speaking, by any instrumentalities proper to be used, and in any assemblies proper to be held.

Needless to say, the powers that be didn't take these demands too seriously. Regardless, the never-cowed Stanton ran for a House seat as an independent in 1866, receiving only 24 of 12,000 votes. Despite her resounding defeat at the polls, Stanton's action set a precedent. Over the next ten years, two women attempted a run for president, both as members of the Equal Rights Party. In 1887, in the town of Argonia, Kansas, the men of the town elected a woman mayor—the first in the country. Seven years later, Colorado men elected three women into the state House of Representatives.

More women followed at the state level in Utah, and in 1900, the first female delegates went to Washington, DC, to attend national party conventions. In 1917, the federal barrier was further broken when Jeannette Rankin of Montana was elected to the US House of Representatives. Rankin served until 1919; notably, she was the only member of Congress to vote against United States entry into World War I.

With the ratification of the Nineteenth Amendment in 1920, women were finally granted the right to vote, and the League of Women

Voters was founded to encourage women's political participation. In 1922, another glass ceiling was cracked when Rebecca Latimer Felton was sworn in as the first female US senator, following the death of the previous officeholder. However, she only served for twenty-four hours before another (male) senator was elected. In 1993, Congress (finally!) added bathroom facilities for women. In 2013, for the first time, a state—New Hampshire—was represented by an all-female delegation.

When looking at an overview of women's political progress over the past decades, it's easy to conclude that gains have been made. From the late 1970s through the 1990s, the number of women seeking—and attaining—political office increased steeply. In contrast, though, the twenty-first century hasn't measured up. In fact, the 2010 congressional election cycle resulted in the first net *decrease* of female representatives since 1978! Furthermore, when the 113th Congress convened in 2013, less than 19 percent of its members were women.

If you're a man, you might not understand the impact of those numbers. To get a better idea of it, imagine for a minute that every single one of your political representatives—from state senators to members of Congress to the president of the United States—is female. Does this make you feel as if your elected officials adequately represent you? Now imagine that 20 percent of those women were replaced by men. Now do you feel adequately represented?

For many women and men living in the United States today, that 20 percent just doesn't seem adequate. The problem is widespread; no class of elected positions in any branch of the federal government is filled by more than 20 percent women. While state governments are slightly more equitable, the overall percentage of elected female officers at the state level is still less than 25 percent as of 2013, according to the National Women's Political Caucus.

The inequality problem in the United States is even more glaring when compared with the rest of the world. The Inter-Parliamentary Union's 2013 statistics on the percentage of women serving in national parliaments ranked the United States seventy-seventh in the world, below countries such as Rwanda, Cuba, Nicaragua, Uganda, Angola, Kazakhstan, China, and South Sudan, not to mention every Western European country with the exception of Ireland. (But Ireland gets deserved recognition as the first nation to legalize gay marriage.) Even Afghanistan and Saudi Arabia, nations not known for their forward-thinking policies on gender equality, soundly beat the United States in percentage of women serving in higher office, ranking at thirty-sixth and sixty-seventh, respectively. However sobering these statistics may be, though, they still represent a vast improvement over the past.

FEMALE POLITICIANS IN THE MEDIA

Ironically, for a segment of the population that's chronically underrepresented in the political process, women certainly aren't underrepresented in media coverage of politics. Why is this, and what effect does the media have on women's political participation and representation? As it turns out, the media's impact is large—and biased.

Media coverage emphasizing superficial characteristics of female candidates—such as hairstyles, clothing choices, and weight—both contributes to a reduction in women's political participation and influences election results. Although a focus on personal traits has little to no effect on male candidates, emphasis on female candidates' appearance always results in detrimental effects. Consider the uproar over vice-presidential candidate Sarah Palin's wardrobe during the 2008 elections or the kerfuffle over then-Senator Hillary Clinton's cleavage during a Senate hearing on education. (Of course, women weren't even allowed to wear pants on the Senate floor until the 1990s, so perhaps the wardrobe fixation isn't so surprising!)

A 2013 study from political advocacy organization Name It. Change It. found that neutral, positive, and negative descriptions of a female candidate's appearance *all* had detrimental effects on voters' perception of her favorability and likability and significantly decreased their likelihood of voting for her. Even complimentary descriptions harmed female candidates because voters were much less likely to view them as in touch, qualified, confident, likable, or effective. Only when the candidate directly addressed the media coverage—such as by stating that appearance or fashion choices are irrelevant to the race—was she able to regain any lost ground.

No matter how professionally our female politicians present themselves, the media gets all hot and bothered every time Clinton changes her hairstyle; apparently, her tresses have their own Twitter account. An op-ed by Maureen Dowd breathlessly described Clinton's latest 'do as "shimmering," "sleek," "glamorous," and lending her the "air of a K.G.B. villainess in a Bond movie"—and also mentioned the potential presidential candidate's clothing choices (hot pink jacket). The press was similarly obsessed with right-wing senator Michele Bachmann's evolving ($4,000 plus) hairdos.

In contrast, this sort of coverage doesn't affect male candidates. With a few exceptions—the mini-scandal surrounding vice-presidential-hopeful John Edwards's überexpensive haircuts, then-candidate Obama's choice to not wear an American flag lapel pin, and snarky jabs at New Jersey governor Chris Christie's weight—media coverage of male politicians doesn't have the same focus.

In fact, studies indicate that not only does media coverage focus on irrelevant personal traits such as appearance, it also tends to hold female politicians responsible for the actions of their husbands and children in a way that it does not do for male candidates—think Hillary Clinton and her husband (and former president) Bill. In addition, the media often spotlights female candidates' home lives, such as marital status and children, in a way that plays on stereotypical gender biases and affects voter perception. It's safe to say that no male politician has ever been asked to enter into a cookie recipe contest, as Hillary Clinton and former First Lady Barbara Bush were in a 1992 edition of *Family Circle* magazine. Twenty years later, the First Lady cookie bake-off continues to be a "political pacesetter," as the magazine puts it, firmly putting women in their place: the kitchen.

Sexist coverage isn't limited to op-ed pages and online articles. Editorial cartoons offer a graphic, overt way to measure bias. A 2010 study by Eileen Zurbriggen at the University of California, Santa Cruz, and Aurora Sherman of Oregon State found that political cartoons from the 2008 presidential election represented Hillary Clinton as smaller in size, uglier, and more violent than her male counterparts

Barack Obama and John McCain. Even more disturbing, a statistically significant number of cartoons showed Clinton being the *target* of violence, and much more than the male candidates.

This study supports the findings of a substantial body of research measuring sexism and gender bias in the media's political coverage. Studies show that, in contrast to coverage of male politicians, media coverage of female politicians tends to

- cover political issues less frequently;
- focus on issues such as education, poverty, and health care rather than the economy, the military, or foreign relations;
- discuss gender, marital status, and children more often;
- perpetuate dominant social constructions and gendered stereotypes; and
- reinforce female candidates' "otherness" by presenting them as outside of the mainstream.

A 2011 study in the *Analyses of Social Issues and Public Policy* journal examines media treatment and voter reactions to candidates Clinton and Palin and posits that media bias—and general prejudice—against female politicians is correlated to how closely those politicians conform to typical gender stereotypes. The researchers found that when voters view candidates as more stereotypically feminine (acting sympathetic, nurturing, weak, dependent, and having a traditionally feminine appearance, e.g., wearing makeup and skirts), they tend to like them more, while at the same time viewing them as less competent than candidates who present less stereotypically feminine characteristics (demonstrating logic, strength, reason, agency, and focusing less on appearance, e.g., wearing pantsuits or having short hair).

Essentially, this places women in a no-win situation. They can be masculine, strong, competent, and capable of leading—yet unlikable, like Clinton—or they can be feminine, pretty, and likable—thus incompetent and incapable of leading, like Palin. (Of course, many would reasonably argue that Palin's reputation results from her actions, not her appearance.)

These trends are nothing new. When news anchor Tom Brokaw presented vice-presidential candidate Geraldine Ferraro to the Democratic National Convention in 1984, he introduced her as "Geraldine Ferraro, the first woman to be nominated for vice president . . . size 6!" The media reported that she was "pushy, but not threatening," described her personality as "feisty," and asked her if she could bake blueberry muffins.

In discussing how women compete in the political arena in *Breaking the Political Glass Ceiling*, Barbara Palmer and Dennis Michael mention New York representative Susan Molinari, who visited the war-torn regions of southeastern Europe in the 1990s. Molinari noted, "There I'd be, in a war zone in Bosnia, and some reporter—usually female— would comment on how I was dressed, then turn to my male colleague for answers to questions of substance."

Biased media coverage doesn't do female political candidates—or voters—any favors. Analyses of voter response to gender-biased articles indicate that issue-focused media coverage provided male candidates with a clear advantage; furthermore, voters rated female candidates as less viable than men after exposure to biased coverage.

MALE OPPOSITION: THE GOOD OL' BOYS CLUB

Along with these status quo–promoting media trends, women's progress into politics has also been continuously challenged by the good ol' boys club: male politicians.

In the early 1970s, Patricia Schroeder, a Democratic representative from Colorado, was appointed to the Armed Services Committee. As Palmer and Simon document in their book, *Breaking the Political Glass Ceiling*, the seventy-two-year-old committee chairman, F. Edward Hébert, wasn't happy that a woman was on his committee. He was also quite peeved that an African American representative, Ron Dellums of California, was appointed as well. After announcing that "women and blacks are only worth half of one regular member," Hébert forced Schroeder and Dellums to share a single chair at the table.

Examples like this aren't limited to the prefeminist past. During the 2012 election cycle, Illinois Republican Joe Walsh ran for a House seat against Tammy Duckworth, an Iraq veteran and Black Hawk helicopter pilot who lost both of her legs during the war. A *Huffington*

Post article on the subject revealed that, while on the campaign trail, Walsh frequently made comments that attempted to portray his opponent as a silly little girl only concerned with fashion, making comments such as "the only debate Ms. Duckworth is actually interested in having is which outfit she'll be wearing," and "I was marching in a parade in Schaumburg, Sunday, two days before the Democratic convention, when Tammy Duckworth was on a stage down in Charlotte . . . picking out a dress for her speech Tuesday night."

In 2013, Texas State senator Wendy Davis filibustered to prevent the passage of a very stringent—and very unpopular—antichoice bill. One of her colleagues, Republican Bill Zedler, later tweeted, in a grammatically incorrect message, no less, that she was acting as a terrorist in the Senate. Characterizing Davis as an out-of-control terrorist—that is, "hysterical"—is par for the course for many male politicians; in a 2013 appearance on the Sunday talk show circuit program *This Week*, John McCain described Hillary Clinton's behavior at a Benghazi hearing as "emotional," again, a code word for hysterical.

Then, of course, there's the image burned into every American feminist's retinas: George W. Bush giving Chancellor Angela Merkel—leader of the most powerful country in Europe—an impromptu, unrequested, and totally inappropriate backrub at the 2006 G8 summit. Needless to say, Merkel didn't look pleased by the unwanted physical contact.

Some of the most visible opposition to women's political progress stems from outside the Beltway, however. Antifeminist backlash has spawned a pundit class that seems to grow louder by the day. From Ann Coulter, who has stated that women shouldn't have the right to vote; to Fox commentator Liz Trotta, who, while speaking of sexual assault in the military, asks what enlisted women "expected to happen"; to Bill O'Reilly, who stated that a raped and murdered eighteen-year-old "asked for it" by wearing a miniskirt and halter top out at night; the world of political punditry isn't exactly known for its pro-women stance. However, the vitriol spewed by some right-wing commentators has been especially over the top in recent years. Many believe it's a reaction that's a direct result of women's political progress.

Perhaps no incident better sums up the climate than Rush Limbaugh's 2012 attack on Georgetown law student Sandra Fluke. After Republican representative Darrell Issa refused to let Fluke testify before an (all-male) panel at a congressional hearing about contraceptive coverage, the Democrats held an unofficial hearing. Fluke testified that her university's health care system—which refused to provide contraception on religious grounds—harms female students economically and physically because some contraception is used to treat reproductive medical conditions.

Limbaugh responded on his show by calling Fluke a "slut" and a "prostitute," accusing her of asking the government and taxpayers to subsidize her sex life. He further said, as noted in a timeline in *The Week*, that she was "having so much sex that she couldn't afford contraception" and suggested that she make some money to pay for the pill by posting online videos of herself having sex. The public outcry from the left was immediate. Responding to negative pressure from advertisers, Limbaugh eventually "apologized" by stating that he had "acted too much like the leftists who despise me." The public outrage grew and led to a boycott; his show lost several commercial sponsors, totaling a $5.5 million loss, according to the Wire. Although Limbaugh is still on the air, the boycott's success points to a growing intolerance for sexist behavior.

However, whether on TV, in the paper, on the radio, or in the blogosphere, the antiwoman rhetoric in the atmosphere has increased to such a point that the media has dubbed it the "war on women." But this war isn't confined to the airwaves; it's spilling over into politics and legislation, making it a battle that women can't afford to lose.

THE WAR ON WOMEN

For as long as women have been fighting for equal representation and rights, those who wish to maintain the status quo have been fighting back. And while misogynistic political punditry is certainly offensive and harmful, the effects of sexism are most pronounced and concrete in policies and legislation that affect women's rights. In recent years, the war on women—an alliance of activist organizations, religious groups, and political leaders that's been simmering for several decades—has reached a boiling point.

As the women's liberation movement took shape through the country during the 1960s and 1970s, opposition groups formed and increased in political influence. In one early example, the first African American congresswoman, Shirley Chisholm—who ran under the slogan "un-bought and un-bossed"—brought an activist approach to her seat. Before being elected to Congress, she cofounded the political advocacy group the National Organization for Women (NOW) with noted feminist Betty Friedan. NOW was instrumental in the creation of the Equal Rights Amendment (ERA), which guaranteed equality of rights under the law, regardless of gender. Congress approved the ERA in 1972, and thirty-five states ratified the amendment. However, an effort by conservative activist Phyllis Schlafly of the Eagle Forum prevented the amendment's passage; the Stop ERA movement used scare tactics such as citing that the ERA would end gender-specific protections for women, like Social Security payment for dependent wives and exemptions from military service.

Antifeminist groups such as the Eagle Forum, Concerned Women for America, the Liberty Council, Focus on the Family, and the nonprofit Thomas More Law Center represent a conservative movement against women's progress into the political sphere. Though such groups have been around since the early days of suffrage, the antifeminist movement became prominent on the political stage as a counterpoint to the women's liberation and civil rights movements in the 1960s and 1970s. In recent years, many such organizations have branched out into efforts to restrict women's reproductive rights, falling into bed with both conservative politicians and religious groups in an attempt to gain more political leverage.

In the latest incarnation of kickback, some women have actually co-opted feminism itself. Perhaps the most high-profile examples include vice-presidential nominee Palin, who famously described herself as "a conservative feminist"; and former presidential candidate and state representative Bachmann, who advised women to submit to their husbands. This new brand of conservative "feminism" is closely tied to evangelical Christianity. Its adherents tend to hold decidedly unfeminist views, many espousing antichoice, anti–birth control, and anti-LGBT platforms on the political stage. Marie Griffith, the Director of Washington University's Center on Religion and Politics, said in a *Huffington Post* op-ed: "Palin and Bachmann decidedly do not lean left. What is 'feminist' about them, for those who want to use that descriptive, is their belief that God calls women no less than men to fight His battles against Satan on earth. Women hold awesome power as spiritual warriors, in this worldview; they're not doormats, nor should their godly duties be confined to the domestic sphere. This is its own sort of egalitarianism, to be sure, but it is one far more compatible with the complementarian theology of arch-conservative Protestantism than with the feminism of liberal religion."

Politicians such as Palin and Bachmann provide options for women who don't identify with certain aspects of the feminist movement such as left-leaning political tendencies, preference toward secularism, acceptance of LGBT rights, and (especially) focus on reproductive choice.

This emphasis on restricting reproductive choice is the most visible manifestation of the antiwoman cultural trend. The 2012 election season was characterized by offensive, misleading, false, clueless, and downright bizarre comments on subjects such as reproduction, birth control, rape, and the female anatomy—all uttered by male Republican politicians. To the delight of comedians across the country, the comments just kept coming. Many observers, however, viewed these as confirmation of the archaic, sexist, and misogynist worldview held by many on the right end of the political spectrum. Among the most face-palm-inducing remarks are the following:

- Senate candidate Todd Akin stated that pregnancy rarely results from rape because "if it's a legitimate rape, the female body has ways to try to shut that whole thing down."
- Representative Michael Burgess felt that Roe v. Wade should be overturned because fifteen-week-old fetuses masturbate in the womb, thus proving that they feel pleasure as well as pain.

- Representative Trent Franks argued against allowing abortion in cases of rape or incest because "the incidence of rape resulting in pregnancy are very low."
- Representative Roger Rivard's opinion on rape is that "consensual sex can turn into rape in an awful hurry . . . All of a sudden a young lady gets pregnant and the parents are madder than a wet hen and she's not going to say, 'Oh, yeah, I was part of the program.'"
- Former congressman Joe Walsh felt that "when we talk about exceptions, we talk about rape, incest, health of a woman, life of a woman. Life of the woman is not an exception."
- Senate candidate Richard Mourdock believed that "even when life begins in that horrible situation of rape, that it is something God intended to happen."
- State senator Chuck Winder hoped that when a woman goes to her doctor with a "rape issue," that the doctor will ask her "about perhaps her marriage, was this pregnancy caused by normal relations in a marriage, or was it truly caused by a rape."
- Senate candidate Tom Smith compared pregnancy due to rape to pregnancy out of wedlock and suggested to women, "Put yourself in the father's situation. Yes, it is similar."
- Representative Henry Aldridge noted that "the facts show that people who are raped—who are truly raped—the juices don't flow, the body functions don't work, and they don't get pregnant. Medical authorities agree that this is a rarity, if ever."
- Representative Steve King stated that he'd never heard of such a thing as a pregnancy caused by rape.
- Representative Don Pridemore suggested that women in abusive marriages shouldn't divorce, but should "refind those reasons and get back to why they got married in the first place."
- Presidential candidate Mitt Romney felt that the contraception coverage mandate is "an assault on religion unlike anything we have seen."
- Presidential candidate Rick Santorum was very concerned about "the dangers of contraception in this country. . . . Many of the Christian faith have said, well, that's okay, contraception

is okay. It's not okay. It's a license to do things in a sexual realm that is counter to how things are supposed to be."

- Gubernatorial candidate Clayton Williams advised rape victims that "as long as it's inevitable, you might as well lie back and enjoy it."

But making bizarre, offensive, and patently false comments about rape, abortion, and contraception is one thing; passing laws that restrict rights is another. Since 2010, when midterm elections swept a wave of Tea Party politicians into the House, women's rights have come under attack across the nation, with local, state, and federal legislatures all introducing and passing more laws restricting abortion rights than any other issue!

Between 2012 and 2015, as documented by People for the American Way, right-wing politicians have

- blocked the passage of the Violence Against Women Act because it contained protections for LGBT people and immigrants;
- blocked a provision of the Affordable Healthcare Act requiring religiously affiliated organizations to provide contraceptive coverage in their employee health care plans;
- attempted to overturn Griswold v. Connecticut, which decriminalized contraceptive sales;
- attempted to defund Planned Parenthood;
- attempted to repeal Title IX (equal rights for women at colleges receiving federal government funding and research projects);
- attempted to pass laws that define fertilized eggs as "persons";
- passed laws that permit medical staff at state institutions to refuse medical training related to abortion without risk of losing their accreditation;
- introduced legislation that imposes criminal penalties for aborting a female or minority fetus;
- introduced bills that define single parenthood as a major contributor to child abuse and neglect;
- passed state laws that allow gender-based pay discrimination in spite of the federal passage of the Lilly Ledbetter Fair Pay Act;

- introduced more than 100 provisions restricting women's access to contraceptives; and
- passed legislation requiring women to get medically unnecessary ultrasounds and transvaginal probes.

Despite vehement denial from the conservative wing of American politics, virtually every offensive in the war on women has come from the political right. Republicans love to point to examples of successful female politicians (such as Palin, Bachmann, and presidential candidate Carly Fiorina) to prove that their "big tent" has enough room for women to squeeze in with all those old white guys. However, a quick rundown of the numbers is all it takes to invalidate the Republican Party's claims of inclusivity and gender neutrality when it comes to policies that affect women. Whether the issue is equal pay for equal work, access to reproductive health services, or rights for victims of sexual assault, this timeline—compiled by the Rad Campaign—summarizes just a few of the Republican Party's more egregious attempts to keep women down over the past few years:

- **2008:** Republicans attempt to pass the "personhood" amendment, which defines a fertilized egg as a person under the law. This amendment would make abortion a criminal act under any circumstances, with no exceptions for rape or incest, and ban many forms of birth control, in-vitro fertilization, and stem cell research.
- **2009:** President Obama signs the Lilly Ledbetter Fair Pay Act; 211 of 219 Republicans vote against it.
- **2011:** Republicans pass 92 antiabortion laws in twenty-four states, setting a new record; however, they *attempt* to pass almost one thousand antiabortion laws out of all forty thousand laws introduced in 2011.
- **2011:** With the strong support of religious groups such as the US Conference of Catholic Bishops and the Family Research Council, House Republicans pass H.R. 328, which allows physicians to "exercise their conscience" by letting pregnant women die rather than providing them with an abortion.

- **2011:** The House Republican Party attempts to redefine the federal definition of rape in order to limit abortion coverage to cases in which "forcible rape" could be proved.
- **2011:** Republicans in the House Committee on Appropriations tie federal funding for "abstinence-only" education to the 2012 budget, despite scientific evidence that such policies actually backfire and lead to more unplanned pregnancies.
- **2012:** House Republicans refuse to re-fund the Violence Against Women Act, which would provide federal money to investigate and prosecute violent crimes against women.
- **2012:** Senate Republicans block a vote on the Paycheck Fairness Act, which seeks to eliminate pay disparity based on gender.
- **2012:** Georgia Republicans pass H.B. 954, which criminalizes abortion at twenty weeks with no exceptions for incest or rape and forces women to carry stillborn or fatally ill fetuses to term.
- **2012:** Arizona Republicans pass H.B. 2036, which defines pregnancy as starting at the first day of the last menstrual period, rather than at the actual time of conception, effectively limiting the legal abortion period to several weeks before most women find any problems with a fetus.
- **2012:** Republicans in six states pass legislation allowing insurers or businesses to legally deny women contraceptive or sterilization coverage under their employee insurance plans.
- **2012:** In its final session of the year, Congress spends fifty-two days discussing legislation that limits women's rights. It costs $4.8 million per day to run Congress, meaning these fifty-two days cost taxpayers $249.6 million.

In 2013 alone, conservative politicians attempted to pass forty-three federal laws restricting women's access to abortion, contraceptives, and other reproductive health services, according to GovTrack. Since then, the number of laws introduced to restrict women's access to health care through Planned Parenthood and to eliminate access to abortion have dominated the Republican-led Congress and state legislatures. Many have provocative names such as Health Care Conscience Rights Act, the Pregnant Women Health and Safety Act, the Sanctity of Human Life Act, and the Pain-Capable Unborn Child Protection

Act. Of course, female politicians don't always represent the most progressive or well-informed points of view; some of these bills have female (Republican) sponsors. In an even more shockingly uninformed display described by the Wire, Texas Republican representative Jodie Laubenberg attempted to block an abortion exemption for rape by explaining that rape kits stop unwanted pregnancies, claiming, "In the emergency room they have what's called rape kits where a woman can get cleaned out."

Republican strategists attempted to turn the war-on-women charge around on Democrats, pointing to the scandals surrounding New York City mayoral candidate Anthony Weiner's sexting habits and San Diego mayor Bob Filner's sexual harassment case. Both of these Democrats' behavior is certainly inappropriate and offensive; there's a huge difference, however, between an individual engaging in sexist or unseemly acts toward a few individuals and a powerful political party making laws that negatively affect the rights of millions of women.

THE TURNING TIDES: WOMEN IN POLITICS

Until the attacks on women got ugly and aggressive in the past several years, women were perfectly willing—even eager—to partner in building a gender-neutral future. Many female politicians on the left listened to, respected, and often voted for more conservative viewpoints.

The radicalization of women's rights politics by the right, however, is unleashing a backlash that men will suffer from for decades and which is contributing to a less than appealing future for men. Women, once relegated to the kitchen and the bedroom, are mounting a political crusade that ultimately will embarrass and destroy those politicians who rail against their rights. While women were very influential in both the 2008 and 2012 presidential election, it may take another presidential election cycle or even two before we experience the *full* impact of the female vote, but it will be felt—and it will be a political tsunami.

As more female politicians run for office and win—as they will—they are going to come into power at the local, state, and national level on a platform focused on equal pay for equal work, reforming immigration laws that will legalize millions of immigrant women in the next several years, assuring that voting rights are extended to as many people as possible, and addressing all forms of discrimination. They will also prioritize dismantling the laws preventing abortion and rebuilding the mandate of Roe v. Wade (regardless of Supreme Court decisions), renewing protection of birth control and funding of Planned Parenthood, and extending maternity and paternity leave and protection of women in business.

There will undoubtedly be retaliation. Views abound similar to those of former Florida congressman Allen West, who stated that "all of these women have been neutering American men and bringing us to the point of this incredible weakness . . .We are not going to have our men become subservient," reported ThinkProgress.

A *Huffington Post* article quoted Katherine Spillar of the Feminist Majority Foundation summing up the damage caused by the multitude of antifemale legislation introduced by conservative lawmakers:

> The war on women being waged by lawmakers in Congress and state capitols across the country is not only an attack on women and girls in the U.S., but its reach circles the globe. Dangerous restrictions on abortion access and cuts in family planning budgets here at home turn deadly when translated into U.S. policies globally in the form of draconian cuts and restrictions on international family planning programs. The result: every 90 seconds of every day a woman or girl dies from complications of pregnancy or childbirth and unsafe abortions. Almost all of these deaths are preventable. The death toll mounts while mostly male politicians debate their next battle in the war on women.

When Texas State senator Wendy Davis's filibuster singlehandedly prevented the passage of one of the most restrictive antichoice bills in the nation, the spectacle lit up the Internet as supporters followed the debate on social media and filled the Texas capitol with their cheers. Despite the outpouring of support for Davis, the Republican-controlled legislature managed to pass the bill a few weeks later. Democrats, how-ever, promised court challenges.

The Texas situation illustrates the battle raging across the country as women fight to add their voices to a political process long dominated by males. Other female Democratic politicians attempting to pass leg-islation of their own that would benefit women include the following:

- Colorado representative Crisanta Duran, who introduced a bill supporting comprehensive sex education
- San Francisco city supervisor Jane Kim, who is working to stop the use of misinformation and scare tactics by the Crisis Pregnancy Centers
- Vermont representative Jill Krowinski and Senator Sally Fox, who champions equal pay legislation
- Missouri representative Stacey Newman, who sponsored the Compassionate Assistance for Rape Emergencies Act
- New York representative Carolyn Maloney, who reintroduced the Access to Birth Control Act

These women represent just the advance guard; more females are entering office every day and organizing to respond aggressively to the male-led war on women. In a *US News & World Report* interview about her book *You've Come a Long Way, Maybe: Sarah, Michelle, Hillary, and the Shaping of the New American Women*, Republican strategist Leslie Sanchez notes that in the 2008 election cycle, women were just as willing as men to attack one another personally rather than engage in debate over ideas, and that there are few safe spaces for women in the political arena. In particular, as written in the *US News & World Report* article, Sanchez described Palin's vice-presidential run as "watching a woman in high heels crossing an icy road—you just really never know what's going to happen."

WOMEN FIGHT BACK

Women are fighting back and, with appropriate recruitment, support from major political parties, and adequate financial support, the pool of potential female politicians is growing and will continue to do so in the future—a development that has implications for women and men alike.

As more women enter the political arena, especially younger and more feminist ones like Sandra Fluke, they are overwhelmingly Democratic and progressive—of the 20 women in the US Senate, 16 are Democrats and 4 are Republicans. Of the 78 women in the House of Representatives, 59 are Democrats and 19 Republicans. State legislatures also reflect women's tendency toward liberal politics, with 1,137 female Democrats serving in state senates and houses, compared with 636 Republicans, according to the Congressional Research Service. Barack Obama was elected and reelected on the strength of his numbers with women, especially single and young women. Women voters had a profound impact in getting many female leaders into elected offices across the nation in 2012, when the number of women elected to major political offices—both on a state level and a national level—eclipsed the records previously set in 1992. While success in the 2014 election failed to set new records, the political power of women has reached an unprecedented stage and will continue to grow.

The only generation that increasingly identifies itself as Republican (and claimed by Donald Trump as his primary constituency) is what's known as Richard Nixon's Silent Generation—those born between 1925 and 1945—who are becoming less and less relevant at the polls. Older white voters (who tend to vote Republican by significantly higher margins) are dying off and being replaced by younger generations who don't share the same views on issues such as women's roles and rights and, most important, tend to vote for Democratic candidates in higher numbers. If that weren't enough, women will dominate future elections even more due to the growing importance of Hispanic voters.

In addition to these demographic trends, women continue to make inroads into the working world, influencing corporate politics, fundraising, and political activism. Women are now a majority in the workforce and the electorate, and gender roles and "traditional" families are changing rapidly. Women are increasingly the financial decision makers, a fact that has broad political implications. Issues that were once considered to be limited to men's domain—the economy, energy costs, and so on—are now women's issues, too, along with traditional women's issues such as reproductive rights, health care, and education.

Given these stark economic realities, it seems nonsensical that conservatives continue to cling to some idealized vision of the "way things ought to be": Mom staying home (wearing a dress and string of pearls) and taking care of the two children and the dog, going out shopping for home décor and appliances every now and then, dressing up for church on Sunday, and having dinner ready and on the table when Dad comes home from working all day to support his family.

In this version of reality, when Mom gets raped while out taking a stroll, her body will magically act to "shut it down" and prevent pregnancy—as long as it's a legitimate rape, of course. In this reality, Mom and Dad's teens won't have sex before marriage and need an abortion; after all, they were taught abstinence in high school or in their home schooling. Additionally, free-market forces work just as they should, and women wouldn't expect or ask for equal pay for equal work because they wouldn't be in the workforce in the first place. Most important, women in this world keep their mouths shut and don't interfere in what's obviously a God-given man's job: runnin' the country (which typically includes sending the young men to die in war).

Of course, these ideals and their associated trends may not remain static over time. The Republican Party may overcome its demographic challenges and attract more minority and female voters—but in order for that to happen, they'll have to curtail their insistence on attempting to pass laws that restrict access to reproductive health care, blocking laws that protect women from violence, opposing laws that would end the gender pay gap, supporting laws that discriminate against LGBT people, and enacting harsh anti-immigration policies.

It's unlikely to happen. These exclusive, misogynist, and often racist policy stances aren't just the result of a few shrill voices within the party. Rather, these views represent the essential belief system that forms the foundation of the entire party platform. For instance, the official 2012 and 2014 Republican Party platforms included a total ban on abortion, with no exceptions in cases of rape, incest, or to save the life of the mother: not a woman-friendly policy stance in any reality.

Some of the few moderate conservatives left standing in the right wing of American politics seem to realize this, as evidenced by comments like those of senior Republican strategist John Weaver, who, when speaking of Senator Todd Akin's comments about legitimate rape, noted that the comments "did not seem like outliers . . . They did not seem foreign to our party. They seemed representative of our party," reported the *New York Times*.

As Buffy Wicks, senior fellow at the Center for American Progress Action Fund, states in a *Daily Beast* column, "Bad policy is bad policy, and women voters can see through this . . . Sadly, today's Republican Party lacks any understanding of the struggles women face today." Until the conservative wing of American politics figures this out, they're not likely to attract many women to their side.

FEMALE ROLE MODELS IN POLITICS

But party platforms aren't the only factors that influence women's participation in politics. Regardless of political persuasion, the fact that women have now been on the national stage as potential—and viable—presidential and vice-presidential candidates is huge. For the first time in US history, millions of young women have seen members of their own gender breaking through that previously uncracked ceiling.

Studies back up this common-sense assertion. The British Psychological Society's *Research Digest* report on a 2013 study found that the presence of female political role models has a significant effect on other women. Study subjects, both male and female, were asked to present a persuasive speech in one of four rooms. Rooms either had a poster of Hillary Clinton or Angela Merkel, or Bill Clinton or no poster. Women who spoke in a room with a poster of one of the women spoke up to 49 percent longer—and presented higher quality speeches—than did women in a room with a Bill Clinton poster or no poster, indicating that presence or awareness of a female role model acted to empower women. Interestingly, that 49 percent difference in speech time made the female subjects' speeches as long as the male subjects' speeches.

Referring to the impact of women's participation in the 2008 election, Dr. Barbara Palmer of Baldwin Wallace University concurred and is quoted in *American Magazine* saying, "We're a very visually oriented society. It's all about the television image. The visual of a woman running, whether it's for vice president or president, affects us in ways that we're not even aware of." A 2012 Gallup poll reported by the American Enterprise Institute supported Palmer's statement, finding that 96 percent of adults said they would vote for a qualified woman presidential candidate.

Not only did media exposure of Hillary Clinton and Sarah Palin expose millions of women and girls to the idea of women in national leadership, it also sparked debate about the role of women in politics. Perhaps the more important question, however, is how these new attitudes are borne out in reality. A 2013 article entitled "Girls Just Wanna Not Run" revealed that the upcoming generation of women (ages eighteen to twenty-five) has just as little interest in entering politics as their older counterparts working in the upper levels of traditional "feeder" occupations such as law, business, and education.

However, it's likely that as young women graduate college and begin to experience the realities of a male-dominated political culture and the ramifications on their personal rights and freedoms, they will become more vocal and politically tuned-in. With the encouragement of colleagues and recruitment efforts by women's organizations, the gender gap in political ambition will shrink.

A higher percentage of women than men already vote. Women hold the edge in the population and a large advantage in education, making them the more likely voters. As women's involvement in the political process—both as voters and as candidates—continues to grow, so will women's influence. Given the current state of US politics, the media's treatment of female politicians, and the gender gap in political ambition, the process will be slow, but it will accelerate as women command the same power at the polls that they are gaining across almost all other sectors of society.

These changes will undoubtedly benefit our government as a whole. It doesn't seem like much gets done in Washington these days; however, when it does, you can usually thank the women of the Senate.

In the heat of the early 2014 pre-election partisanship, Senator Amy Klobuchar wrote in a *Huffington Post* piece that "during a time when Congress is synonymous with gridlock and obstructionism, the women are showing we can move past the partisanship, roll up our sleeves and get things done."

History, furthermore, shows women are virtually an unstoppable force once they throw their time, talents, and energy into supporting a cause. Dedicated efforts from outspoken female leaders in the late years of the nineteenth century and early years of the twentieth century helped women everywhere gain the right to vote. Further efforts brought about better pay and working conditions in the workplace and opened the doors for women to pursue higher education. Women also gained greater control over their bodies, earning legal protection allowing them to make decisions on bearing and raising children.

The war on women is likely doomed to meet the same fate as battles waged against women in past generations. Women have proved resilient in advocating for causes and getting favorable results in the end; there's no reason to believe history will not repeat itself.

While the numbers of women running for office have not grown at a rate commensurate with their growing influence at the polls, it is a safe assumption that an increasing number of women will successfully run for elected national, state, regional, and local political offices. It's a safer assumption that the old guard of dominant men will see their power base diminished. All politicians will recognize that taking up arms against a sea of women leads to political doom. The political currents are clearly moving in one direction, and although there is a powerful undercurrent, it will soon be overwhelmed by the tidal wave of the women's vote.

Young men will unfortunately suffer from the sins of their fathers. Conservative lawmakers are scaling back on federal and state funding for education at all levels, restrictions that are doing more harm to boys and men than to women, since men need all the financial encouragement they can get to attend college. As women proactively battle to recapture rights they've lost or that have been jeopardized by conservative right-wing politicians, they will simultaneously fight and win other protections and advantages for women and minorities.

Ultimately, the scales will balance, but it will take decades. By then, the traditional dominance of men (especially white men) in politics and government will be a distant memory, and the current repressive antifemale, antimulticultural period in American politics will be looked back at with scorn, disdain, and ridicule.

CHAPTER 21

HOW MEN CAN ADAPT TO THE NEW WORLD

What is it about women that makes them such fierce competitors in today's workforce and contributes to their growing success in politics? The truth is, women are better at many things than men, and both employers and voters have begun to realize that the skills that women offer are at times a better fit for their needs. What does that mean for men who are struggling to find reliable, gainful employment? Must men simply concede, allowing women to become the higher wage earners in certain industries? Should they just take the backseat and let women take over at the things they are naturally better at? Alternatively, can a man "borrow" the skills that women naturally have in order to become more valuable, more employable in his chosen industry, and more electable at the polls?

The answer to the last question is yes: a man can absolutely consciously adopt methods that are more natural to women to become more efficient on the job without sacrificing his masculinity. Men can take a few pages out of womankind's book, working better, faster, and harder while still offering an employer all the skills associated with being a man.

LEARN TO MULTITASK

A 2013 study published by the University of Hertfordshire in the United Kingdom and described by *BBC News* revealed that women were able to "significantly outperform" men when tested on their multitasking abilities. The test required participants to complete several different tasks at once, including using maps, working out math problems, and answering the phone. Subjects were given two tasks to work on at a time; those who excelled were given a third task, such as the phone ringing while they were doing something else. Researchers measured participants by their ability to accomplish both or all of these tasks. The women showed greater competence in handling up to three or four tasks at a single time than the men in the study.

It's not hard to understand how having the ability to do several things at once would have a positive effect on the ability to perform a job well. For example, if a woman can work on her smartphone, process a document, and acknowledge a customer all at the same time, she might be a better candidate than a man for several roles in a company. An employee who can multitask accomplishes more for their employer for the same compensation—and employers know it. There is a clear advantage to hiring a person who can get more done in a set time frame.

Does this mean that men are excluded from jobs that require multitasking? Not exactly. In an article originally published in *Psychological Review* by world-renowned psychologist George A. Miller in 1956, the human brain's short-term memory has the capacity to store between five and nine things at any given time. The operative word here is *human*; although women may inherently be better at multitasking, it does not scientifically follow that multitasking is beyond the mental capabilities of a man. Brains can be exercised like any other muscle. Try multitasking at home: work on two things at once as often as possible until you are comfortable with doing so. Then try three or four. You may not be able to juggle nine things all at the same time, but you will increase your ability to multitask, thereby making you a more valuable addition to any company.

When learning how to multitask, try using these excellent suggestions, including tips from *Entrepreneur*'s "How to Train Your Brain to Multitask Effectively," on how to get better at doing more than one thing at a time:

- **Group related tasks together and work on them simultaneously:** It is far easier to work on a group of tasks that are similar than to work on a group of tasks that are completely unrelated. Art Markman, author of *Smart Thinking*, suggests that when people work on several unrelated tasks in the same time frame, they are changing the state of their brains multiple times.

- **Use apps that organize tasks:** There are several apps and computer-based programs that can assist you in organizing multiple tasks and managing them effectively. Review the best-selling time management apps and select the one or two that are most likely to meet your needs.

- **Use a to-do list:** Sure, to-do lists may seem cliché, but they've been around this long for a reason. Create a list of the most important and most crucial tasks first, followed by tasks that you have more time to work on or that are less imperative. When you are constantly referring back to your to-do list, it reminds you which tasks need to be done first; you can then continually redirect yourself to work on the most important things. Once those are finished, work your way down the list. You will often find when using a to-do list that you are much better at multitasking and working quickly: you always know what you need to be doing, how you need to be doing it, and when you need to be doing it.

- **Take time to re-review information:** You may only have had a few minutes in the morning to review the meeting minutes, but you might have more time on your lunch break. Using downtime to do other things can help you learn how to multi-task effectively—and will make your time as useful as possible. Instead of playing your favorite smartphone game while you're on mass transit or riding as a passenger in a car, use that time to check your e-mail messages and get through as many as you can. If you're always using your downtime to do something productive, it won't be long before you become a pro at doing more than one thing at a time.

ADMIT MISTAKES AND TELL THE TRUTH

For whatever reason, women have an easier time admitting when they're wrong and when they have made a mistake. They are also far more likely to tell the truth than men when confronted with an uncomfortable situation or inappropriate action. As discussed in Chapter 5, men are preprogrammed to lie as a tool to avoid conflict—even in anticipation of conflicts that may not materialize. Men struggle with lying, either due to pride issues or because they simply do not believe that what they did was wrong.

Many men also believe that emotions don't belong at work and that admitting a mistake is an unacceptable display of feelings. Unfortunately, if an employer believes that you made a mistake, he or she expects you to fix it—and is paying you to do so. Furthermore, if the mistake is sexist or sexual, men are far more likely to be compromised by disclosure (more married men engage in infidelity than women). As many, many men have discovered in the past two decades, forms of harassment in the office are no longer tolerated, and the worst action to take when challenged is denial. Despite this, men continue to compulsively lie and are far less likely than women to admit errors. This is unacceptable; men must change these behaviors.

A woman is more likely to confess a mistake and correct it in the way the employer prefers. When she makes an error, she is more inclined to study and understand what she did wrong and use that knowledge to avoid future problems. Although this may seem like an easy fix, it can be difficult for some men to move through the process of understanding the fault. Men often rely instead on defensiveness and aggressiveness, two surefire ways to lose a job. However, *Entrepreneur* reported that according to Guy Winch, author of *Emotional First Aid*, admitting when you've made a mistake is "a sign of strength."

The next time an employer points out a mistake, follow these easy steps from *Entrepreneur* to help you admit your wrongdoing and get back on the right track:

- **Never make excuses:** While you may be tempted to explain what happened or give reasons for why you acted the way you did, your employer is simply going to see that as an excuse. Apologize immediately instead of arguing about why you felt what you did was right. Once you own the problem, you can own the solution.

- **Don't fake it:** Just as women can smell a lie and a fake apology, so can employers (and everyone else for that matter). In fact, they're already looking for it. Professor of managerial leadership at Washington University Kurt Dirks suggests that your audience will be on the watch for "stiff delivery" of your apology or other signs that you don't really mean what you're saying. If you want to rectify your mistake, your apology needs to be genuine. Apologies aren't a sign of weakness; they are a sign that you have the guts to admit when you've done something wrong—which we all are guilty of sometimes.

- **Take the initiative to make a change:** Ask your employer to clarify what it is that he or she would like you to do differently, and then put in an honest effort to do it. Your employer should be impressed by your ability to correct your behavior. If you are a leader in your workplace, you can begin proactively changing your behavior by giving your employer a specific example of what you've already done to rectify the situation and explaining how you plan to do things differently in the future.

LEARN TO ASK FOR HELP

You've probably heard the old saying that when men get lost, they never stop and ask for directions. Although this isn't always true, men do exhibit a tendency to try to handle things on their own before asking for assistance. That's not always a bad thing—in some cases, it can be the best solution—but there are other issues that can prevent a man from looking for or accepting a helping hand. It may not always be clear right away to a man when assistance is needed; he may not realize it until the situation has escalated into a much larger problem. Women, however, typically have no qualms about asking for help when it's needed, especially in the workplace.

For many men, asking for help is a weakness. Self-reliance is considered a strength. When a man is able to solve a problem on his own, he enjoys the "pleasures of being self-reliant, such as increased feelings of accomplishment and confidence in figuring something out for oneself," said Dr. Daniel Seidman, creator of a popular stop-smoking program, in a *Huffington Post* article. Men continue working on a problem that they can't solve far longer than is acceptable, holding out for that moment in the future when they finally find the solution and are praised for their ability to see something difficult through to the end.

Unfortunately, while men may see forgoing asking for assistance as a strength, employers often consider it a liability. Here are a few simple steps to asking for help, as suggested by *Forbes*:

- **Try everything you can first:** Although women have no qualms about asking for help, they usually exhaust other options first. It's important to make sure you've crossed everything you know how to do off your list before you reach out.

- **Know when to stop trying:** This may seem like it directly conflicts with the above advice, but there's no need to be a martyr when you're struggling with something. If you've tried everything you know of and still can't find a solution, go ahead and ask for help.

- **Think about potential solutions before you ask for assistance:** You may have tried as much as you can to solve a problem at work to no avail, but it's still bad form to ask for help without having at least one more solution in mind. Women will often approach their employer with a few more ideas when asking for help, sending the message that they're not just giving up—they simply want more hands on deck.

Consciously making the effort to ask for help may be uncomfortable for you at first, but the more you do it, the more natural it will feel.

PAY ATTENTION TO DETAILS

A 2013 study by Citi and LinkedIn revealed that women are more likely to think of themselves as detail-oriented and collaborative than men, reported Business Wire. In many professions, details are absolutely critical, and missing one or more of them could result in disaster. So what can a man who struggles with the ability to notice fine details do to help himself pay better attention to the small things?

Learning to listen is key. Men aren't naturally as good at listening as women are, but fortunately, it's a skill that can be learned. Make eye contact with your employer and colleagues, turn toward him or her when he or she is speaking, and take notes. Most important, start listening and stop thinking primarily about the next thing you are going to say and how you can best attract the attention back to you and your ideas.

As you learn to listen better, you will begin to notice more in what people say. You'll pick up on things you never did before—all because you're watching the conversation as much as you're hearing it. As you begin to perceive details in what people are saying, you will do the same in the work environment around you, resulting in a higher level of efficacy on your part. You won't miss nearly as many things, and you won't have to go back and ask about the specifics of a project later.

SHOW CONCERN FOR COWORKERS

In general, women are caring; they're natural givers. *Forbes* contributor Glenn Llopis notes that women are constantly encouraging and lifting one another up in the workplace. A woman is less concerned with what is going on in her corner of the office than she is about her coworkers; she shows genuine concern for others and wants them to perform at their best. She treats them with respect, kindness, and compassion, Llopis writes in his piece, "The Most Undervalued Leadership Traits of Women."

While men may not naturally be as predisposed to showing concern for others as women are, that doesn't mean that they can't learn to care more for the people they work with. If a coworker appears to be having a difficult day, ask if you can support them in any way; you might be able to take a task off their plate. Today's strong workforce is about teamwork and collaboration.

From *Reader's Digest*, here are more easy ways to show that you care for your coworkers:

- Greet your coworkers with enthusiasm.
- Ask your coworkers what they think about something.
- Don't be shy about handing out compliments.
- Make an honest effort to answer calls and e-mails.
- Respect your coworkers' time.

USE MORE WORDS TO COMMUNICATE, AND THINK ABOUT OTHER PEOPLE'S FEELINGS

Women are better at using words to communicate their thoughts, feelings, and needs than men are. Women reportedly use an estimated thirteen thousand more words in a day than men, according to Louann Brizendine's *The Female Brain*, the *Huffington Post* said. Although you might assume that this is a negative thing in a work environment, the opposite is in fact true.

The ability to effectively communicate is a highly sought-after skill. Better communication skills lead to more accurate, more efficient work performance. Equally important is the ability to effectively communicate via e-mail, a medium that tends to communicate unintended messages. If you're not very language-oriented, consider taking a course that will allow you to increase your vocabulary and better communicate at work. Make a habit of looking up words that you don't know or understand and take some time every day to read.

CHAPTER 22

THE FUTURE OF MEN (AND WOMEN) GLOBALLY

Women-owned businesses represented approximately 37 percent of enterprises globally in 2012, reported the *Harvard Business Review* in its coverage of Global Entrepreneur Monitor data. The entrepreneurship study cited found that 126 million women started or own new businesses, and 98 million women are running established businesses that have been in operation for more than three and a half years. That is a total of 224 million women affecting the world's economy—and the survey included only 67 of 188 countries counted by the World Bank.

Around the world, the "battle between the sexes" rages on. Some countries acknowledge that women are a valuable resource and that equal treatment can lead to a better life experience for everyone. These nations, such as Iceland and Norway—which took the top two rankings in the World Economic Forum's *Global Gender Gap Report 2011*—make it easier for women to navigate and build economic and political power in a traditionally patriarchal environment. Others fear women's strength, seeking to keep women down by limiting their use of education, paid work, participation in politics, and even control over their own bodies. Still others believe that women do not deserve consideration.

Worldwide, this appears as a process with definable stages. All countries are headed in the same direction, even if some have made more progress than others. First, women begin to seek education in greater numbers than men. Second, they use their education to find parity in the workplace in their own countries—and if they cannot find it there, they go abroad. Third, they exert their power in education and employment to influence politics in their favor. This often leads to a backlash by men, who attempt to rein women in using violence and cultural pressure. Despite this, however, the tides are turning across the planet. Even in personal relationships, women are increasingly taking control.

This trend toward women's empowerment has both positive and negative effects for men, depending on their own attitudes and biases. Unsurprisingly, the countries with the most even-handed approach to men and women rank highest in their overall standard of living. Nations that treat women as people worthy of respect have robust economies and compete well on the world stage. Regions that do not encourage women's empowerment or rights find that their development is stagnating. Men who think they are still on top are left behind.

WOMEN'S ASCENDANCE IN EDUCATION

The process starts with education. In all the world's regions, the number of women attending institutions of higher education is increasing faster than that of men. Even in regions where men are more likely to attend college, the averages are nearly even. In Europe, women keep pace or outnumber men in nearly every country. In Asia, the Middle East, and North Africa, the ratio varies widely from country to country. Some think this change is great; other times, men's reactions to this improvement in women's social mobility turns violent.

In Europe (as in the United States) women attend college in greater numbers than men. In a 2011 report from the Institute for Social and Economic Research and Policy at Columbia University, Anne McDaniel cross-referenced data from a variety of sources in an attempt to discover the reason. She argued that, when adjusted for the individual backgrounds of those studied, men do not outnumber women in any European country. McDaniel noted that, while men and women in higher education have gender parity in twenty-two countries studied, women far outpace men in fifteen others. She concluded that women are 50 percent more likely than men to complete college in European countries.

The outcome of McDaniel's analysis showed how dramatically society is turning against men. She contended that having a wide gender gap in education may make women even less likely to marry undereducated men, dropping low birthrates even further. In an Associated Press interview, *Date-Onomics* author Jon Birger confirmed that in the United States "among millennials, there are four college-grad women for every three college-grad men. In fact, the lopsidedness is actually worse in some rural states like Montana and West Virginia than it is in urban states like California and New York." In her paper, McDaniel stated that researchers and advocates must change the way they look at gender and higher education, claiming that "the comparative study of gender inequalities in higher education must be considered a gender issue, not a women's issue."

Because of the focus on women's concerns, McDaniel suggested that people do not pay enough attention to the reasons that men do not attend or finish college the way women do. She believed that a typical upbringing draws women to take after their mothers, whereas men take after their fathers, especially in regard to education. A man is more than twice as likely to drop out of school if his father was absent from the family. This can create a very large difference in attendance; for example, 2007 data from the Centre for Research and Development of Education indicates that women now make up 70 percent of medical school students in the Netherlands.

Asia, particularly in the southeast, is well known for its strong (and occasionally disastrous) cultural preferences for men over women. Even in this region, however, women are attending college at a higher rate than ever before. The United Nations Educational, Scientific and Cultural Organization (UNESCO) Institute of Statistics, which maintains records of college enrollment for twenty-six countries in Asia, reported that in 2010 and 2011, women's enrollment in higher education was on the rise, and this trend is continuing. In about one-third of countries, women outnumber men in college attendance. In some countries, such as Myanmar, Sri Lanka, and Brunei, the number of women far exceeds the number of men.

In other countries, such as Afghanistan, male leaders try to stem the tide of educated women taking over. Compared with its neighbors Iran and Pakistan, Afghanistan is positively backward; Iran reached gender parity in 2011 and Pakistan nearly so, while there are only three to four Afghan women in college for every ten Afghan men, according to 2010 United Nations (UN) data presented in the *Guardian*.

Even in Pakistan, women must continue to battle for rights. In 2012, teenage Pakistani activist Malala Yousafzai was shot for advocating broad educational reform for girls. Yousafzai's experience reflects the exceptional power of social media in forcing change at the national level. When her story went viral, people all over the world began to demand better treatment for girls in conservative sovereignties. By trying to silence her, men turned Yousafzai into a herald for women's education worldwide and a Nobel Peace Prize winner.

In the Middle East and North Africa, the numbers vary widely. Overall, university women outnumber men in two-thirds of Middle Eastern countries, as stated in 2012 UN data covered by *CNN*. In countries such as Kuwait, Qatar, and the United Arab Emirates, women's enrollment outstrips men's by nearly two to one. However, in Iraq and Yemen, the numbers are completely reversed.

In Middle Eastern and North African countries where women dominate education, they often use college to find a better life. They have fewer rights than men, so university becomes a form of passive resistance against the men who rule their lives. Nawar Al-Hassan Golley, a literary professor at the American University of Sharjah in the United Arab Emirates, told *CNN* that many cultures encourage education while maintaining a strict gender hierarchy. For many women, college may be the easiest way to escape the culture entirely. In 2012, *BBC News* covered a *Chronicle of Higher Education* report that said women represent two-thirds of international students worldwide.

WORKFORCE PARTICIPATION

As women take over the realm of education, they expect to assume a greater role in the labor force as a means to gain a bigger share of the economic pie. This step, however, is not as easy for them to achieve. Even men who are happy to send wives and daughters to school often have a very different view about women gaining power in the workplace. As a result, in some countries women's participation in education is inversely proportionate to their contribution to employment. Western countries, as a rule, lead the way in women's greater access to equity in the workplace, but many regions ignore the potential that an educated female workforce presents to a growing economy. Without that awareness, these countries suffer when their women leave for a better life abroad.

As in higher education, the most starkly contrasting statistics come out of the Middle East and North Africa. In many countries in the region, women obtain a significant majority of bachelor's degrees, yet represent less than one-third of the workforce. Women in the region make up only 20 percent of employed adults, lower than in any other area; for example, Lebanese women represent 54 percent of university students but only 26 percent of paid labor according to the 2003 UN Statistics Division report, "Empowering Women, Developing Society."

The answer, Dima Dabbous-Sensenig, former director of the Institute for Women's Studies in the Arab World at the Lebanese American University, told *CNN*, lies in a culture that restricts both men and women. In many countries, women are largely barred from entering the public sphere. When women do not or cannot work, the pressure increases on men to provide. Men are less likely to obtain degrees in the Middle East and North Africa in large part because they need to earn money and cannot do so effectively while they are full-time students.

In South and East Asia, the workforce gender gap increased significantly during the global economic crisis of 2002–2007, reaching nearly 50 percent in some Asian countries, reported the International Labour Office in *Global Employment Trends for Women 2012*. The types of jobs women seek are the largest determiner in their employment, said the report. In Asia, women are most likely to engage in unpaid labor in the home; if they are paid, it is often within small family businesses, which are more vulnerable to economic changes. In Bangladesh, only one woman in ten is paid for work. Women are expected to stay home and support the family physically, not monetarily. The International Labour Office argues that these stereotypes, upheld by both men and women, create a cycle that is difficult to break and puts pressure on both parties to stay within those norms.

Even in Europe, college-educated men still outnumber women in the workplace. In a 2012 study, the Organisation for Economic Co-operation and Development noted that in European countries, only 69 percent of women with higher education were employed, compared with 84 percent of men. In the Slovak Republic, Hungary, and Portugal, the ratio is nearly equal; in the Netherlands and Germany, many more college-educated men than women work.

Although 69 percent sounds like a lousy number, it does at least show that the gender gap is closing. Education cannot solve everything, of course, but when studies consider women's part-time participation in the workforce, as well as their increased dominance of specialized education, the numbers come much closer. The European Commission, the executive body of the European Union, argues that men's contributions are often taken more seriously. Regions that overlook women's economic potential, however, risk losing their contributions entirely.

WOMEN'S RIGHTS AND "BRAIN DRAIN"

In any nation, administrators and politicians want to keep the educated population in the country; for many regions, keeping women from leaving is extremely difficult. Governments pay to educate young people locally or even internationally, and then those students seek greener pastures upon graduation.

Human capital migration, more commonly known as "brain drain," can be a scourge on any local economy. If education only drives citizens to leave, the country itself cannot take advantage of a person's improved skill set. The Organisation for Economic Co-operation and Development reported that in Africa, the Middle East, Southeast Asia, and even Europe, many countries have more than 20 percent of their educated population living abroad.

Women especially want to leave countries that are frequently torn by war, famine, or poverty. Maryam Naghsh Nejad at the Institute for the Study of Labor (IZA) wrote in "Female Brain Drains and Women's Rights Gaps" that she had discovered a perfect correlation between countries with poor treatment of women and the likelihood that women would leave those countries when they graduate from college. On average, college-educated women are 17 percent more likely than men to seek work abroad. Migration is a dangerous venture for anyone, particularly for women, but Naghsh Nejad argued that women living in regions with limited economic and political rights are more willing to accept those risks to escape an unsatisfying home life. Once these women are gone, the remaining men are left with a lower national level of education, making them unable to compete with stronger markets.

POLITICAL EMPOWERMENT

Worldwide, men tend to restrict women's access to the workplace, feeling that women belong in the private sphere. If women struggle to gain power in the labor force, their entrance into the most public of public spheres, politics, is even more challenging. Despite this, women globally are taking every opportunity they can to wield political power. If they cannot use money to apply influence, they vote in greater numbers than men to alter who sits in government. As women's power in the workplace and their determination to control politics grows, so does their share of political positions.

Women represent a small portion of politicians for now. The organization UN Women tracks such statistics. Worldwide, only slightly over one in five parliamentarians are women (21.8 percent). While that number (from 2013) seems small, it has nearly doubled from the 11.3 percent it was in 1995, showing that the tide is starting to turn. In some places, women have all but taken over the government; the central

African state of Rwanda heads the pack with 63.8 percent of seats in
the lower house taken by women. Other regions hang onto tradition
with every bit of strength; only 8 percent of Lebanese legislators and
senior officials are women.

The differences by region are wide, UN Women statistics reveal.
Nordic countries have 42.1 percent women parliamentarians, compared with 25.8 percent in the Americas, 23.7 percent in non-Nordic
Europe, 22.6 percent in sub-Saharan Africa, 19 percent in Asia, 17.8
percent in the Arab states, and a paltry 13.4 percent in the countries
of the Pacific. The correlation is obvious between states with greater
dedication to gender equality by law and the trend toward parity of
women in political office.

At the ballot box, researchers have realized that men do not
appreciate the right to vote as much as women do. The International
Institute for Democracy and Electoral Assistance indicated in their
Voter Turnout Since 1945: A Global Report that women are more likely
to report voting in almost every category. Women with limited access
to primary school were much more likely to vote than men of a similar
education; furthermore, the largest positive difference between women
and men at the voting booths came among those with disabilities.

As the population gets older and men and women gain greater
access to education, however, researchers suspect that the gap will be
eliminated across the board. Men cannot continue to rely on voting
power to keep men's issues at the forefront of politics, particularly as
the oldest and most conservative in current society pass on.

Men's control of money significantly affects a woman's ability to
improve her lot, no matter the region. Economic freedom, especially
in less-developed regions of the world, is tied as much to politics as it is
to a woman's ability to fulfill any particular job. For example, according
to UN Women, in Southeast Asia, women are far more likely than men
to work in agricultural jobs than in the more lucrative industrial and service sectors. As these regions push away from agriculture-based economies, women are finding that no jobs are available as a replacement.

If women are given the opportunity, however, they will take advantage of it, improving the entire nation in the process. Certain North
Asian countries, particularly from the former Soviet Bloc, commonly

employ more women than men. The *Statistical Yearbook for Asia and the Pacific 2011* showed that in regions with more protections for workers, more women participate in the paid labor force.

WOMEN'S CONCERNS: THE BEST, THE WORST, AND THE EXCEPTIONALLY DANGEROUS

All countries have a level of awareness of their relationship with women and how their approaches compare to other regions. Most are aware that women are gaining power relative to men in many areas; some react positively, promoting equity in health care, education, employment, and politics to the betterment of all. Nordic countries show their dedication to improving women's lives, which pays off for everyone through a solid economy and a higher standard of living. In contrast, most developing nations continue to struggle to realize the benefits of equality. A few holdouts of the past—dominated largely by men—encourage girls and women to marry and have children very young. They attempt to limit women's opportunities and violently silence their dissent as a means to hinder women's progression into dominance.

Pregnancy is the most common barrier between women and full participation in society, said UN Women. For thirty to forty years of their lives, women can expect to be fertile and anticipate pregnancy resulting from unprotected sex. As such, access to pregnancy prevention, prenatal care, and maternity leave is crucial to maintaining women's ability to remain a functional part of the workforce. Unfortunately, many regions in the developing world do not make these provisions available to women, and some that do, including the United States, fall short of targets. The United States is currently the only developed country that offers only unpaid maternity leave.

Unfortunately, the influence of US-based evangelicals who have advocated in Africa and other undeveloped nations against any form of birth control including condoms has had a significant effect on the medical care of the developing world. Decades of overseas influence by men with no education or proper context on the situation created a health crisis in Africa: faith-based organizations, many of which were founded in the United States, provide 40 percent of the health care in sub-Saharan Africa. The World Health Organization notes that several of these organizations ignore established worldwide standards for treating conditions; for example, according to a 2007 World Health Organization document, faith-based organizations may advise against using condoms for safe sex, citing that sex within marriage requires no protection and that sex outside of marriage is forbidden. In countries such as Botswana, where almost one in four adults has HIV (with women disproportionately affected), this counsel has had disastrous effects, according to the AIDS prevention organization AVERT.

Anywhere in the world, women are at greater risk than men for violence and subjugation. In South Asia and sub-Saharan Africa, men arrange for their young daughters to wed men who may be decades older, often as an economic trade. The nonprofit CARE reported that more than 64 million girls have been married off as child brides; considering that pregnancy complications are the leading cause of death for girls aged fifteen to nineteen years worldwide, this is a concerning statistic. The younger a girl is at marriage, the less likely she is to be educated or have a means to support herself independently.

Men use other methods to keep women and girls in line as well. Female genital mutilation has been performed on at least 140 million girls worldwide, with catastrophic and sometimes deadly side effects in addition to the horror of the procedure itself. Despite this, some families in Westernized nations send their daughters abroad to have the procedure done to avoid interference from local authorities.

In developing nations, even girls who avoid the knife cannot escape other sexual violence. Women and girls make up 98 percent of all sex trafficking victims worldwide, in operations primarily orchestrated by men, said the organization Equality Now. Even women who grow up in safe, industrialized countries are not immune. The UN estimates that at least one in three women worldwide will experience an unwanted sexual attack during her lifetime.

Thankfully, some countries have taken a more egalitarian view to the gender gap. The World Economic Forum (WEF) creates a yearly international report measuring the gender gap related to access to education and health care, as well as participation in politics and the workforce. In 2013, for the fifth year in a row, Iceland topped the list, followed by all Nordic countries, the Philippines, New Zealand, and Nicaragua. These countries have reached gender parity in health outcomes and education and have dramatically increased the number of women in politics and the labor force. The WEF notes that the Nordic countries often come out on top in lists like this because of their high income levels; however, even when WEF researchers factor out actual income and consider data showing access to work and income, the Nordic countries still rank highest. The WEF attributes those countries' dedication to effective primary education and generous benefits to working mothers as a few of the reasons these countries have such robust economies and rising birthrates. In other words, countries that treat all groups with humanity are generally happier, stronger, healthier, and richer.

Unlike the best countries for both men and women, the worst countries are inconsistent. The WEF stated that Southeast Asia ranks last in women's health and survival, but leads the way in political empowerment. By the WEF's rubric, countries in the Middle East and West Africa fare the worst: Yemen ends the list, preceded by Pakistan, Chad, Syria, and Mauritania.

There is no doubt that women and men alike will fare worse in countries that are war-torn or regions with traditional views that do not make allowances for modern perspectives. Without a concrete plan to improve the lives of women, regions suffer in many different ways.

STORIES FROM A
WOMAN'S HEART

CHAPTER 23

REALITY FROM A FEMALE POINT OF VIEW

While I was conducting research for *The Future of Men*, several women who learned about the project reached out and shared their stories, expressing a clear desire that their experiences be included in this book. They wanted other women to know they're not alone, that there are solutions and opportunities to grow. They also hoped that their experiences could help men, especially young men, understand the impact and implications of their actions and behavior.

Over the past couple of years, as I told people about my plans to write a book about the future of men, women were typically engaged, interested, and eager to share their stories and to read the book and find out what I had discovered. The feedback from a large majority of men, however, was a simple and glib one-liner: "You mean we have a future?"

Yes, men do have a future, but for young men it will require a greater understanding of the conflicts and contradictions between what was expected and accepted in the past and what will be accepted and increasingly expected in the future. In this context, it's helpful to hear the words from women. These are actual narratives told by real women in their own words. These are just a handful of stories, but combined with those shared earlier in this book, they reflect the realities of many people.

CHAPTER 24

LARA'S STORY: IT'S NO LONGER A MALE-DOMINATED WORLD

"We're going to the Caribbean," my mom said. No one should sound as unhappy as she did saying those words. I walked into my backyard, since I felt that our phone conversation was about to get a little more serious.

"Wasn't the Italy trip next?" I asked. "You've been taking those language classes for a year."

No. My father, she told me, had spent that year's vacation funds on a cruise, so that was where they were going. They hadn't gone to Italy the year before either.

I'd been on my own for a few years at this point, as had my younger sister. My mother still worked at the job she had taken to help defray college costs back when my sister and I were teenagers, despite the fact that we were well out of school. My parents were winding down their careers and spent a few weeks traveling every year, and ever since I was little, my Italian-American mother had talked about her desire to visit the place her ancestors had come from and to meet relatives who still lived there.

"Why not take a cheaper trip to Italy?" I asked her. She replied that my dad wouldn't be up for it. I floated the idea of using her hard-earned paychecks to go without him. In the end, unfortunately, it came down to her accepting his authority and not feeling confident going on her own.

My mom came of age at the peak of the 1960s women's movement. The movement, though, didn't reach every woman in the same way and at the same time. While Betty Friedan was talking about the vague but persistent dissatisfaction of housewives in *The Feminine Mystique*, my mom was waiting to join my dad on base in the Air Force. What we historically see as a massive, universal change in the way that men and women relate in the workplace and at home actually happened in fits and starts.

My mom was a full-time stay-at-home parent until both my sister and I were in grade school. After that, she only took jobs that matched our schedules. For many women, the social change of the women's liberation movement would not find fertile ground for a generation or two, and for many women today, women's liberation remains an oxymoron.

My mom would occasionally bitterly observe that it was a man's world. Men had the power; men made the decisions. That observation definitely reflected our family reality. When my dad switched to a job with more travel that would leave my mom solely responsible for the house and kids for weeks at a time, he made the choice without consulting her. Similarly, few of my aunts worked outside the home. Even if both members of a couple were retired, the men watched football at holiday gatherings while the women washed dishes and scrubbed down the kitchen.

It wasn't until I was an adult that I really examined the roles that my parents played and the power structure of their marriage. At that point, I started to understand why my mom pushed me to do well in school with the ominous threat that if I didn't get a good education, I'd wind up a housewife. I was a reasonably bright kid, but somehow didn't put it together that that had been her main vocation and that she didn't want that for me.

While quietly taking a backseat in her own relationship, she raised me and my sister to be able to take the wheel on our own. It helped that I grew up in an era when women's magazines had as many articles about careers as they did about hair and makeup and that most of the dating tip articles started with the premise that, on a first date, you went dutch.

Growing up in this environment, I was naturally primed for a more equal relationship. When I had live-in boyfriends in my twenties, we both worked full-time, and household chores were handled more like we were roommates than like we were married. (Also, seeing that we were in our twenties, it often meant they weren't really handled at all until absolutely necessary.)

When I got married to a wonderful guy after sharing a house for five years, this dynamic still held. It's funny: he and my father had upbringings that were very similar in some ways. Both were raised by working single mothers; both were called on early to be "the man of the house." However, the differences in the times they were raised made them very dissimilar men. While a working mom was unusual in my father's childhood, it was the norm by the time my husband was a kid. It was common for him to see women in professional places every-where, from his teachers to his pediatrician to the woman who did his mom's taxes.

We are partners. We happily (and mostly smoothly) slip back and forth between roles. That's not to say it's a relationship with no resem-blance to traditional gender roles. I tend to cook because I enjoy it and I'm better at it and ditto for grocery shopping and laundry. We split household cleaning fifty-fifty, but he is usually the one to mow the lawn and take out the trash. The handling of large spiders is done by neither of us (we're both terrified of them) but instead by my preternaturally cool fifteen-year-old daughter.

Our relationship is, of course, not every relationship. Just as women were invading the workplace during my mom's time, other women are now proudly defending their right to be the submissive partner in their own relationship. All in all, I do feel that there is more freedom of choice, and I'm grateful to the ones who sacrificed to provide it.

CHAPTER 25

NICKY'S STORY, AS TOLD BY HIS MOM: WHAT ARE WE TEACHING OUR SONS?

We were standing in line for the antique car ride at Storybook World when it happened.

Let me set the scene for you: my son and daughter had just declared a truce in their squabble over who would get to "drive" and had joined forces in trying to guess whether we'd get a red, blue, or yellow car based on the order of the cars on the track and our place in line. It was one of the final days of August, following a brutal length of time during which our family had endured a number of financial setbacks related to my husband's job, the government sequester, and my own poor planning. On the upside, we'd recently received some promising news, my feuding offspring were in rare alignment, and the school year was about to begin, bringing with it relief from the relentlessness of parenting during ten weeks of school vacation. In other words, my spirits were higher than they'd been in months.

The kids and I had received passes to a nearby amusement park for Christmas the previous December. In former years, we hadn't thought twice about buying the passes for ourselves; we'd taken both access and proximity to Storybook World for granted. This year, though, we'd needed help, and I was thankful to be there. I'd even saved up some money to treat the kids to pizza and ice cream inside the park (as opposed to the peanut-butter-and-jelly-sandwich picnic lunches I'd been packing for outings throughout the rest of the season).

As we inched forward in the very long line, I heard a male voice behind us rise above the delighted shrieking, background music, and popcorn munching. "No son of mine will ever have long hair," the voice declared. "If he does, I'll cut it right off."

My six-year-old son, Nicky, standing mere feet away, had long hair. Although my inner tiger mom wanted to turn and roar at the heartless stranger, sense trumped sensitivity. I'd observed the man a few minutes earlier tossing his infant high into the air and catching him while the baby's mother smoked a cigarette under a No Smoking sign. The baby, about three months old, was clad in a onesie that read, "All My Mommy Wanted Was a Backrub." Keeping in mind my mother's oft-imparted "consider the source" rule, this was clearly not someone with whom I could expect to reason, let alone silence with a glare.

Instead, I turned my attention to my son, studying him for a reaction to the man's outburst. Nicky was staring straight ahead at the winding track punctuated with brightly colored vehicles and animatronic livestock. He didn't say anything. I didn't even know if he'd heard. The line moved faster. We got the yellow car; Nicky drove. It was a breathtaking end-of-summer day.

While eating his oatmeal the next morning, Nicky was uncharacteristically quiet before setting down his spoon and announcing, "I want to get my hair cut."

This is the same child who steeled his jaw, clenched his fists, and refused to cry following a bike crash that resulted in eight stitches. This is also the same child who, within days of that accident, was inconsolable for hours after a snail he'd found clinging to the underside of a leaf was unceremoniously crushed by an older cousin. A dynamic blend of virile and vulnerable, my son is committed to asserting his independence—and yet is deceptively fragile. The careless seed planted by the jerk behind us—because that's exactly what he was—had taken root and grown into an invasive weed. My heart broke at Nicky's words.

The combined product of being the younger sibling of a sister and my own efforts not to assign gender stereotypes to either child, Nicky had until that moment gone through life happily wearing pink hand-me-downs and cooking sunny-side-up eggs in the play kitchen. That's not to say we hadn't seen plenty of indications of nature's handiwork: his relentless love of all things with engines since the age of eighteen months and a recently acquired ability to turn everything—from a cucumber to a toy guitar—into a pretend weapon. Long hair, fuchsia snow boots, and all, my son has been frequently declared "all boy" by loved ones and strangers alike.

While I've also made a large effort not to validate my children based on appearance, I'd slipped up in one regard: my son's magnificent mane. Since he was a baby, Nicky's wavy blond locks were admired nearly every day by a certain kind of mom. In retrospect, I suppose his hair may also have been scorned daily by a different kind of mother, but those types of comments weren't typically made within my earshot. Nick's surfer-chic, tousled hair naturally achieved what had been carefully cultivated by countless 1980s-era prep school boys and modern-day Disney Channel heartthrobs. Women similarly would pay hundreds of dollars at the beauty salon to replicate his natural flaxen color.

But there we were: my previously unflappable, long-haired son wanted his hair cut, and I realized how deeply opposed I was to satisfying his request. Had my daughter asked for Anne Hathaway's pixie cut, I likely would have acquiesced without a second thought. Did my resistance to allowing Nicky to have short hair make me any better than the man standing behind us in line at Storybook World that day?

My hairy problem was, at least in the short term, resolved by a well-timed viewing of the movie *Hercules*, in which the übermasculine hero has long, flowing locks. (I suppose I could have taken it a step further and shared the story of Samson and Delilah, but that was farther than I was ready to go!) I've been spared the haircut for now, but the underlying issue remains: had my son persisted in demanding that haircut—and he may still; Nicky is nothing if not persistent—what lesson would I be teaching him in refusing to honor his request? While Nicky's long hair indeed serves as a personal reminder of days gone by, I have admitted that it is also a matter of principle for me, as it has been for generations before me. Does long or short hair, then, become passed on as a matter of principle to my son and, for that matter, the airborne baby in the offensive T-shirt? Something else to think about: I don't want my daughter to be defined by her hairstyle, so why would I wish that on my son?

Since that day at Storybook World, I've become increasingly aware of the fact that although we frequently discuss ways to improve our daughters' paths to adulthood by stressing the importance of promoting positive body image; encouraging them to opt in to studies in math, sciences, and technology; and teaching them to advocate for themselves and for one another, we sometimes trust too much that the path for our sons will be simpler. In assuming that they can and will fend for themselves, it's easy to lose sight of the fact that they shouldn't have to.

Girls are encouraged daily to reach beyond traditional societal constraints and are applauded for doing so. I can't help but wonder: we are working so hard to teach our daughters that they can be anything they want to be, but what are we as a society working hard to tell our sons?

CHAPTER 26

MICHELLE'S STORY: BEING A PERFECT 1950S GIRL . . . IN THE 1990S

With blond pigtails and little-girl dimples, I stood on a stool in my mom's country kitchen and mashed the potatoes, surrounded by blue-checked wallpaper and ceramic ducks. On other days, I would peel boiled eggs, knead dough, or stir homemade gravy to prevent it from scorching. After dinner, my sister and I would argue about who would wash and who would dry the dishes.

On Saturday mornings, my job was to dust the living room furniture and scrub the bathtub while cartoons played on the big console TV, and my sister's was to vacuum the shag carpet and clean the mirrors with newspaper. It sounds like a typical 1950s upbringing—but I was a child of the 1980s. The women's rights movement was long past. Women were already shattering the glass ceiling in nearly every field. However, I grew up in rural southeast Texas, and the area was a bit slower to catch up to most modern ideas.

Household duties and cooking were not chores in our home: they were education and vocational training. Through every task, my mother (a stay-at-home mom) stood nearby to critique me and help improve my domestic skills. Spelling, multiplication, and (eventually) computer skills were all seen to, but training to be a housewife was the most important part of my education. I was taught that while a few unlucky women might have to take on jobs, a woman was always primarily a wife and mother.

At church on Sundays, we sat on wooden pews in our tiny Baptist church. The pastor stood behind the pulpit and preached that "the liberals" wanted people to think that a woman should be in the workforce, not at home making cookies. He went on to say that he liked cookies and the women who made them. Moreover, women who joined the workforce were taking something away from their husbands and decreasing the quality of life for their families. A woman was to be submissive to her husband and a helper to him.

Glancing around that Baptist church, what I saw didn't work with what I was hearing. Many of the women in our church and community held jobs. Very few of those jobs could be described as "careers"; most women only took them reluctantly. However, for many families, economic realities drove women from the stove and vacuum to retail or secretarial jobs.

In high school, my education in "women's work," as I often heard household duties called, took a more formal turn. At my mother's insistence, I enrolled in home economics as one of my electives. The class, taught by a sweet lady well past retirement age, was made up entirely of girls. We spent the first semester on cooking and the second on sewing and child-rearing. The goal of the class was to add structure to the work of caring for a home and family. Lessons were aimed more at augmenting and adding to the skills we had already been taught at home rather than teaching new concepts.

When I entered college in 1997, my parents wanted me to study hard, do well, and graduate. More important, though, they wanted me to find a husband. A college degree, something neither of my parents had, was looked at as something to "fall back on"—it was more important to get my "MRS degree."

College began to open my eyes to a different reality. When I went to my first class, I shared it with more women than men. Up until then,

I had thought myself a bit of a rebel by planning a career and life that didn't focus on home and family. Knowing that more women than men had attended college since the late 1970s would have shocked me. It was a revelation to find that I had left small-town Texas far behind and was now surrounded by smart, capable women. They were working on much more than fallback plans and finding husbands—and they weren't limiting themselves to becoming paralegals or nurses. They were working on degrees in everything from medicine to art, all while serving on student government and interning at major corporations. Their energy and passion inspired me. I began to work harder and dream bigger.

And every few days my mother would call and ask if I was dating anyone.

To me as a woman, marriage meant turning away from my own goals and focusing on my husband and starting a family. That wasn't what I wanted. I had worked hard to earn my degree, and I was excited about building my career. I couldn't fathom shoving aside my dreams and focusing on making babies and keeping house.

Fortunately, when I met and fell in love with my future husband, I realized that it didn't have to be that way. Marriage was not, as I had always assumed, the end of my independence. Contrary to what I had been taught, my husband was not looking for a subservient helper; he was looking for a partner. He didn't need another mother or someone to cook for him and clean up after him; he needed someone to tackle life with and someone to have adventures with. He wanted to, and still does, support my career. He views my goals and aspirations as equal to his own.

It shouldn't have been surprising. According to the Bureau of Labor Statistics, in 2003 (the year that I married) 60 percent of adult women held either full- or part-time jobs. That number has risen significantly in my lifetime; in 1979 (the year that I was born) less than 50 percent of adult women were employed.

Throughout our marriage, I have certainly put my husband's support to the test. I have worked full-time, part-time, and overtime. I have worked for large corporations, government agencies, nonprofit organizations, and now for myself. Throughout it all, his support has been unwavering, even when I struggled with finding any sort of balance. After a few years in a job that I found to be both profoundly rewarding and extremely exhausting, I woke up one morning knowing my time there was done. I shook my still-snoring husband awake and said, "I think I'm giving my notice today at work."

To be honest, I expected a discussion. I know my mother never would have made a decision this size alone. In marriages of my parents' generation, decision were made by the husband and carried out by the wife. But my husband never once doubted me and never questioned my decisions. To him, as with most modern couples, a woman's place is where she wants it to be.

CHAPTER 27

AVA'S STORY: COMMUNICATION VERSUS CONFRONTATION

I was born in 1985. From the earliest I can remember, my parents fought—not just about the big decisions, but over even the smallest details. I remember them arguing over a shade of blue they were painting on the wall of my old bedroom. I was young enough to still feel free to yell, "Stop fighting!" as I shut myself in the closet. I remember my dad opening the door and explaining to me that they weren't "fighting," they were "discussing." Well, to a three-year-old, it sure seemed a lot like fighting. I was pretty sure if my brother and I had been using those tones with each other, we would have been told to stop.

Over the years, my mom and dad would have discussions that led to full-fledged arguments and an ongoing, raging battle of wills. My dad would get really intense, and my mom would be really emotional. I hated it.

My dad always told us that honest couples fought. He said that the details were too important to just let go, and to be the best you can be, you needed to get all the wrinkles ironed out. The thing was, I didn't feel like any wrinkles were being ironed out for them. After well over twenty years of marriage, things seemed just as disagreeable as ever.

I learned a lot from my parents that I didn't want to carry with me into my own relationships. As a kid, I felt guilty when my parents fought. There wasn't anything I could have done, but I wanted it to stop. Arguments made it feel like a gray fog had settled over the whole house, and the forecast predicted no change any time soon. My brother and I always said we would be different. We promised that when we grew up we would have conversations—real conversations—instead of arguing. We swore that if we couldn't come to a solution with our spouses, we would just let it go rather than continuing to fight about the same things for years on end.

I guess confrontation is common with our parents' generation, but my generation just isn't that way. We noticed that our parents didn't become happier because of their strong-headed approach. We decided compromise was better than conflict and communication better than confrontation. Best of all, when it comes to communication, my generation is able to connect unlike any other previous generation. The Internet, e-mail, cell phones, blogs, and numerous social media sites have us expecting immediate interaction. Our communication is frequent and ongoing; there are no curfews on the Internet.

CHAPTER 28

TINA'S STORY: YOU CAN'T CHANGE A MAN

When I was young, I didn't have many conversations with my mother about men. She seemed untrusting of and a bit peeved by them. One of the few tidbits of information I did glean from her was that it didn't matter if there was something about a man I didn't like—I could change him. Well, that seemed interesting. If I didn't like who he hung around, his hobbies, or the way he dressed or acted, she made it seem that he would easily change his entire lifestyle because I, his woman, requested it.

At the tender age of nineteen, when I was first married, I found out how very wrong she was. That marriage lasted five long years, and there wasn't a single thing about him (or the relationship) that he changed for me. He didn't change the yelling or the violence, nor did he change seeing his girlfriend after we were married. If anything, he stepped all those things up a notch. He didn't stop the mood swings, he didn't suddenly start doing things to help around the house, and he didn't become a nicer guy. Nothing swayed his opinions, his lifestyle, or anything about him. Being with him was my own damn fault. I should have known that you need to be with someone who you want just as they are, not who you think they could be if they changed this or that.

When that marriage finally came to its end, I remarried. My second marriage has lasted twenty years, and I realize now that sometimes men can change. My husband has flaws, and there have been times that I really wanted things to change—and he has been open to and accepting of my requests. I love him for who he is; he's a man who is willing and capable of changing certain aspects of himself. I realized, though, that he's not changing for me; he's changing because he cares about being a better husband, a better father, and a better man.

Going into relationships with the belief that you can change a man is wrong. Men are men: love them for who they are and not who you believe you can make them. If they truly love you, and if they know how to love you, they will listen to your needs, express their own, and makes the changes in their lives necessary to show you their love. Unfortunately, these men seem few and far between; fortunately, more and more young men are approaching relationships with less need to establish their dominance and impose their will on their partners.

CHAPTER 29

MARY M.'S STORY: HEY, MAN, IT'S NOT ALL ABOUT YOU

My husband, Ed, built an ice skating rink in our backyard last winter. Even while enduring sixty-hour-plus work weeks during the stressful, sequester-induced nose-dive of his company, he made time for weeks of online research, followed by wood sourcing, framework construction, tarp distribution, and days of hammering. Evenings were spent filling the rink, then letting it freeze; filling, then freezing: a mathematically optimized process for the formation of ideal ice. He even engineered a homegrown Zamboni out of a garden hose and some PVC pipe. And midnight after midnight—no matter how cold, dark, or late it felt—Ed headed out into the Vermont winter to groom the ice.

It was a worthwhile endeavor: he spent countless hours out there with our kids. In the morning before school and evenings afterward, Ed coached Clementine through back crossovers and James on his power turns as I watched out the kitchen window. That's the kind of dad he is.

He's the kind of husband, however, who didn't realize that an at-home ice rink would yield unfortunate consequences for a work-at-home mom who had relied on quiet afternoons alone while the rest of the family enjoyed their weekly hours-long skating/pizza/slush Sunday routine. Now, instead of sending them out the door with a wave and a banana—pulse pounding faster at the thought of a few hours at my computer catching up on work—I spent my time putting on and removing my coat; traipsing back and forth to the rink to tie and tighten skates; delivering hot chocolate; and serving as on-call witness for all rink-related feats, antics, and impromptu performances. It was only a matter of time before our backyard became a neighborhood destination, at which point the demands on my time increased to include witnessing the semi-amazing feats of whoever stopped by that day.

A backyard skating rink, as it turns out, is not all twinkle lights and toe jumps. Either because he hasn't been broken down by the sheer repetition of the life of the stay-at-home mom or because his constitution withstands on-call demands better than mine, my husband to this day remains blind to the increased demands imposed on me by his prized creation. Would I rather Ed be an uninvolved "bring me my pipe and slippers" stereotype of a dad? Absolutely not. Do I value and appreciate his involvement, despite his occasional cluelessness? Yes, I do. Does it still frustrate me to no end? Yes, that too.

This is just one of a series of incidences during our married life that highlighted an unexpected divide. Another happened more recently, but rose to the surface in a more immediate way. Actually, "rose to the surface" may be a bit of an understatement—it more burst forth like a massive underwater projectile missile.

I'd just completed writing a piece detailing the work and financial troubles affecting our family. I wouldn't say that we had fallen on hard times, but due to a combination of corporate cutbacks and lack of fiduciary foresight, we were certainly in the act of stumbling. I'd been asked to write an autobiographical account of how Ed's salary cut, along with my resulting return to the workforce as a freelance writer, had affected our family.

This was not an easy time for us or for our children, but it was an eye-opening one—and ultimately, one that put Ed and me on the same page after years of being in entirely different books. Writing the piece was an act of honesty and therapy. I was proud of it, but—as Ed pointed out later—not proud enough to tell him I was writing it. In my defense, we rarely discussed what I was working on, as product descriptions for jewelry catalogues and cosmetic dentistry content don't usually engage his curiosity or interest.

When my editor asked if I preferred that the piece be published under a byline or a pseudonym, I surprised myself by preferring the former. It was a positive representation of our situation and my feelings, and I felt I was in a position to own it. As a courtesy to Ed and our family, I shared it with him first. And that's when the lurking submarine hurtled up through the still, murky waters.

To explain why this shook our marriage so deeply, I'll need to share our background.

My husband and I met as undergraduates at a highly ranked university known for its intense, academically rigorous environment. I majored in creative writing, with a minor in partying, while Ed was in the übercompetitive five-year BS/MS degree program of the school's elite biomedical engineering (BME) department. The English department held a cookout for our graduation reception, whereas the BMEs got a top-shelf open bar with sushi, crab cakes, and a raw bar.

Ed is the smartest person I know, and he naturally continued directly into the doctoral program in BME. It took him ten years to get his degree—not because he was lazy or unfocused, but because he was committed to getting it right. He wanted to accomplish the best PhD in the history of PhDs, and he wasn't going to settle for anything less. It goes without saying: that's a lot of pressure (not an uncommon state of being for my husband).

For the past ten years, Ed has thrown the same level of perfectionism into his job as vice president and chief strategy officer for a small software engineering start-up company, while I stopped working to stay home with our young children. A recent funding shake-up due to the government sequester put us in new and unfamiliar territory: with salaries slashed company-wide and a dimming future as cuts continued to stall progress, I reentered the workforce, and every member of our family had to adjust to a new (and possibly permanent) way of life.

What I couldn't begin to conceive of when I was younger—and am just barely beginning to understand now as I emerge from raising two children—is the degree to which the responsiveness of full-time parenting can tear away at you without the right support mechanisms in place. I was not prepared for the rigors of stay-at-home mother-hood. That's not to say I was unwilling to do it or ungrateful to have the opportunity: I was both willing and grateful, but also unprepared, exhausted, and (more than occasionally) resentful.

Years ago, I read something about how in every relationship, there is a gardener and a flower: one person who tends and the other who flourishes. (Okay, I didn't actually read it; I saw it on an episode of *Will & Grace*.) Regardless of the source, I took the point to heart and kept it with me through the years. In balanced relationships, these roles fluctuate. For many stay-at-home moms, however, I suspect that the role of nurturer becomes fixed. This was certainly the case for me. Prior to having children and while we were both working, Ed and I had a balance of responsibilities. When mothering became my job, I assumed the additional role of full-time gardener, tending constantly to my familial bed of flowers. I knew how hard my husband worked and the pressures he faced daily at the office, and I worked hard to satisfy his needs and the needs of our children. I attempted to take on every household role, including managing the family finances (a task to which I was remarkably unsuited!).

Regardless of the challenges, much of what I read touted the many benefits of work-from-home jobs or part-time telecommuting, both of which are great for families, company finances, and the environment. Despite that, I had been hard-pressed to find a full-time telecommut-ing job for a mother of two in Vermont who has been out of the work-force for the past decade. What I stumbled on, however, was a thriving freelance writing career with seemingly endless opportunities to use the skill that best suits my nature and talents. While the pay is variable (and less than if I held a full-time office job), the hours are flexible, and the work can be carved out around my children's schedule. Through dogged perseverance, I have been able to cobble together a roster of clients who appreciate my work and offer critical flexibility in terms of hours and workload. Being a stay-at-home mom, though immensely valuable, doesn't bring in a dime—and the electric company doesn't trade in the currency of full-time parenting.

My return to work has not been easy on any of us. Only in doing so, though, have I realized just how much—both physically and emotionally—goes into being a stay-at-home parent. Your time is no longer your own. My brain, previously content to wander, became a roiling mass of carpooling plans and scheduling, as well as the other million needs that make up modern childhood. My husband works hard at his job, giving it everything he's got, and I still ask him to leave work early on days when our daughter needs to be picked up from ballet class at five o'clock—the same time that our son needs fetching from hockey all the way across town.

Even after busy days when I'm shuttling kids around, hosting house-wrecking play dates, and rushing off after breakfast and not returning until dinnertime because of one kid's event after another, he still gets annoyed if dinner isn't on the table and the laundry isn't done. And now that I am a member of the workforce—freelance writing, but with full-time hours—I see even fewer ways to make time for relentless domestic pursuits. And to be honest, I don't want to. Nor do I want to return to being a full-time stay-at-home mom—at least not just yet. I aspire to reach a time when I fully appreciate the privilege, but I also want to be appreciated for the effort.

During this uneasy period, I have become much more vocal about identifying and expressing my needs. After all, for the past ten years, my needs have been about fulfilling those of others, which is not a sustainable way to live. My husband, meanwhile, is good at expressing his needs but bad at explaining his rationale. Part of our problem is that we can't read minds, and obviously, we're not alone in that: our marriage stumbled into the classic "men are from Mars, women are from Venus" scenario without us even knowing it. Guessing at each other's motivations was excessively destructive, as we have since realized. My husband can constantly surprise me with his stubbornness but also with his adaptability. And the ability to surprise each other—in a good way—is what keeps our relationship alive.

"Choosing battles" has long been a bone of contention between my husband and me. I think this is likely the case in most families where one parent is the primary caregiver and the other is decidedly less present. By necessity, I choose my battles every day. If my son wants to walk barefoot into the supermarket, he automatically loses a battle. For his safety, and out of respect for the store rules, the answer is no. However, if he wants to wear pajamas for a quick trip to the store on a rainy morning, I see no reason to decline. My husband, however, is horrified when James spends the day in his pajamas. Why the difference in perspective? Because so many battles are waged every day in the life of the stay-at-home parent that we don't even notice half of them anymore.

Moms who are used to positive affirmation in the workplace can struggle with the switch to staying home with kids. Unless you have a particularly empathetic spouse, positive affirmation becomes a thing of the past when you become a stay-at-home mom to a self-serving toddler. While I am lucky to have a supportive network of mom friends, it's not the same; how they feel about me bears no impact on whether there's accord where I need it most: in my home. Just like everyone else, I require validation, the occasional pat on the back. My husband—wonderful in many other ways—fails at this. We are not a "push present" or even a Valentine's Day card sort of family. The Christmas present, if one makes it under the tree, may be a new vacuum cleaner, and I'm certainly not sporting any birthday bling.

Although I used to fantasize about being a stay-at-home mom, I now fantasize about the opposite: a workplace life free of the daily routine of keeping track of everyone's needs but my own. As a freelance writer, I enjoy certain scheduling freedoms, but with that come the expectations of availability. My first year, with a full roster of freelance clients and high hopes of putting in a full work week, has been a frustrating revelation. The time I expected to magically appear when the kids headed off to school simply doesn't exist.

My grand vision for the school year made magnificent use of the six hours when the kids were at school. The plan (don't laugh) went something like this: two hours of freelance work, followed by an hour of exercise, followed by two hours of working on that ever-elusive novel, followed by an hour designated—generously, I thought—for miscellany. So far, my experience has flipped that vision on its head. If I squeeze in one hour of writing among all the miscellaneous tasks, it's a miracle. In the end, as much as I can aspire to a full-time freelance schedule, I still own all of the other thankless tasks and housework that need to be done.

I have nothing but respect for mothers in the workforce who can keep up with domestic demands and kids' schedules while also urging me via Facebook to cheer them on during their latest run. I also have nothing but respect for moms who stay home while managing to maintain a sense of cheer and optimism: the ones who lament the end of summer because they have enjoyed all that unadulterated time with their kids. The only one I don't respect is myself, apparently. I am unable to pursue a full-time career out of feelings of obligation and circumstance but equally unable to appreciate how lucky I have been to get to stay home.

Ed has, meanwhile, tried to step up his game, but there are slip-ups now and then. Last week, for example, when he referred to "watching the kids *for me*," the perception gap widened with the implication that that their care is primarily my responsibility, while his involvement is more akin to that of the goofy bachelor uncle who burps at the dinner table.

Unfortunately, Ed and I don't fight clean. We've lost the leeway to dance around issues and instead just get straight to the metaphorical hair-pulling, eye-gouging heart of it. Either one of us will grab whatever is in reach and pull as hard as we can. It's not something I'm proud of, and we are working on it. I'm half Italian and half Irish, and he's an only child; neither of us effectively learned to resolve issues peacefully.

This isn't the life we envisioned together back in our midtwenties when Ed received his PhD from the best BME program in the country. It wasn't the life I pictured at sixteen, when I opened an envelope to learn I'd scored a perfect eight hundred on my verbal SATs. We didn't anticipate that we'd have to keep a plastic bowl underneath our dishwasher because it leaks whenever we run it, or that we'd still have the same 1997 Subaru Outback—only now with 180,000 miles on it and a trunk that can only be opened from the inside.

Although the future of my husband's company looks at best uncertain at this point, a month ago, I might have said the same about our marriage. We have both been learning that true communication is the only way to serve each other and our family, no matter how the household and extracurricular division of power breaks down. It is finally obvious to me that happiness is a choice we can make together, but it is a choice that requires constant effort and vigilance on all parts.

Ultimately, I agreed that my biographical family story would be published without a byline and that our names would be changed in the story. Unfortunately, too many family disagreements require a winner and a loser; compromise is often not an option. I'm not sure if Ed ever recognized—or even tried to understand—my desire to be seen, my need to be heard. That disconnect runs to the heart of our reality.

CHAPTER 30

CAROL'S STORY: MANAGING FROM A WOMAN'S PERSPECTIVE

Carol, based in New York City, is a forty-five-year-old executive director of a major financial institution. She manages forty employees, and there is a 60/40 percent male/female split. The world in which she has built her success always had female role models in high places.

I treat all my employees—male and female—equally and have never experienced sexism as I worked my way up. Young women are more successful here out of the gate. They seem to feel a greater urgency, which is missing in the young men, to be successful quickly. Today's society is breeding super-people: women who are capable of a career and a family and who are successful at both.

We have begun now to support our male workers in the same way that we have been supporting our women, giving them time off for family commitments. Men have to play catch-up in response to women's early success, so supporting men's lives outside the office helps.

Twenty years ago, I was required to dress in a conservative style. The flannel business suit was the norm. That has changed. Today's working environment allows women to dress in a feminine fashion. Men can feel challenged by both the physical presence of a self-assured woman as well as by her intellect. Feminine fragrance and appearance has long stirred a call to action in men; sensitivity training to recognize proper behavior is required.

Those born in a world of shared leadership roles find it easiest to conform to today's mores. The young men just coming into business grew up in this world, both online and in college. They're more adaptive, but they need to learn that the current male leaders in the companies they're joining are rarely role models. These young men are better served, in fact, by looking to women as leadership models.

CHAPTER 31

LIZZ'S STORY: MEN DON'T WANT WOMEN WHO ARE TOO OPINIONATED

A piece of advice that I got from my mother as a young woman was that men didn't want women who had all of the opinions I did. They wanted good listeners who would hear their stories and rarely chime in with opinions—unless, of course, it was to agree. Having opinions about everything—and being so vocal about them—was sure to turn men off, my mother told me. Men wouldn't want to debate with a date. They would just want to hear about how smart and funny they were.

It sounded to me as if it might have been true, but it was advice I simply couldn't follow. Even if it meant fewer dates, I couldn't pretend to be someone I wasn't.

There may still be mothers giving their daughters that kind of advice when they start dating, but it's doubtful that many girls are following it. Today, taking my mother's advice would be detrimental. Doing so would likely attract boorish men who like to dominate a woman, men who are simply out of step with society and with women.

In today's educational and romantic climate, both women and men are expected to have their own points of view, and neither has to change theirs to conform to their partners' expectations. An inherent expectation of equality permeates relationships. If one person comes into a relationship without having the confidence to share his or her own thoughts and ideas, the relationship is unlikely to last.

In the same way, women may still be telling political pollsters they're voting for a candidate favored by their husbands, but in the privacy of the polls, they're voting on the issues relevant to them. The dynamic of equality leads to power sharing in the modern relationship; the days when the educated, sophisticated man led the household and made the decisions on behalf of the family are over.

THE FUTURE
OF MEN

CHAPTER 32

WHAT CAN WE LEARN FROM THE LAST MATRIARCHAL TRIBE?

THE MOSUO OF SOUTHWEST CHINA

In most societies worldwide, social scientists would describe the family gender dynamic as patrilineal: men play the central role in earning money, owning property, making inheritance decisions, and determining the family's surname. This framework continues to influence the religious right and gender relationships in the United States, although it is slowly changing toward a more egalitarian balance of power for many families. If women do eventually displace men as breadwinners and leaders in business, traditions could shift, ironically making them more similar to an ancient society currently living in rural Southwest China—but with origins stemming from more than two thousand years ago.

While the concept of a matriarchal society may be more familiar to most as the Amazonian tribe of ancient Greek myth, trained in war and agriculture, a living example resides today near Tibet, below the Himalayan Mountains (at an elevation of 8,858 feet) and along the shores of Lake Lugu. The Mosuo women are the leaders of their families, controlling the agricultural work and earning the money that sustains them. The men only participate in fishing, hunting, and tasks that require heavy lifting. Even more unusually, there is no marriage in the Mosuo society.

After a woman attains maturity, the community standard allows her to have sexual encounters with one man or multiple men throughout a lifetime, but she does not marry and continues to remain in her mother's home. Children born from these unions remain with the mother's family, while the men who sire the children remain with their own mother's family, helping to care for their nieces and nephews.

While in China a one-child policy that favored boys was in place until 2015, most Mosuo women (an ethnic minority outside of the immediate concern of the government) have as many as three children, and girls are preferred because they eventually transition into sharing the family leadership.

Anthropologists have suggested that because the Mosuo are geographically isolated, the family dynamics developed naturally, influenced by Buddhist values that emphasized harmony and un-encumbered by the conventions of modern romantic partnerships that have yet to reach the Himalayan-area villages. Furthermore, the Mosuo, an ethnic group composed of nearly fifty thousand people, had no violence, crime, jails, or dissent for most of their history.

In the 1950s and 1960s, the Chinese communist government forced the Mosuo men and women to legally marry. As couples began to share practical everyday experiences that replaced the solely romantic and sexual love that had characterized the relationships previously, their harmonious existence fragmented. They argued and struggled to negotiate the new connections and power dynamics in a unified household, compromising their culture to conform to demands by the Mao Zedong administration.

Eventually, through organized resistance and China's governmental shifts, the Mosuo were able to return to their traditional customs. Starting in the 1980s, the media began to broadly reveal to the rest of the world the Mosuo way of life, spurring an insurgence of tourism to the area that has inspired a few lifestyle changes. The basic family construct, however, remains the same.

The collaborative approach to work and relationships that allowed the Mosuo women to lead and relegated men to a less important role has demonstrated compelling advantages for the society, including a completely peaceful existence. However, the result was achieved only by separating men and women in the family structure, a structure that is unfeasible today. However, as men in the United States and around the world continue to fall behind as the primary successful players in business, it is worth examining the instinctive motivations that led the Mosuo women to rule the society without male involvement.

CHAPTER 33

SUMMARIZING MASCULINITY IN THE TWENTY-FIRST CENTURY

To end on a personal note, as a man, I'm personally excited about the opportunities this new age offers me. Over the past four decades, I have been accurate at envisioning technological, organizational, cultural, and societal shifts well before they are recognized as trends. As described in my book *Hooked Up*, I was the first to grasp the emergence of a new generation of leaders, identifying a young millennial cohort that is just now entering business, politics, education, and adult society and on their way to becoming what I believe will be the most important generation of this century. More recent articles, books, and research from multiple sources are reinforcing the thesis I put forward in *Hooked Up*.

The ideas and perspectives shared in *The Future of Men* are almost entirely factual and most are apparent. The conclusions about their future impact are mine. They seem to me to be incontrovertible, yet I know they will be debated. Many men and women may have problems with the female-centric future I describe; the disruption of the status quo is always challenging to those who stand to suffer from a new order of things. But it is future generations that will be most affected. The full implications of the societal transformation from male to female dominance will not be fully realized until well into the third decade of the twenty-first century. But they will be realized, will become progressively more evident in business, education, politics, culture, society, and families, and will transform the future of America and the world.

So, what is the future of men? I do not believe it is a downward spiral into a subservient role in society, culture, and business—and I hope it is a new and elevated stature gained through personal growth, greater balance of work and personal lives, positive role models, and newly defined perceptions of masculinity. There is a road back from the genetic progression toward the top of the endangered species list.

Well into the twentieth century, man accepted the compliance of woman as his due. His role was that of a provider and a protector. His control over his family, his workplace, and his church was absolute. To what extent his authority extended over women was dependent on the individual man and woman, his society and culture, and his childhood upbringing. Man's dominion over the women in his life was largely left unchallenged in all arenas.

Many people remain lodged in this past, retaining outdated and outmoded policies and behavior. Nevertheless, the shifts in gender roles are having an enormous effect on how society values the roles of both sexes within the culture—and how men and women relate to each other both individually and within communities.

As men wrestle with the enormous changes they have had to absorb since the end of World War II, they are struggling with the fundamental conflict between trying to make more emotionally honest connections and reasserting their pride and maintaining their self-respect. Society today is more challenging for men than ever before. Once upon a time, men were confident about their ability to meet expectations—whether in politics, business, or personal relationships—simply because they were male, and frankly, employers, voters, and women encouraged this attitude. Modern-day men are hardwired from thousands of years of the traditional roles to avoid intimacy: providers, protectors, and decision makers—the modern equivalents of hunters, warriors, and defenders of home and hearth—need not show affection.

Now, men are facing fresh issues. Newly empowered women are demanding more intimacy. Although somewhat relieved of the constant pressure to prove their masculinity, men now have to cope with new expectations of honesty, compassion, and learning how to understand and communicate their feelings and express their love. It will take years of education and enlightenment for men to learn how to respond appropriately in the bedroom and the boardroom to women's needs and desires for intimacy and honesty and to appropriately fulfill women's expectations that men will still be the aggressor in situations when *they* (the women) consider it to be appropriate.

The vast majority of men do not want to turn back the gains of the women's movement. In fact, studies have shown that men are even more loath than women to see women return to their traditional place. Clearly, societal shifts will persist as men and women continue to grapple with their new positions, what is expected of them, and whatever changes in their relationships are on the horizon.

Just as women are turning to women's cohort groups for support and to have their needs met, men must learn to rely on one another for reinforcement, affirmation, and help with day-to-day struggles. Men need a positive and profemale place, both in-person and online, where they can connect on a practical, emotional, and spiritual level. Although there are many organizations focused on fostering assistance for women in advancing their careers, there is no available data on how many of such groups exist for male teachers, secretaries, nurses, and so on. Men need to be as proactive in forming and facilitating these kinds of groups as they have been in forming women's advocacy and career development organizations in every major industry and business community.

In recent history, when men held steady as the business leaders, a person's technical skills, intelligence, and membership in the old boys' network were the most influential factors in success. Today, according to the Carnegie Institute, as detailed in *Forbes*, 85 percent of career success is due to communication, negotiation, and leadership skills; only 15 percent is attributed to technical abilities and intelligence. There is no question that the paradigm shift has occurred, and taking into account the growing numbers of college-educated women entering and becoming instrumental in the workplace, they are clearly positioned to dominate executive leadership in the future as the glass ceiling becomes a distant memory.

Stay-at-home dads also need visible communities and their own networks of support. While media coverage of homemaking dads has expanded, their working female partners have come together in bonds of sisterhood through organizations such as Lean In, SheSpeaks, Ellevate, the 3% Conference, and WomenAdvancing.org.

Organizations focused on positively supporting males are needed to update resources and programs for education, careers, and relationships. Schools can introduce gamification, video, and remote learning programs at all educational levels; invest in arts and home economics programs; and encourage both genders to participate in those programs.

Men, in short, need a new set of rules, guidelines, and skills. A new narrative needs to be developed and communicated to support young men who are emerging into their adult years. Marketers' messages and media stereotypes need to be updated to embrace the future rather than reflect the past.

Men must also stop stereotyping themselves. Many sociologists report that women have adapted much better to society's changes than men in part because men are reluctant to pursue traditionally female occupations and family roles. "As a society, we haven't really changed men's roles to the same extent that we have women's roles," professor of psychology Sarah Murnen told the *Kenyon College Alumni Bulletin*.

Married or not, parents should make special efforts to expose their sons to positive, happy relationships. They must cultivate friendships with adults who have made romantic relationships work so that by the time these boys are men, they have seen many different examples of positive bonding. Parents must emphasize intimacy-building traits, such as cooperation and putting a group ahead of self-interest, as positive traits in men. They must expand definitions of manhood to encompass every type of man, instead of using just the narrow ideals of strength and power.

Only when our society becomes more comfortable with current expressions of both heterosexual and LGBT lives will we learn new and more egalitarian ways to work together. On most college campuses today, there are support organizations serving a wide spectrum of gender definitions, expanding beyond the standard LGBT cohorts. The same holds true for multicultural organizations. Caucasian heterosexual males are typically prevented by culture and college regulations from forming their own support groups where they can engage in positive and constructive preparation for a future in which they no longer have their customary power base, with a focus on healthy relationships and career development. The conventional concept of fraternities needs to be completely discarded; they need to be reinvented around a redefined purpose and support structure that enables young men to come together around topics other than sex, sports, gaming, TV, drugs, and alcohol. Perhaps that's an unfair generalization of young men, but it's one that resonates as accurate with most people. The large numbers of men, of all gender and cultural definitions, who are not going to college also have few places where they can be welcomed, embraced, supported, and educated.

More fathers are embracing caregiving and equitable marriages, exploring the hopes and dreams that inform their choices, and analyzing economic and social developments that are restructuring their traditional rung on the career ladder, but there is nowhere near the number of support groups for them as exist for their working wives and ex-wives.

It is a corporate and societal imperative that we focus resources and capital on initiatives that help men prepare for, adapt to, and learn to succeed in the organization and family of the present and future. The future roles of men and women in society, culture, and business will take decades to evolve, but the future itself has already been ordained. Look around: in the middle and junior ranks of most organizations, in politics, in families, and in the media, women are a dominating force, and men are slowly adapting to the upheaval that is radically transforming society, culture, business, politics, and religion.

Some of my conclusions about the future of male–female relationships will be met by many with derision, debate, and dismissal. Many men and women are suffering from a heavily challenged sense of self. It is difficult, however, not to look around and see the writing on the wall.

Both men and women who grew up with a fundamental belief in traditional male/female roles will hold on for dear life to their prescriptive place in the world—a world in which a man has dominance over his kingdom, exerting physical, financial, and emotional control over his family and workplace. But it's a serious error to assume that the same dynamics that formed the male and female realities of the past one hundred plus years will be those that inform the next hundred.

We are entering a new age of female dominance and a reshaping of the male psyche, the male libido, and the male ego. This is the new reality, and it will gain greater and greater momentum. Nothing in the history of humanity can prepare us for this newly upside-down world. We cannot look to the past or even the present for rules to help us navigate the future. We can only accept or fight the inevitable ascendency of women and the dramatically shifting roles of men. We can, it seems, rely on the genetic stability of women to guide us into the future, collaboratively and cooperatively with men, to achieve a more stable and healthier gender balance.

ACKNOWLEDGMENTS

Researching and writing *The Future of Men* has both triggered and accompanied a period of great personal exploration and growth. We are living through a period of historic transformation, not only of the move from male to female dominance but of transformation across almost every aspect of the social, cultural, political, educational, and business spectrum of our lives. The first Internet browser was introduced in 1993, which marked the beginning of a thirty-to-forty-year period of disruption and change unequaled since the transformation from the agrarian age to the Industrial Age in the late 1800s and early 1900s. As we move through the shift from the industrial and information ages to the relationship age (a term I coined and trademarked in 1998), we can't even begin to measure or fully understand the many ways our relationships are being affected.

Gender relationships are at the forefront of changes in society, with women rising up to proclaim, exert, and implement their rights. My mom, Gert Myers, was never a vocal part of the women's rights movement, but her life personified its goals and many of its realities. She began working when I was two and started her college education at night when I was nine, ultimately receiving her master's degree in accounting and becoming one of the US Air Force's highest ranking civilian computer programmers. My sister, Sandra Adirondack, was battling for civil rights with the Congress of Racial Equality in the 1960s and has devoted her career to supporting nonprofit and global rights initiatives. Many effects, both positive and negative, come from having these two women as prominent forces in my life. Their forceful presence lives throughout this book. Also embedded throughout *The Future of Men* is the positive energy and love of my daughter, Ariele, who influences me more than she can ever imagine. This book's dedication focuses on my children and grandchildren as well as all future generations: every word of every page was written with the future of Leo and Jonah Tritt and Aaron Myers in mind. I deeply love and cherish them, as I do my son-in-law, Dori Tritt; my sons, Andy and Dan; and their respective spouses, Dominique and Janie. They give me and my life meaning far beyond what any career achievements can represent.

Also giving my life immense value and meaning is Ronda Carnegie, who is lighting, with love and her positive spirit, the journey into the future that we are on together.

Norah Burden and her daughters, Izzy and Claire, have made an indelible contribution to my life and my books. I look back at our time together with affection, love, and happy memories. My journey the past several years has been aided and enhanced immeasurably by my confidante and guide Nicole Janssen, to whom I owe great thanks. All those in whom I've confided over the past few years have made important contributions as I progressed through my personal journey.

Maryann Teller has been my colleague and friend for nearly twenty-seven years and has been an integral and incredibly important partner as we navigated through the choppy waters of business and life. I owe her more than gratitude and thank her husband, Rich, and son, Ryan, for allowing me to share her time and commitment.

Connor Zickgraf joined me as an intern to assist in writing the publishing proposal for *The Future of Men*. Since then, as the book's project manager and producer, she has become a leading expert on men's issues and the emerging men's movement. Without question, Connor has been my most important partner in advancing *The Future of Men* platform. I'm extremely grateful to the team at MyersBizNet, who have empowered me to embrace my passion even as we simultaneously expanded our business and launched MediaVillage. Thanks especially to Ed Martin and Charlotte Lipman.

I'm grateful to Jeffrey Hayzlett for introducing me to my publisher, Inkshares, and to the team there, led by Adam Jack Gomolin, Matt

Kaye, and Avalon Radys. Inkshares's innovative publishing platform provides unique and relevant opportunities, and I appreciate their support. The editing support of the team at Girl Friday Productions has made a meaningful contribution and enhanced the book immeasurably. Thanks to Devon Fredericksen, Christina Henry de Tessan, Ryan Boudinot, Amanda O'Brien, and Monique Vescia.

My colleague Ian Wishingrad at BigEyedWish has been a thoughtful and valuable friend and contributor throughout the writing and editing process, as have Matt Fried and Jacqui Rossi. Thanks to the team at MediaPlace, led by Jeremy Hopwood and Scott Kushner, for their valuable work. I am confident that Bryn Freedman will be a valuable collaborator in advancing *The Future of Men* story. Thanks to Douglas Dicconson, Karol Martesko-Fenster, Damon Smith, Nelly Petit, and Alexandra Rosen of Cinelan; and Morgan Spurlock and Jeremy Chilnick of Warrior Poets. The collaboration with our public relations and publicity team at Hilsinger-Mendelson has been very productive, and the contributions of Sandi Mendelson, Deborah Jensen, Margaret Rogalski, and Amrit Judge have been and will continue to be greatly valued. I've received important and appreciated advance publication support from Mike Walsh, Merrill Brown, Andrew Ferebe, Alex Manley, AskMen, Walter Sabo, Shelley Zalis, Jackie Kelley, and Janet Stilson. *Men's Health* editors Bill Phillips and Peter Moore, publisher Ronan Gardiner, writer Ben Court, and Rodale executive Renee Appelle are welcome collaborators and supporters.

The early endorsements from my friends and colleagues Morgan Spurlock, Ken Burns, Contessa Brewer, Dr. Jane Greer, Larry Kramer, Sydney Fulkerson, Charlie Collier, Kendall Allen, Ross Martin, Alan Cohen, Ken Dychtwald, Mitch Joel, Jeffrey Hayzlett, David Houle, and Keith Reinhard mean more to me than a simple acknowledgment can express. Thanks also to Ellen Archer and Gail Tifford and her colleagues at Unilever. In anticipation of their support and contributions to the success of *The Future of Men*, I'm grateful to my many colleagues in the media business who I know will assist in generating public awareness and advancing our multiplatform publishing goals.

Throughout the research process required for *The Future of Men*, WriterAccess has been an invaluable resource. I'm grateful to Byron White, Kristin Schiff, and to all the researchers and contributors.

I'm sure I've failed to acknowledge the contribution and support of many who should know that I sincerely regret my lapse and promise to make it up with recognition in my next book, which I know I'll eventually write. So to all of you who should be included here but aren't, know that you are inspiring and motivating me. And to all of you who have read *The Future of Men*, I hope you've gained a new understanding of the evolving gender realities we all are confronting and are committed to true gender equality without bias. Please share your stories and your comments at www.futureofmen.com or with me personally at jm@jackmyers.com.

ABOUT THE AUTHOR

Photo © 2015 Doug Goodman

The Future of Men is Jack's fifth book focusing on advancing the health of business, culture, and humanity. Jack is a cultural, economic, and technological visionary; award-winning documentary film producer (*Hank Aaron: Chasing the Dream* and *GE Focus Forward Films*); author; chairman of MyersBizNet; and publisher of MediaVillage. com, a community of more than two hundred leading global companies. His last book, *Hooked Up: A New Generation's Surprising Take on Sex, Politics and Saving the World*, won the International Book Award for Youth Issues and was a finalist for the USA Book Award for Pop Culture. Jack is founder of Women Advancing, a seventy-five-hundred–member all-women's dual-mentoring support group, and he passionately believes that society needs to recognize how successful the women's movement has been and will continue to be and identify and address the implications for men, especially young men and boys. Jack's career includes management positions at CBS, ABC, and Metromedia. He is a board member of the Newhouse School of Public Communications at Syracuse University and served on the advisory board for the Steinhardt School of Culture, Education, and Human Development at New York University where he studied media ecology with Dr. Neil Postman. He is chairman of the board of the IRTS Foundation, which works to build future leaders through access, education, and diversity initiatives.

BIBLIOGRAPHY

CHAPTER 1

Smith, Jed. "New Study Demolishes One Major Myth About How Attached Men and Women Are to Their Relationships." Independent Journal Review, June 10, 2015. http://www.ijreview.com/2015/06/342044-new-study-demolishes-one-major-relationship-myth-men-women.

CHAPTER 2

"About Forté." Forté Foundation. Accessed September 24, 2015. http://www.fortefoundation.org/site/PageServer?pagename=about#.VgSssGRViko.

Banks, Beth, and Ros Usheroff. "How Men and Women Communicate Differently at Work." Business Know-How. Accessed September 24, 2015. http://www.businessknowhow.com/growth/gendercommunication.htm.

Blackman, Stacy. "More Women Head to School for M.B.A.s." US News & World Report, August 19, 2011. http://www.usnews.com/education/blogs/mba-admissions-strictly-business/2011/08/19/more-women-head-to-school-for-mbas.

Bosker, Bianca. "Fortune 500 List Boasts More Female CEOs Than Ever Before." Huffington Post, May 7, 2012. http://www.

huffingtonpost.com/2012/05/07/fortune-500-female-ceos_n_
1495734.html.

"Building the Foundation: Business Education for Women at Harvard
University: 1937–1970." Harvard Business School. Accessed
September 24, 2015. http://www.library.hbs.edu/hc/wbe/
exhibit_mba-program.html.

Caliper Corporation. *The Qualities That Distinguish Women Leaders.*
Princeton, NJ: Caliper Corporation, 2005. http://www.
calipermedia.calipercorp.com/whitepapers/us/Qualities-in-
Women-Leaders.pdf.

Carnevale, Anthony, Nicole Smith, and Jeff Strohl. *Help Wanted:
Projections of Job and Education Requirements Through 2018.*
Washington, DC: Georgetown University Center on Education
and the Workforce, 2010. http://files.eric.ed.gov/fulltext/
ED524310.pdf.

Damast, Alison. "Extra Effort Lures Women MBAs." Bloomberg Business,
November 20, 2008. http://www.bloomberg.com/bw/stories/
2008-11-20/extra-effort-lures-women-mbasbusinessweek-
business-news-stock-market-and-financial-advice.

"Data & Statistics: MBA Students." Harvard Business School. Accessed
September 24, 2015. http://www.hbs.edu/recruiting/data/
Pages/default.aspx.

Dickler, Jessica. "Best-Paid Executives: The Gender Gap Exaggerated."
CNNMoney, October 3, 2007. http://money.cnn.com/2007/
10/02/news/newsmakers/mpwpay/.

Dorning, Mike. "Obama Fails to Stem Middle-Class Slide He
Blamed on Bush." Bloomberg Business, April 30, 2012.
http://www.bloomberg.com/news/articles/2012-05-01/
obama-fails-to-stem-middle-class-slide-he-blamed-on-bush.

Eaves, Elisabeth. "In This Recession, Men Drop Out." *Forbes*, April 10,
2009. http://www.forbes.com/2009/04/09/employment-men-
women-recession-opinions-columnists-gender-roles.html.

"Femininity." *Wikipedia*. Accessed September 24, 2015. https://
en.wikipedia.org/wiki/Femininity.

Gannon, Drew. "How Men and Women Differ in the Workplace."
The Fiscal Times, May 25, 2012. http://www.thefiscaltimes.com/

Articles/2012/05/25/How-Men-and-Women-Differ-in-the-Workplace.

Gnaulati, Enrico. "Why Girls Tend to Get Better Grades Than Boys Do." *Atlantic*, September 18, 2014. http://www.theatlantic.com/education/archive/2014/09/why-girls-get-better-grades-than-boys-do/380318.

The Great Mancession of 2008–2009: Statement Before the House Ways and Means Committee Subcommittee on Income Security and Family Support On "Responsible Fatherhood Programs." (June 17, 2010) (statement by Mark J. Perry, professor of economics at the University of Michigan-Flint and Visiting Scholar at the American Enterprise Institute). https://www.aei.org/wp-content/uploads/2011/10/GreatMancessionTestimony.pdf.

Harjani, Ansuya. "Male or Female Bosses? The Majority Prefers . . ." *CNBC*, November 11, 2013. http://www.cnbc.com/2013/11/11/employees-prefer-a-male-boss-over-female-poll.html.

Huffington, Christina. "Women And Equal Pay: Wage Gap Still Intact, Study Shows." *Huffington Post*, April 9, 2013. http://www.huffingtonpost.com/2013/04/09/women-and-equal-pay-wage-gap_n_3038806.html.

Isidore, Chris. "7.9 Million Jobs Lost." *CNNMoney*, July 2, 2010. http://money.cnn.com/2010/07/02/news/economy/jobs_gone_forever/index.htm.

Jones, Del. "Women CEOs Slowly Gain on Corporate America." *USA Today*, January 2, 2009. http://usatoday30.usatoday.com/money/companies/management/2009-01-01-women-ceos-increase_N.htm.

Livingston, Gretchen. "The Rise of Single Fathers: A Ninefold Increase Since 1960." Pew Research Center, July 02, 2013. http://www.pewsocialtrends.org/2013/07/02/the-rise-of-single-fathers.

Lockhard, Brett, and Michael Wolf. "Occupational Employment Projections to 2020." *Monthly Labor Review* 128, no. 12 (2012): 84–108. http://www.bls.gov/opub/mlr/2012/01/art5full.pdf.

"No News Is Bad News: Women's Leadership Still Stalled in Corporate America." Catalyst, December 14, 2011. http://www.catalyst.

org/media/no-news-bad-news-womens-leadership-still-
stalled-corporate-america.

"One-Third of Fathers with Working Wives Regularly Care for Their
Children, Census Bureau Reports." *Newsroom Archive*, US
Census Bureau, December 5, 2011. https://www.census.gov/
newsroom/releases/archives/children/cb11-198.html.

Pappas, Stephanie. "'Mancession' Shifts Gender Roles." Live Science,
August 23, 2011. http://www.livescience.com/15695-mancession-
recession-shifts-gender-roles.html.

"Pyramid: Women in S&P 500 Companies." Catalyst, November 15, 2012.
http://www.catalyst.org/knowledge/women-sp-500-companies.

Rigoglioso, Marguerite. "Researchers: How Women Can Succeed in
the Workplace." Stanford Graduate School of Business, March
1, 2011. https://www.gsb.stanford.edu/insights/researchers-
how-women-can-succeed-workplace.

Rosin, Hanna. "The End of Men." *Atlantic*, June 8, 2010. http://www.
theatlantic.com/magazine/archive/2010/07/the-end-of-
men/308135.

Sandberg, Sheryl. "Sheryl Sandberg Pushes Women to "Lean In."
60 Minutes video, 12:31. *CBSNews.* March 10, 2013.
http://www.cbsnews.com/videos/sheryl-sandberg-pushes-
women-to-lean-in-3.

Scott, Robert. "Manufacturing Job Loss: Trade, Not Productivity,
Is the Culprit." Economic Policy Institute, August 11, 2015.
http://www.epi.org/publication/manufacturing-job-loss-
trade-not-productivity-is-the-culprit.

Smith, Jeremy Adam. *The Daddy Shift: How Stay-at-Home Dads,
Breadwinning Moms, and Shared Parenting Are Transforming
the American Family.* Boston: Beacon Press, 2009.

US Bureau of Labor Statistics. "Employment Projections: 2010–20
News Release." *Economic News Release*, US Bureau of Labor
Statistics, February 1, 2012. http://www.bls.gov/news.release/
archives/ecopro_02012012.htm.

US Bureau of Labor Statistics. "Household Data Annual Averages:
Employed Persons by Detailed Occupation, Sex, Race, and

Hispanic or Latino Ethnicity." Current Population Survey, 2014. http://www.bls.gov/cps/cpsaat11.pdf.

US Bureau of Labor Statistics. "How Women Spend Their Time." *Spotlight on Statistics*, US Bureau of Labor Statistics, March 2011. http://www.bls.gov/spotlight/2011/women.

US Bureau of Labor Statistics. "The Recession of 2007–2009." *BLS Spotlight on Statistics*, US Bureau of Labor Statistics, February 2012. http://www.bls.gov/spotlight/2012/recession/pdf/recession _bls_spotlight.pdf.

US Bureau of Labor Statistics. "Table 3. Employment by Major Industry Sector, 2002, 2012, and Projected 2022." *Economic News Release*, US Bureau of Labor Statistics, December 19, 2013. http://www.bls.gov/news.release/ecopro.t03.htm.

US Bureau of Labor Statistics. "Table 4. Fastest Growing Occupations, 2012 and Projected 2022." *Economic News Release*, US Bureau of Labor Statistics, December 19, 2013. http://www.bls.gov/ news.release/ecopro.t04.htm.

US Bureau of Labor Statistics. "Table 7. Employment by Summary Education and Training Assignment, 2012 and Projected 2022." *Economic News Release*, US Bureau of Labor Statistics, December 19, 2013. http://www.bls.gov/news.release/ecopro. t07.htm.

US Bureau of Labor Statistics. "Table 8. Occupations with the Largest Projected Number of Job Openings Due to Growth and Replacement Needs, 2012 and Projected 2022." *Economic News Release*, US Bureau of Labor Statistics, December 19, 2013. http://www.bls.gov/news.release/ecopro.t08.htm.

US Bureau of Labor Statistics. "Women." *Labor Force Statistics from the Current Population Survey*, US Bureau of Labor Statistics. Accessed September 24, 2015. http://www.bls.gov/cps/ demographics.htm#women.

US Bureau of Labor Statistics. "Women and Employment by Industry." *Economics Daily*, US Bureau of Labor Statistics, January 7, 2009. http://www.bls.gov/opub/ted/2009/jan/wk1/art03.htm.

US Bureau of Labor Statistics. "Women in the Labor Force: A
    Databook." *BLS Reports* 1040, February 2013. http://www.bls.
    gov/cps/wlf-databook-2012.pdf.
US Bureau of Labor Statistics. "Women as a Percent of Total Employed
    in Selected Occupations, 2011." *Economics Daily*, US Bureau
    of Labor Statistics, May 1, 2012. http://www.bls.gov/opub/
    ted/2012/ted_20120501.htm.
US Census Bureau. *Statistical Abstract of the United States: 2012.*
    Washington, DC: US Census Bureau and US Department
    of Commerce, 2012. http://www2.census.gov/library/
    publications/2011/compendia/statab/131ed/2012-statab.pdf.

CHAPTER 3

Sykes, Bryan. *Adam's Curse: A Future Without Men.* New York: WW
    Norton, 2004.

CHAPTER 4

Hamon, Katherine. "No Sex Needed: All-Female Lizard Species Cross
    Their Chromosomes to Make Babies." *Scientific American*,
    February 21, 2010. http://www.scientificamerican.com/article/
    asexual-lizards.
Hamzelou, Jessica. "Men's Y Chromosome Is Not About to Go Extinct."
    New Scientist, February 22, 2012. https://www.newscientist.
    com/article/mg21328535-100-mens-y-chromosome-is-not-
    about-to-go-extinct.
Holland, Stephanie. "Marketing to Women Quick Facts." She-conomy,
    May 7, 2008. http://she-conomy.com/facts-on-women.
Perry, Mark. "Stunning College Degree Gap: Women Have Earned
    Almost 10 Million More College Degrees than Men since 1982."
    American Enterprise Institute, May 13, 2013. https://www.aei.
    org/publication/stunning-college-degree-gap-women-have-
    earned-almost-10-million-more-college-degrees-than-men-
    since-1982.

Sykes, Bryan. *Adam's Curse: A Future Without Men*. New York: WW Norton, 2004.

CHAPTER 5

Clinton, Bill. *My Life*. New York: Knopf, 2004.

Deutsch, Linda. "OJ Simpson Murder Trial: 'If It Doesn't Fit, You Must Acquit.'" *NBC Los Angeles*, June 11, 2014. http://www. nbclosangeles.com/news/local/OJ-Simpson-20-Years-Later-Glove-Fit-Darden-Dunne-Murder-Trial-of-the-Century-262534821.html.

Kundera, Milan. *The Unbearable Lightness of Being*. New York: Harper & Row, 1984.

Mustich, Emma. "A Weinergate Timeline." *Salon*, June 1, 2011. http:// www.salon.com/2011/06/01/weinergate_timeline.

Solin, Ken. "The Truth About Emotional Honesty." MariaShriver. com, April 20, 2012. http://mariashriver.com/blog/2012/04/ truth-about-emotional-honesty.

Zychik, Joe. *The Most Personal Addiction: How I Overcame Sex Addiction and How Anyone Can*. SexualControl.com, 2002. http://www.sexualcontrol.com/images/stories/the-most-personal-first-48.pdf.

CHAPTER 6

"Internet Pornography Statistics." TopTenReviews. Accessed September 24, 2015. http://internet-filter-review.toptenreviews.com/ internet-pornography-statistics.html.

Gross, Alan E. "The Male Role and Heterosexual Behavior." *Journal of Social Issues* 34, no. 1 (2010): 87–107.

Hearing on Pornography's Impact on Marriage and the Family Subcommittee on the Constitution, Civil Rights and Property Rights Committee on Judiciary United States Senate, November 10, 2010 (2010) (testimony of Jill C. Manning, MS). http:// s3.amazonaws.com/thf_media/2010/pdf/ManningTST.pdf.

Herkov, Michael. "What Is Sexual Addiction?" Psych Central, December 10, 2006. http://psychcentral.com/lib/what-is-sexual-addiction.

"Statistics and Other Reference Resources on the Impact of Pornography to Marriages, Families, and Society." Prodigals International. Accessed September 25, 2015. http://prodigalsinternational. org/statistics-on-sexual-addiction.html.

Weiss, Robert. "Who Is a Sex Addict?" Psych Central, January 30, 2013. http://psychcentral.com/lib/who-is-a-sex-addict/.

CHAPTER 7

Always. "Always #LikeAGirl." YouTube video, 3:18. June 26, 2014. https://www.youtube.com/watch?v=XjJQBjWYDTs.

BetterBrandsSC. "Bud Light 'Johnny, I Love You Man' 1995." YouTube video, 0:30. December 12, 2012. https://www.youtube.com/watch?v=Xglqe2UhJME.

Boogaart, Judith. "Maintaining the Image." *Amaranthus* 1996, no. 1 (1996): 31–34. http://scholarworks.gvsu.edu/cgi/viewcontent. cgi?article=1068&context=amaranthus.

"The Calvin Klien Ads That Made Marky Mark Famous." Marky Mark Fan Club, 1997. Accessed September 25, 2015. http://markyadvertising.tripod.com.

"Case Study: Old Spice Response Campaign." D&AD. Accessed September 25, 2015. http://www.dandad.org/en/old-spice-response-campaign.

Debord, Guy. *The Society of the Spectacle*. New York: Zone Books, 1994.

Dodge. "Official 2015 Dodge Super Bowl Commercial | Wisdom | #DodgeWisdom." YouTube video, 1:01. January 31, 2015. https://www.youtube.com/watch?v=JKKlqMs19tU.

Dos Equis. "The World's Most Interesting Man: Dos Equis Commercials." Dos Equis. Accessed September 25, 2015. http://www.dosequis.com/Videos/dos-equis-commercials.

Elliott, Stuart. "Commercials With a Gay Emphasis Are Moving to Mainstream Media." *New York Times*, June 25, 2013. http://

www.nytimes.com/2013/06/26/business/media/commercials-with-a-gay-emphasis-are-moving-to-mainstream-media.html.

Elliott, Stuart. "Viagra and the Battle of the Awkward Ads." *New York Times*, April 24, 2004. http://www.nytimes.com/2004/04/25/business/viagra-and-the-battle-of-the-awkward-ads.html?pagewanted=all.

Garfield, Bob. "Cue the Breasts, It's Miller Time: A Beer Company's Abomination of a Commercial." *Advertising Age*, January 20, 2003. http://adage.com/article/ad-review/garfield-s-adreview-miller-lite-s-catfight-ogilvy/36645.

Garfield, Bob. "Heineken 'DraftKeg': The Most Sexist Beer Commerical Ever Produced?" *Advertising Age*, August 27, 2007. http://adage.com/article/ad-review/heineken-draftkeg-sexist-beer-commerical-produced/120078.

Grinspan, Izzy. "A&F Quarterly: The Story of Abercrombie's Highbrow, Controversial, Sort of Amazing Magalog." Racked, October 1, 2014. http://www.racked.com/2014/10/1/7574879/a-and-f-quarterly-abercrombie-magazine.

Groshoff, David. "Eat This, Man Up, or Just Put a Scarf In It." *Huffington Post*, January 2, 2012. http://www.huffingtonpost.com/david-groshoff/man-up-gender-stereotypes_b_1173578.html.

Infante, Dave. "Remembering the Swedish Bikini Team, Beer Advertising's Forgotten First Ladies." Thrillist, August 12, 2014. https://www.thrillist.com/drink/nation/swedish-bikini-team-old-milwaukee-beer-history-story-behind-the-sexiest-beer-commercials.

Kane, Leslie. "Spectacle." University of Chicago: Theories of Media Keywords Glossary. Accessed September 25, 2015. http://csmt.uchicago.edu/glossary2004/spectacle.htm.

Kilbourne, Jean. *Can't Buy My Love: How Advertising Changes the Way We Think and Feel*. New York: Simon & Schuster, 1999.

Kirk, Jim. "'Real Men' Ads Move onto TV May Be Genius." *Chicago Tribune*, October 15, 2003. http://articles.chicagotribune.com/2003-10-15/business/0310150167_1_bud-light-radio-campaign-radio-spots.

Kroker, Arthur. "Television and the Triumph of Culture: Three Theses." *Canadian Journal of Political and Social Theory* 9, no. 3 (Fall 1985): 37–47. http://journals.uvic.ca/index.php/ctheory/article/view/14054/4827.

Lazarus, George. "The Answer To 'Whassup': Budweiser Sales." *Chicago Tribune*, May 26, 2000. http://articles.chicagotribune.com/2000-05-26/business/0005260409_1_grand-clio-metropolitan-pier-client-and-agency.

Lepitak, Stephen. "Diet Coke Hunk's Return Cleared by ASA over 'irresponsible' Complaint." Drum, July 17, 2013. http://www.thedrum.com/news/2013/07/17/diet-coke-hunks-return-cleared-asa-over-irresponsible-complaint.

"Marketing Beer." Marketing-Schools.org. Accessed September 25, 2015. http://www.marketingschools.org/consumer-psychology/how-to-market-beer.html.

Messner, Michael A., and Jeffrey Montez De Oca. "The Male Consumer as Loser: Beer and Liquor Ads in Mega Sports Media Events." *Signs: Journal of Women in Culture and Society Signs* 30, no. 3 (2005): 1879–909. doi:10.1086/427523.

Nudd, Tim. "10 Sexist Ads Made by Total Pigs." *AdWeek*, July 13, 2011. http://www.adweek.com/adfreak/10-sexist-ads-made-total-pigs-133401.

Old Spice. "Old Spice | The Man Your Man Could Smell Like." YouTube video, 0:32. February 4, 2010. https://www.youtube.com/watch?v=owGykVbfgUE.

O'Reilly, Terry. "Sex in Advertising." *Under the Influence with Terry O'Reilly*. CBC Radio, April 21, 2012. http://www.cbc.ca/radio/undertheinfluence/sex-in-advertising-1.2801858.

Parvaz, D. "Nudity, Sex Articles in Abercrombie & Fitch 'Magalog' Draw Fire." *Seattle Post-Intelligencer*, December 2, 2003. http://www.seattlepi.com/lifestyle/article/Nudity-sex-articles-in-Abercrombie-Fitch-1131136.php8.

Sacks, Glenn. "Protest Anti-Father Verizon Commercial." GlennSacks.com. November 7, 2004. http://www.glennsacks.com/campaign.php?id=4.

Schultz, EJ. "Top Ad Campaigns of the 21st Century: Budweiser: Whassup." *Advertising Age*, March 29, 1999. http://adage.com/lp/top15/#whassup.

Stein, Jeanine. "An Intoxicating Mix of Celebrity: Rob Fitzgerald Is the Lying Loser Who Can't Beg a Brew in Beer Commercials but Those Spots Have Made Him a Winner with Television Viewers." *Los Angeles Times*, January 25, 1996. http://articles.latimes.com/1996-01-25/entertainment/ca-28306_1_rob-fitzgerald.

Strate, Lance. "Beer Commercials: A Manual on Masculinity." In *Men, Masculinity, and the Media*, edited by Steve Craig, 78–92. Newbury Park, CA: Sage, 1992.

Sunset, Bali. "I Love You, Man Campaign." *Marketing Campaign Case Studies*, February 19, 2008. http://marketing-case-studies.blogspot.com/2008/02/i-love-you-man-campaign.html.

"Top 10: Worst Male-Bashing Ads." Masculine Heart, January 14, 2008. http://masculineheart.blogspot.com/2008/06/top-10-worst-male-bashing-ads.html.

Toyota USA. "My Bold Dad | Presented by the Bold New Camry | Toyota." YouTube video, 1:14. February 1, 2015. https://www.youtube.com/watch?v=Un6uP6cykgo.

"USA: Budweiser 'Whassup?!' Ads Win Grand Prix in Cannes." Just-drinks.com, June 27, 2000. http://www.just-drinks.com/news/budweiser-whassup-ads-win-grand-prix-in-cannes_id75820.aspx.

"Videos." Old Milwaukee. Accessed September 25, 2015. http://oldmilwaukee.com/videos.

Wolf, Barnet D. "Anheuser-Busch's 'Real Men of Genius' Ad Campaign Wins Accolades." *Columbus Dispatch*, May 19, 2004. http://www.highbeam.com/doc/1G1-118267913.html.

Wong, Venessa. "Diet Coke Brings Back Hunk Ad; Viewers Yawn." Bloomberg Business. January 30, 2013. http://www.bloomberg.com/bw/articles/2013-01-30/diet-coke-brings-back-hunk-ad-viewers-yawn.

CHAPTER 8

"AskMen and Cosmopolitan.com Unveil Survey Results on Gender
    Differences." IGN Entertainment, July 20, 2010. http://corp.
    ign.com/press/2010/askmen-and-cosmopolitancom-unvel-
    survey-results-on-gender-differences.
Chapman, Gary. "Understanding the Five Love Languages." Focus
    on the Family. Accessed September 25, 2015. http://www.
    focusonthefamily.com/marriage/communication-and-
    conflict/learn-to-speak-your-spouses-love-language/
    understanding-the-five-love-languages.
Cohen, Shiri, Mark S. Schultz, and Emily Weiss. "Eye of the Beholder:
    The Individual and Dyadic Contributions of Empathic
    Accuracy and Perceived Empathic Effort to Relationship
    Satisfaction." *Journal of Family Psychology* 26, no. 2 (2012):
    236–245. doi:10.1037/a0027488.
"Do Women and Men Communicate Differently?" Curiosity, December
    22, 2008. https://curiosity.com/playlists/do-women-and-men-
    communicate-differently-jR9LHhia/?utm_source=dsc&utm_
    medium=rdr&utm_campaign=rdrwork#intro-playlist.
Gwynne, Rori. *Have the Relationship You Want*. Raleigh, NC: Lulu.
    com, 2006.
Harman, Justine. "The Underreported Pressures of Being Born Male
    in the U.S." *ELLE*, February 23, 2015. http://www.elle.com/
    culture/movies-tv/news/a26944/the-mask-you-live-in-film.
Heller, Kalman. "Sexuality and Marital Intimacy." Psych Central,
    January 30, 2013. http://psychcentral.com/lib/sexuality-and-
    marital-intimacy.
Lenhart, Amanda, and Maeve Duggan. "Couples, the Internet, and
    Social Media." Pew Research Center, February 11, 2014.
    http://www.pewinternet.org/2014/02/11/couples-the-internet-
    and-social-media.
"Online Dating Statistics." Statistic Brain Research Institute, March 18,
    2015. http://www.statisticbrain.com/online-dating-statistics.
Pearse, Damien. "Facebook's 'Dark Side': Study Finds Link to
    Socially Aggressive Narcissism." *Guardian*, March 17, 2012.

http://www.theguardian.com/technology/2012/mar/17/
facebook-dark-side-study-aggressive-narcissism.

Raye, Rori. "How to Date Smart for Lasting Love." eHarmony.
Accessed September 25, 2015. http://www.eharmony.com/
dating-advice/dating/how-to-date-smart-for-lasting-love/#.
VgXkf2RViko.

Sherwood, Susan. "10 Ways Men and Women Communicate
Differently." *Jadin Best's Blog*, October 21, 2014. https://
jadinbest.wordpress.com/2014/10/21/10-ways-men-and-
women-communicate-differently.

Weiss, Robert. "Is Male Porn Use Ruining Sex?" *Psychology Today*,
January 20, 2014. https://www.psychologytoday.com/blog/
love-and-sex-in-the-digital-age/201401/is-male-porn-use-
ruining-sex.

Wenner, Melinda. "Sex Is Better for Women in Love." *Scientific
American Mind* 19, no. 1 (2008): 9. doi:10.1038/scientific
americanmind0208-9b.

"What Is Intimacy and Why Is It So Important?" Relationships Australia.
Accessed September 25, 2015. http://www.relationships.org.au/
relationship-advice/faqs/what-is-intimacy-and-why-is-it-so-
important.

"Women with Sexually Addicted Husbands Often Neglected for
Treatment." The Ranch. Accessed September 25, 2015. http://
www.recoveryranch.com/articles/sex-addiction/women-with-
sexually-addicted-husbands-often-neglected-for-treatment.

CHAPTER 9

A., Suzie. "Prince Charming Syndrome." *Suzie the Single Dating
Diva*, May 13, 2013. http://singledatingdiva.com/2013/05/13/
prince-charming-syndrome.

Altman, Alex. "A Brief History of Girlie Mags." *Time*, December 01, 2008.
http://content.time.com/time/arts/article/0,8599,1862878,00.
html.

Bedell, Geraldine. "I Wrote the Story of O." *Guardian*, July 24, 2004. http://www.theguardian.com/books/2004/jul/25/fiction. features3.

Blumberg, Antonia. "What You Need To Know About The 'Quiverfull' Movement." *Huffington Post*, May 26, 2015. http://www. huffingtonpost.com/2015/05/26/quiverfull-movement-facts_n_7444604.html.

Brannon, Linda. *Gender: Psychological Perspectives, Sixth Edition*. New York: Pearson Education, 2011.

Breene, Sophia. "Do We Really Have Sexual Peaks?" Greatist, November 7, 2014. http://greatist.com/happiness/do-we-have-sexual-peaks.

Dirks, Tim. "History of Sex in Cinema: The Greatest and Most Influential Sexual Films and Scenes." AMC Filmsite. Accessed September 28, 2015. http://www.filmsite.org/sexinfilms1.html.

Fraterrigo, Elizabeth. "Taking Stock of Playboy Legacy as Hugh Hefner Tries to Buy Back Rest of Company." *Washington Post*, July 18, 2010. http://www.washingtonpost.com/wp-dyn/content/article/2010/07/16/AR2010071602718.html.

Garber, Megan. "All Unhappy Families: The Downfall of the Duggars." *Atlantic*, May 22, 2015. http://www.theatlantic.com/entertainment/archive/2015/05/the-downfall-of-the-duggars/394013.

Gross, Alan E. "The Male Role and Heterosexual Behavior." *Journal of Social Issues* 34, no. 1 (Winter 1978): 87–107. doi:10.1111/j.1540-4560.1978.tb02542.x.

Kerner, Ian. "Ian Kerner, She Comes First (Episode 382)" The Art of Charm podcast, 53:01. *The Art of Charm*, March 03, 2015. http://theartofcharm.com/podcast-episodes/ian-kerner-she-comes-first-episode-382.

Kerner, Ian. "What Do Women Consider Good Sex?" AskMen. Accessed September 28, 2015. http://www.askmen.com/dating/love_tip/596_what-do-women-consider-good-sex.html.

Moore, Andrew. "Top 10: Things Women Want: The Ten Most Important Qualities Women Are Looking For." AskMen.

Accessed September 28, 2015. http://www.askmen.com/
top_10/dating/top-10-things-women-want.html.

Offen, Karen. "The History of Feminism Is Political History."
American Historical Association, May 2011. https://www.
historians.org/publications-and-directories/perspectives-
on-history/may-2011/political-history-today/the-history-
of-feminism-is-political-history.

Pease, Barbara, and Allan Pease. *Why Men Don't Listen and Women
Can't Read Maps.* London: Pease International, 2003.

New York Times. "Court Lifts Ban on 'Ulysses' Here." *New York Times,*
December 7, 1993. http://www.nytimes.com/books/00/01/09/
specials/joyce-court.html?_r=2.

"Our History." Playboy Enterprises. Accessed September 28, 2015.
http://www.playboyenterprises.com/about/history.

Reid, Danny. "Safe in Hell (1931) Review." Pre-Code.com, September
18, 2012. http://pre-code.com/pre-code-safe-in-hell-1931.

Stern, Marlow. "60 Years of Playboy: The Most Iconic Playboy
Covers, from Marilyn Monroe to Kim Kardashian." *Daily
Beast,* November 30, 2013. http://www.thedailybeast.com/
galleries/2013/11/30/60-years-of-playboy-the-most-iconic-
playboy-covers-from-marilyn-monroe-to-kim-kardashian.
html.

CHAPTER 10

Comedy Central. "Inside Amy Schumer—Last F**kable Day—Uncensored."
YouTube video, 4:57. April 22, 2015. https://www.youtube.
com/watch?v=XPpsI8mWKmg.

Covert, Bryce. "It's Not Just Us: Women Around the World
Do More Housework and Have Less Free Time."
ThinkProgress. March 14, 2014. http://thinkprogress.org/
economy/2014/03/14/3399641/oecd-housework-women.

Fischer, Mary. "Why Women Are Leaving Men for Other Women."
O, the Oprah Magazine, April 2009. http://www.oprah.com/
relationships/Why-Women-Are-Leaving-Men-for-Lesbian-
Relationships-Bisexuality.

Ghose, Tia. "Women's Sexuality May Depend on Romantic Options."
    LiveScience, August 25, 2015. http://www.livescience.com/
    51970-available-options-shape-sexual-orientation.html.

Goodman, Lizzy. "Leaving It All or Having It All? A Closer Look at
    Once Straight Women Who Are Leaving Their Husbands
    for Other Women." *ELLE*, November 18, 2013. http://
    www.elle.com/life-love/sex-relationships/advice/a13868/
    exploring-female-sexuality.

Gunn, Tim, and Ada Calhoun. *Gunn's Golden Rules: Life's Little Lessons
    for Making It Work*. New York: Gallery Books, 2010.

Hickey, Walter. "Here's How Many Messages Men Have to Send to
    Women on a Dating Site to Be Sure of Getting a Response."
    Business Insider, July 17, 2013. http://www.businessinsider.
    com/online-dating-message-statistics-2013-7.

Jacobs, Tom. "Courtesy Can Be Counterproductive." *Pacific Standard*,
    February 24, 2014. http://www.psmag.com/books-and-culture/
    courtesy-can-counterproductive-75293.

"Kinsey's Heterosexual-Homosexual Rating Scale." The Kinsey Institute.
    Accessed September 28, 2015. http://www.kinseyinstitute.org/
    research/ak-hhscale.html.

Kuttner, Robert. "She Minds the Child, He Minds the Dog." *New
    York Times*, June 25, 1989. http://www.nytimes.com/1989/
    06/25/books/she-minds-the-child-he-minds-the-dog.
    html?pagewanted=all.

Lamoureux, Mack. "This Group of Straight Men Is Swearing Off
    Women." VICE, September 24, 2015. http://www.vice.com/
    read/inside-the-global-collective-of-straight-male-separatists.

Love, Dylan. "Inside Red Pill, the Weird New Cult for Men Who Don't
    Understand Women." Business Insider, September 15, 2013.
    http://www.businessinsider.com/the-red-pill-reddit-2013-8.

Merwin, Hugh. "Brogurt, or Greek 'Yogurt for Men,' Is a Real Thing."
    Grub Street, February 25, 2013. http://www.grubstreet.
    com/2013/02/powerful-yogurt-greek-yogurt-for-men.html.

Meyers, Seth. "Fear of Intimacy in Men: Cause, Relationship
    Problems, Tips." *Insight Is 20/20* (blog), *Psychology Today*,
    April 15, 2013. https://www.psychologytoday.com/blog/insight-

is-2020/201304/fear-intimacy-in-men-cause-relationship-problems-tips.

Mims, Christopher. "Thanks to the 'Mancession,' Metrosexuals Have Become 'Manfluencers™.'" Quartz, October 24, 2013. http://qz.com/138822/thanks-to-the-mancession-metrosexuals-have-become-manfluencers.

OECD. "Balancing Paid Work, Unpaid Work and Leisure." OECD, July 3, 2014. http://www.oecd.org/gender/data/balancingpaidworkunpaidworkandleisure.htm.

Randall, Kay. "Stay-at-Home Dads' Psychological Well-Being Gauged in New Study." UT News, January 07, 2008. http://news.utexas.edu/2008/01/07/fathers.

Theobald, Stephanie. "Lesbianism: Sexual Fluidity Is a Fact of Life for Women." *Guardian*, November 26, 2013. http://www.theguardian.com/lifeandstyle/2013/nov/26/lesbianism-women-sexual-fluidity-same-sex-experiences.

"Tim Gunn Excerpt: 'Gunn's Golden Rules.'" *ABC News*. Accessed September 29, 2015. http://abcnews.go.com/GMA/Books/tim-gunn-excerpt-gunns-golden-rules/story?id=11552513.

CHAPTER 11

Abrams, Lindsay. "Study: Why Straight Women Are Often Close with Gay Men." *Atlantic*, February 21, 2013. http://www.theatlantic.com/health/archive/2013/02/study-why-straight-women-are-often-close-with-gay-men/273353.

Gates, Gary J., and Frank Newport. "LGBT Percentage Highest in D.C., Lowest in North Dakota." Gallup, February 15, 2013. http://www.gallup.com/poll/160517/lgbt-percentage-highest-lowest-north-dakota.aspx.

Mapes, Diane. "Why Straight Women and Gay Men Are Often so Close." *NBC News*, February 28, 2013. http://www.nbcnews.com/id/50981531/ns/health-mens_health/t/why-straight-women-gay-men-are-often-so-close/#.VgoVymRVikp.

Miller, Claire Cain. "The Divorce Surge Is Over, but the Myth Lives On." *New York Times*, December 01, 2014. http://www.

nytimes.com/2014/12/02/upshot/the-divorce-surge-is-over-
but-the-myth-lives-on.html?hp&action=click&pgtype=Hom
epage&module=second-column-region°ion=top-news&WT.
nav=top-news&_r=1&abt=0002&abg=0.

Russell, Eric, Danielle Delpriore, Max Butterfield, and Sarah Hill.
"Friends with Benefits, but without the Sex: Straight Women
and Gay Men Exchange Trustworthy Mating Advice."
Evolutionary Psychology 11, no. 1 (2013): 132–147. http://evp.
sagepub.com/content/11/1/147470491301100113.full.pdf.

CHAPTER 12

Adam, Seth. "Video: VP Biden Says Will and Grace Educated
Americans on Equality." GLAAD, May 06, 2012. http://www.
glaad.org/blog/video-vp-biden-says-will-and-grace-educated-
americans-equality.

Adams, Erik, Phil Dyess-Nugent, Genevieve Koski, David Sims, and
Todd VanDerWerff. "The Episode That Liberated—then
Destroyed—Ellen." AV Club. August 14, 2013. http://www.
avclub.com/article/the-episode-that-liberatedthen-destroyed
ielleni-101551.

Battles, Kathleen, and Wendy Hilton-Morrow. "Gay Characters in
Conventional Spaces: *Will and Grace* and the Situation Comedy
Genre." *Critical Studies in Media Communication* 10, no. 1
(March 2002): 87–105. http://www.csun.edu/~vcspc00g/301/
will%26grace-csmc.pdf.

Capeheart, Jonathan. "From Harvey Milk to 58 Percent." *Washington
Post*, March 18, 2013. http://www.washingtonpost.com/blogs/
post-partisan/wp/2013/03/18/from-harvey-milk-to-58-
percent.

Castiglia, Christopher, and Christopher Reed. "The Revolution Might
Be Televised." In *If Memory Serves: Gay Men, AIDS, and the
Promise of the Queer Past*, 113–144. Minneapolis: University
of Minnesota Press, 2012.

Kissell, Rick. "'Modern Family,' 'Criminal Minds' Win as Season
Wraps." *Variety*, May 23, 2013. http://variety.com/2013/tv/

ratings/modern-family-criminal-minds-win-as-season-wraps-1200486917.

Klemm, Michael D. "Queer as Folk: Six Feet Under." CinemaQueer, September 2001. http://www.cinemaqueer.com/review%20 pages/qafsixfeetunder.html.

Kregloe, Karman. "Are Gay Men More Acceptable Than Lesbians on TV?" AfterEllen.com, July 23, 2010. http://www.afterellen.com/ tv/76507-are-gay-men-more-acceptable-than-lesbians-on-tv.

Kutner, Max. "A Proud Day at American History Museum as LGBT Artifacts Enter the Collections." *Smithsonian*, August 19, 2014. http://www.smithsonianmag.com/smithsonian-institution/ will-grace-affirms-role-american-history-180952400/?no-ist.

Lo, Malinda. "Back in the Day: Coming Out With Ellen" AfterEllen. com, April 08, 2005. http://www.afterellen.com/tv/34682-back-in-the-day-coming-out-with-ellen.

Rotello, Gabriel. "Andrew Sullivan Declares the 'End of AIDS'—Again." *The Blog, Huffington Post*, June 25, 2007. http:// www.huffingtonpost.com/gabriel-rotello/andrew-sullivan-declares-_b_53624.html.

"Will and Grace." World Public Library. Accessed September 29, 2015. http://www.worldlibrary.org/articles/Will_and_Grace.

"Will & Grace: Awards & Nominations." Television Academy. Accessed September 25, 2015. http://www.emmys.com/shows/will-grace.

Wong, Curtis M. "'Will & Grace' Star Eric McCormack Didn't Want To Play Gay, Co-Star Megan Mullally Reveals." *Huffington Post*, October 12, 2012. http://www.huffingtonpost.com/ 2012/10/12/will-and-grace-star-eric-mccormack-playing-gay_n_1959483.html.

CHAPTER 13

Allen, Steve. "The 1990s: The Loss of Shared Experience." In *Encyclopaedia Britannica Online*. Accessed September 25, 2015. http://www.britannica.com/art/television-in-the-United-States/The-1990s-the-loss-of-shared-experience.

Bellafante, Ginia. "Sympathy for the Devil: The Nice-Guy Serial Killer Next Door." *New York Times*, November 22, 2007. http://www.nytimes.com/2007/11/23/arts/television/23dext.html?_r=2&.

Doyle, Sady. "Mad Men's Very Modern Sexism Problem." *Atlantic*, August 2, 2010. http://www.theatlantic.com/entertainment/archive/2010/08/mad-mens-very-modern-sexism-problem/60788.

Eaves, Elisabeth. "In This Recession, Men Drop Out." *Forbes*, April 10, 2009. http://www.forbes.com/2009/04/09/employment-men-women-recession-opinions-columnists-gender-roles.html.

Goudreau, Jenna. "The Changing Roles of TV Dads." *Forbes*, June 15, 2010. http://www.forbes.com/2010/06/15/tv-dads-parenthood-modern-family-forbes-woman-time-dean-mcdermott.html

Grosz, Christy. "Antiheroes at Work." *Los Angeles Times*, June 16, 2010. http://articles.latimes.com/2010/jun/16/news/la-en-antiheroes-20100616.

Leonard, Andrew. "Inside 'Breaking Bad,' TV's Most Exquisitely Agonizing Drama." *Rolling Stone*, June 10, 2011. http://www.rollingstone.com/movies/news/inside-breaking-bad-tvs-most-exquisitely-agonizing-drama-20110610.

Livingston, Gretchen. "Less than Half of U.S. Kids Today Live in a 'traditional' Family." Pew Research Center, December 22, 2014. http://www.pewresearch.org/fact-tank/2014/12/22/less-than-half-of-u-s-kids-today-live-in-a-traditional-family.

Reimers, Valerie. "American TV Sitcoms: The Early Years to the Present." *Cercles* 8 (2003): 114–121. http://www.cercles.com/n8/reimers.pdf.

Rodriguez, Gregory. "The 'Mad Men' Mystique: Were the 1960s All That Great?" *Chicago Tribune*, October 12, 2011. http://articles.chicagotribune.com/2011-10-12/site/ct-perspec-1012-mystique-words-20111012_1_liberation-characters-mad-men.

"U.S. Fatherless Statistics." Fatherhood Factor. Accessed September 25, 2015. http://fatherhoodfactor.com/us-fatherless-statistics.

CHAPTER 14

Kushner, David. "Dungeon Master: The Life and Legacy of Gary Gygax." *Wired*, March 10, 2010. http://archive.wired.com/gaming/ virtualworlds/news/2008/03/ff_gygax?currentPage=all.

Schiesel, Seth. "Gary Gygax, Game Pioneer, Dies at 69." *New York Times*, March 5, 2008. http://www.nytimes.com/2008/03/05/ arts/05gygax.html.

CHAPTER 15

"Edward R. Murrow vs. McCarthyism." The Cold War Museum. Accessed September 25, 2015. http://www.coldwar.org/ articles/50s/Murrowvs.McCarthyism.asp.

Moylan, Brain. "Jon Stewart's Daily Show Skewered the Powerful and Pushed US Satire Forward." *Guardian*, August 5, 2015. http://www.theguardian.com/tv-and-radio/2015/aug/05/ jon-stewart-daily-show-pushed-american-satire-forward.

CHAPTER 16

McBride, Alex. "Landmark Cases: Roe v. Wade (1973)." PBS, December 2006. http://www.pbs.org/wnet/supremecourt/rights/landmark _roe.html.

Tucker, Ken. "The 100 Greatest Moments In Television: 1970s." Entertainment Weekly's EW.com. February 19, 1999. Accessed October 30, 2015. http://www.ew.com/article/1999/ 02/19/100-greatest-moments-television-1970s.

CHAPTER 17

American Psychological Association. *Stress in America: Paying With Our Health*. Washington, DC: American Psychological Association, 2015. doi:10.1037/e511782015-001.

Chuck, Elizabeth. "Juggling Act: Why Are Women Still Trying to Do It All?" *NBC News*, January 14, 2014. http://usnews.nbcnews.

com/_news/2014/01/14/22291797-juggling-act-why-are-women-still-trying-to-do-it-all?lite.

Cohen, Patricia. "Signs of Détente in the Battle Between Venus and Mars." *New York Times*, June 1, 2007. http://www.nytimes.com/learning/teachers/featured_articles/20070601friday.html.

Consoli, John. "Women's Cable Networks Prep for Upfront Battles." *Broadcasting and Cable*, February 4, 2013. http://www.broadcastingcable.com/news/advertising-and-marketing/women%E2%80%99s-cable-networks-prep-upfront-battles/53085.

Drake, Bruce. "Another Gender Gap: Men Spend More Time in Leisure Activities." Pew Research Center, June 10, 2013. http://www.pewresearch.org/fact-tank/2013/06/10/another-gender-gap-men-spend-more-time-in-leisure-activities.

Drexler, Peggy. "Don't Call Him Mr. Mom: The Rise/Reign of the Stay-at-Home Dad." *The Blog, Huffington Post*, June 6, 2012. http://www.huffingtonpost.com/peggy-drexler/dont-call-him-mr-mom-the_b_1573895.html.

Freedman, Mia. "Gastrosexuals. Blame Jamie and Gordon. Or Should We Thank Them?" Mamamia, August 10, 2008. http://www.mamamia.com.au/lifestyle/gastrosexuals-blame-jamie-and-gordon-or-should-we-thank-them.

Fullerton, Horton M. "Labor Force Participation: 75 Years of Change, 1950–98 and 1998–2025." *Monthly Labor Review*, December 1999. http://www.bls.gov/mlr/1999/12/art1full.pdf.

"Future Foundation Studies Show Trend of 'Gastrosexuals' in the Kitchen." *FSR*, April 18, 2013. https://www.fsrmagazine.com/content/future-foundation-studies-show-trend-gastrosexuals-kitchen.

Glasier, Vicki. "One-Third of Fathers with Working Wives Regularly Care for Their Children." *Newsroom Archive*, US Census Bureau, December 5, 2011. https://www.census.gov/newsroom/releases/archives/children/cb11-198.html.

Glover, Eleanor. "Rise of the 'Gastrosexual' as Men Take up Cooking in a Bid to Seduce Women." *Daily Mail*, July 21, 2008. http://

www.dailymail.co.uk/femail/article-1036921/Rise-gastrosexual-men-cooking-bid-seduce-women.html.

Kersten, Andrew Edmund. "'Under the Stress of Necessity': Women and the AFL." In *Labor's Home Front: The American Federation of Labor during World War II*, 100–138. New York: New York University Press, 2006.

Leer, Jonathan. "PhD Thesis on Masculinity in TV Cooking Shows." University of Copenhagen, June 30, 2014. http://news.ku.dk/all_news/2014/06/phd_thesis_on_masculinity_in_tv_cooking_shows.

Leonhardt, David. "Pulling Back from the Crisis: A Roadmap for the Future of the American Economy." In *The Global Economic Crisis and Potential Implications for Foreign Policy and National Security*, edited by R. Nicholas Burns and Jonathon Price, 35–45. Washington, DC: Aspen Institute, 2009.

Livingston, Gretchen. "Less Than Half of U.S. Kids Today Live in a 'traditional' Family." Pew Research Center, December 22, 2014. http://www.pewresearch.org/fact-tank/2014/12/22/less-than-half-of-u-s-kids-today-live-in-a-traditional-family.

Lluch, Alex, and Elizabeth Lluch. "Introduction." In *The Ultimate Guide for Men & Women to Understand Each Other: Improve Your Love, Communication and Friendship*, 5–14. San Diego, CA: WS Publishing Group, 2010.

London, Bianca. "Men Think They Have Conquered the Kitchen—Because They Create More Adventurous Dishes." *Daily Mail*, July 24, 2012. http://www.dailymail.co.uk/femail/article-2178283/Whats-cooking-good-looking-Men-think-Kings-kitchen-according-new-research.html.

Marcotte, Amanda. "Even When They Don't Have Jobs, Men Do Less Housework Than Women." *Slate*, January 6, 2015. http://www.slate.com/blogs/xx_factor/2015/01/06/gender_and_housework_even_men_who_don_t_work_do_less_than_women.html.

"The 1960s-70s American Feminist Movement: Breaking Down Barriers for Women." Tavaana. Accessed September 29, 2015.

https://tavaana.org/en/content/1960s-70s-american-feminist-movement-breaking-down-barriers-women.

OECD. "Balancing Paid Work, Unpaid Work and Leisure." OECD, July 3, 2014. http://www.oecd.org/gender/data/balancingpaid workunpaidworkandleisure.htm.

Rampell, Catherine. "U.S. Women on the Rise as Family Breadwinner." *New York Times*, May 29, 2013. http://www.nytimes.com/2013/05/30/business/economy/women-as-family-breadwinner-on-the-rise-study-says.html?_r=0.

Rampton, Martha. "The Three Waves of Feminism." Pacific University of Oregon, October 23, 2014. http://www.pacificu.edu/about-us/news-events/three-waves-feminism.

Roberts, Soraya. "Pop Culture's House Husbands Lag Behind the Reality in American Homes." *Daily Beast*, June 18, 2013. http://www.thedailybeast.com/articles/2013/06/18/pop-culture-s-house-husbands-lag-behind-the-reality-in-american-homes.html.

Silverman, Rachel Emma. "Dealing With the 'Daddy Track': Men Face Challenges Going Part Time." *Wall Street Journal*, September 1, 2015. http://www.wsj.com/articles/dealing-with-the-daddy-track-men-face-challenges-going-part-time-1441099800?mg=id-wsj.

Sullivan, Patricia. "Voice of Feminism's 'Second Wave.'" *Washington Post*, February 5, 2006. http://www.washingtonpost.com/wp-dyn/content/article/2006/02/04/AR2006020401385.html.

US Bureau of Labor Statistics. "American Time Use Survey Summary." *Economic News Release*, US Bureau of Labor Statistics, June 24, 2015. http://www.bls.gov/news.release/atus.nr0.htm.

US Census Bureau. "Mother's Day: May 13, 2012." *Profile America Facts for Features*, US Census Bureau, March 19, 2012. https://www.census.gov/newsroom/releases/archives/facts_for_features_special_editions/cb12-ff08.html.

US Department of Labor. "Latest Annual Data." Women's Bureau, US Department of Labor. Accessed September 25, 2015. http://www.dol.gov/wb/stats/latest_annual_data.htm.

Wang, Wendy, Kim Parker, and Paul Taylor. "Breadwinner Moms." Pew Research Center, May 29, 2014. http://www.pewsocialtrends. org/2013/05/29/breadwinner-moms.

Wang, Wendy, Kim Parker, and Paul Taylor. "Chapter 3: Married Mothers Who Out-Earn Their Husbands." Pew Research Center, May 29, 2013. http://www.pewsocialtrends.org/2013/05/29/ chapter-3-married-mothers-who-out-earn-their-husbands.

Wang, Wendy, Kim Parker, and Paul Taylor. "Chapter 4: Single Mothers." Pew Research Center, May 29, 2013. http://www. pewsocialtrends.org/2013/05/29/chapter-4-single-mothers.

Wang, Wendy. "The 'Leisure Gap' Between Mothers and Fathers." Pew Research Center, October 17, 2013. http://www.pewresearch. org/fact-tank/2013/10/17/the-leisure-gap-between-mothers- and-fathers.

"When Women Earn More Than Their Husbands." The University of Chicago Booth School of Business, February 18, 2013. http://www.chicagobooth.edu/about/newsroom/news/2013/ 2013-02-18-bertrand.

Yearwood, Lugusta. "Nigella Lawson Is Right. Baking Is a Feminist Act." *Guardian*, May 31, 2011. http://www.theguardian.com/ commentisfree/2011/may/31/nigella-lawson-baking- feminist-act.

CHAPTER 18

Appelbaum, Binyamin. "What the Hobby Lobby Ruling Means for America." *New York Times*, July 22, 2014. http://www.nytimes. com/2014/07/27/magazine/what-the-hobby-lobby-ruling- means-for-america.html.

Duke, Alan. "Timeline to 'Retribution': Isla Vista Attacks Planned over Years." *CNN*, May 27, 2014. http://www.cnn.com/2014/05/26/ justice/california-elliot-rodger-timeline.

Grinberg, Emanuella. "Why #YesAllWomen Took Off on Twitter." *CNN*, May 27, 2014. http://www.cnn.com/2014/05/27/living/ california-killer-hashtag-yesallwomen.

"Every Trafficking Victim in the United States Should Have Access to Justice." Human Trafficking Pro Bono Legal Center. Accessed September 25, 2015. http://www.htprobono.org.

Henderson, J. Maureen. "When It Comes To Workplace Sexism, Millennial Women Suffer Most." *Forbes*, March 11, 2014. http://www.forbes.com/sites/jmaureenhenderson/2014/03/11/when-it-comes-to-workplace-sexism-millennial-women-suffer-most.

Hess, Amanda. "Three New Cases Challenge Sexual Assault on High School and College Campuses." *Slate*, April 22, 2013. http://www.slate.com/blogs/xx_factor/2013/04/22/rape_at_occidental_and_swarthmore_three_new_title_ix_cases_challenging_rape.html.

Hoag, Zach J. "Rape Culture, Bob Jones University and the End of Forgiveness." *The Blog, Huffington Post*, June 24, 2014. http://www.huffingtonpost.com/zach-j-hoag/rape-culture-bob-jones-university-and-the-end-of-forgiveness_b_5518082.html.

Jaffe, Eric. "The New Subtle Sexism Toward Women in the Workplace." Fast Company, June 2, 2014. http://www.fastcompany.com/3031101/the-future-of-work/the-new-subtle-sexism-toward-women-in-the-workplace.

Junkin, Vanessa. "Girl Raped in High School Hallway as Class Goes On." *USA Today*, May 9, 2014. http://www.usatoday.com/story/news/nation/2014/05/07/maryland-high-school-rape/8803161.

Lowder, J. Bryan. "In War on Women, History Matters." *Slate*, March 26, 2012. http://www.slate.com/blogs/xx_factor/2012/03/26/war_on_women_frank_rich_and_amanda_marcotte_show_why_history_matters.html.

"New Efforts to Combat Human Trafficking." *The Diane Rehm Show*, October 3, 2013. http://thedianerehmshow.org/shows/2013-10-03/new-efforts-combat-human-trafficking/transcript.

Slaughter, Anne-Marie. "Why Women Still Can't Have It All." *Atlantic*, July/August, 2012. http://www.theatlantic.com/magazine/archive/2012/07/why-women-still-cant-have-it-all/309020.

Slaughter, Anne-Marie. "Yes, You Can." *New York Times*, March 7, 2013. http://www.nytimes.com/2013/03/10/books/review/sheryl-sandbergs-lean-in.html?pagewanted=all&_r=0&mtrref=undefined&gwh=73223FA657DB5C7C7488C7D894EA98B1&gwt=pay.

Taylor, Paul, Kim Parker, Rich Morin, Rakesh Kochhar, Gretchen Livingston, Rick Fry, and Wendy Wang. "On Pay Gap, Millennial Women Near Parity—For Now." Pew Research Center, December 11, 2013. http://www.pewsocialtrends.org/2013/12/11/on-pay-gap-millennial-women-near-parity-for-now.

Walker-Rodriguez, Amanda, and Rodney Hill. "Human Sex Trafficking." *FBI Law Enforcement Bulletin*, March 2011. https://leb.fbi.gov/2011/march/human-sex-trafficking.

Waltman, Max. "Criminalize Only the Buying of Sex." *New York Times*, updated August 24, 2015. http://www.nytimes.com/roomfordebate/2012/04/19/is-legalized-prostitution-safer/criminalize-buying-not-selling-sex.

Weiss, Sasha. "The Power of #YesAllWomen." *New Yorker*, May 26, 2014. http://www.newyorker.com/culture/culture-desk/the-power-of-yesallwomen.

WYSK. "BOLD Over: Enterprising Women Wow and Inspire at the WE Festival." Women You Should Know, January 17, 2014. http://www.womenyoushouldknow.net/bold-over-enterprising-women-wow-inspire-we-festival.

CHAPTER 19

Anderson, Nick. "Student Loan Default Rate Declines to 13.7 Percent; Federal Government Says the Figure 'Is Still Too High.'" *Washington Post*, September 24, 2014. https://www.washingtonpost.com/local/education/national-student-loan-default-rate-declines-to-137-percent/2014/09/24/d280c8bc-43ee-11e4-b437-1a7368204804_story.html.

Bidwell, Allie. "Student Loan Expectations: Myth vs. Reality." *US News & World Report*, October 7, 2014. http://www.usnews.com/

news/blogs/data-mine/2014/10/07/student-loan-expectations-myth-vs-reality.

Budd, Ashley. "Missing Men: Addressing the College Gender Gap." Higher Ed Admissions Live, January 24, 2012. http://www.higheredlive.com/missing-men.

Casselman, Ben. "Why Men Are More Likely to Drop Out." *Wall Street Journal*, February 22, 2013. http://blogs.wsj.com/economics/2013/02/22/why-men-are-more-likely-to-drop-out.

CCAP. "The Male-Female Ratio in College." *Forbes*, February 16, 2012. http://www.forbes.com/sites/ccap/2012/02/16/the-male-female-ratio-in-college.

Christensen, Clayton M., Michael B. Horn, Louis Caldera, and Louis Soares. *Disrupting College: How Disruptive Innovation Can Deliver Quality and Affordability to Postsecondary Education*. Washington, DC: Center for American Progress, February 2011. https://cdn.americanprogress.org/wp-content/uploads/issues/2011/02/pdf/disrupting_college.pdf.

Day, Lori. "Why Boys Are Failing in an Educational System Stacked Against Them." *The Blog, Huffington Post*, June 27, 2011. http://www.huffingtonpost.com/lori-day/why-boys-are-failing-in-a_b_884262.html.

DiPrete, Thomas A., and Claudia Buchmann. *Gender Disparities in Educational Attainment in the New Century: Trends, Causes and Consequences*. Russell Sage Foundation, July 2013. http://www.s4.brown.edu/us2010/Data/Report/report07172013.pdf.

Dwyer, Rachel E., Randy Hodson, and Laura McCloud. "Gender, Debt, and Dropping Out of College." *Gender & Society* 27, no. 1 (2013): 30–55. doi:10.1177/0891243212464906.

Francese, Peter. "When It Comes to Education, Men Are Getting Schooled." *Advertising Age*, February 15, 2011. http://adage.com/article/adagestat/women-earning-college-graduate-degrees-men/148888.

Francis, David R. "Why Do Women Outnumber Men in College?" National Bureau of Economic Accessed September 25, 2015. Research. http://www.nber.org/digest/jan07/w12139.html.

Goldin, Claudia, Lawrence F. Katz, and Ilyana Kuziemko. "The Homecoming of American College Women: The Reversal of the College Gender Gap." *Journal of Economic Perspectives* 20, no. 4 (Fall 2006): 133–156. http://www2.econ.iastate.edu/classes/econ321/orazem/goldin_college.pdf.

Gurian, Michael. "Disappearing Act." *Washington Post*, December 4, 2005. http://www.washingtonpost.com/wp-dyn/content/article/2005/12/02/AR2005120201334.html.

Kingkade, Tyler. "Student Debt Repayment Causes Concern Among Many Borrowers." *Huffington Post*, June 26, 2013. http://www.huffingtonpost.com/2013/06/26/student-debt-repayment_n_3500251.html.

Lewin, Tamar. "At Colleges, Women Are Leaving Men in the Dust." *New York Times*, July 08, 2006. http://www.nytimes.com/2006/07/09/education/09college.html?pagewanted=all&_r=0.

Logan, Tim. "Student Loan Debt Curbs Housing Market by $83 Billion, Study Says." *Los Angeles Times*, September 22, 2014. http://www.latimes.com/business/realestate/la-fi-student-loan-debt-housing-market-20140922-story.html.

OECD. "Education and Skills: New Entrants by Sex and Age." OECD. Stat. Accessed September 25, 2015. https://stats.oecd.org/Index.aspx?DataSetCode=RNENTAGE.

OECD. "Education." OECD Better Life Index. Accessed September 25, 2015. http://www.oecdbetterlifeindex.org/topics/education.

OECD. *Gender Equality in Education, Employment and Entrepreneurship: Final Report to the MCM 2012*. Paris: OECD, 2012. http://www.oecd.org/employment/50423364.pdf.

Russell Sage Foundation. "The Rise of Women: Seven Charts Showing Women's Rapid Gains in Educational Achievement." *RSF Review*, February 21, 2013. http://www.russellsage.org/blog/rise-women-seven-charts-showing-womens-rapid-gains-educational-achievement.

Sacks, Glenn. "Why Males Don't Go to College." GlennSacks.com, November 13, 2002. http://www.glennsacks.com/column.php?id=68.

Schmidt, Peter. "Men's Share of College Enrollments Will Continue to Dwindle, Federal Report Says." *Chronicle of Higher Education*, May 27, 2010. http://chronicle.com/article/Mens-Share-of-College/65693.

Schmitt, John, and Heather Boushey. *The College Conundrum: Why the Benefits of a College Education May Not Be So Clear, Especially to Men*. Washington, DC: Center for American Progress, December 2010. www.americanprogress.org/wp-content/uploads/issues/2010/12/pdf/college_conundrum.pdf.

"Table 303.10: Total Fall Enrollment in Degree-granting Postsecondary Institutions, by Attendance Status, Sex of Student, and Control of Institution: Selected Years, 1947 through 2023." *Digest for Education Statistics*, National Center for Education Statistics, July 2014. http://nces.ed.gov/programs/digest/d13/tables/dt13_303.10.asp.

US Census Bureau. *Statistical Abstract of the United States: 2012*. Washington, DC: US Census Bureau and US Department of Commerce, 2012. http://www2.

US Department of Education Institute of Education Sciences and National Center for Education Statistics. "Fast Facts: Title IX." National Center for Education Statistics. Accessed September 25, 2015. http://nces.ed.gov/fastfacts/display.asp?id=93.census.gov/library/publications/2011/compendia/statab/131ed/2012-statab.pdf.

Vincent-Lancrin, Stéphan. "The Reversal of Gender Inequalities in Higher Education: An On-going Trend." In *Higher Education to 2030, Volume 1, Demography*, by OECD and the Educational Research and Innovation, 265–298. Paris, France: OECD, 2008.

"The Weaker Sex." *Economist*, May 30, 2015. http://www.economist.com/news/leaders/21652323-blue-collar-men-rich-countries-are-trouble-they-must-learn-adapt-weaker-sex.

CHAPTER 20

Abad-Santos, Alexander. "Sponsor of New Texas Anti-Abortion Bill Thinks Rape Kits Are Contraceptives." The Wire, June 24, 2014.

http://www.thewire.com/politics/2013/06/new-texas-anti-abortion-bill-rape-kits/66531.

"Abortion." GovTrack. Accessed September 25, 2015. https://www.govtrack.us/congress/bills/subjects/abortion/5897.

An Examination of the Impact of Media Coverage on a Candidate's Appearance. Name It. Change It. 2010. http://wmc.3cdn.net/63fa94f234fe3bb7eb_g4m6ibsyr.pdf.

Baird, Julia. "Must Read: From Seneca Falls to … Sarah Palin?" Council on Foreign Relations, September 13, 2008. http://www.cfr.org/world/must-read-seneca-falls-sarah-palin/p17207.

Bassett, Laura. "Chuck Winder, Idaho Lawmaker, Suggests Women Use Rape As Excuse For Abortions." *Huffington Post*, March 20, 2012. http://www.huffingtonpost.com/2012/03/20/chuck-winder-rape-abortions_n_1366994.html.

Bassett, Laura. "Trent Franks: 'The Incidence of Rape Resulting in Pregnancy Are Very Low.'" *Huffington Post*, June 12, 2013. http://www.huffingtonpost.com/2013/06/12/trent-franks-rape-pregnancy_n_3428846.html.

Bendery, Jennifer. "Michael Burgess: I Oppose Abortion Because Male Fetuses Masturbate (VIDEO)." *Huffington Post*, June 18, 2013. http://www.huffingtonpost.com/2013/06/18/michael-burgess-abortion_n_3459108.html.

Bennett, Dashiell. "Steve King Never Heard of Anyone Getting Pregnant by Statutory Rape." The Wire, August 21, 2012. http://www.thewire.com/politics/2012/08/steve-king-never-heard-anyone-getting-pregnant-statutory-rape-incest/56014.

Bowman, Karlyn, and Jennifer Marscio. "The Past, Present, and Future of the Women's Vote—AEI." American Enterprise Institute, October 4, 2012. http://www.aei.org/publication/the-past-present-and-future-of-the-womens-vote.

Bump, Philip. "The New Congress Is 80 Percent White, 80 Percent Male and 92 Percent Christian." *Washington Post*, January 5, 2015. http://www.washingtonpost.com/news/the-fix/wp/2015/01/05/the-new-congress-is-80-percent-white-80-percent-male-and-92-percent-christian.

Coleman, Korva. "Life of the Mother: Never a Reason For Abortion, Congressman Says." NPR, October 19, 2012. http://www.npr.org/sections/thetwo-way/2012/10/19/163239925/life-of-the-mother-never-a-reason-for-abortion-congressman-says.

"Declaration of Sentiments and Resolutions, Seneca Falls: Stanton and Anthony Papers Online." *The Elizabeth Cady Stanton and Susan B. Anthony Papers Project*, Rutgers University. Accessed September 25, 2015. http://ecssba.rutgers.edu/docs/seneca.html.

Dowd, Maureen. "Can We Get Hillary Without the Foolery?" *New York Times*, April 06, 2013. http://www.nytimes.com/2013/04/07/opinion/sunday/dowd-can-we-get-hillary-without-the-foolery.html?src=me&ref=general&_r=0&mtrref=undefined&gwh=CB2CC6E2AF772EE9BC1BBDE5C605B93D&gwt=pay&assetType=opinion.

Family Circle. "Presidential Cookie Recipes." *Family Circle*. Accessed September 25, 2015. http://www.familycircle.com/recipes/desserts/cookies/presidential-cookie-recipes.

Frank, Adrienne. "Women in Politics: One of Anything Is Never Enough." *American Magazine*, December 15, 2008. http://www.american.edu/americanmagazine/features/december2008-women-politics-election.cfm.

Givhan, Robin. "Hillary Clinton's Tentative Dip Into New Neckline Territory." *Washington Post*, July 20, 2007. http://www.washingtonpost.com/wp-dyn/content/article/2007/07/19/AR2007071902668.html.

Goff, Keli. "Worst Political Gaffes: Rape Jokes to the N-Word." *Root*, August 22, 2012. http://www.theroot.com/blogs/blogging_the_beltway/2012/08/worst_political_gaffes_rape_jokes_to_the_nword.html.

Griffith, Marie. "The New Evangelical Feminism of Bachmann and Palin." *The Blog, Huffington Post*, July 6, 2011. http://www.huffingtonpost.com/marie-griffith/evangelical-feminism_b_891579.html.

Hana, J. "Coulter Culture." *Observer*, October 2, 2007. http://observer.com/2007/10/coulter-culture.

Harding, Luke. "Bush Rubs Merkel up the Wrong Way." *Guardian*, July 28, 2006. http://www.theguardian.com/news/blog/2006/jul/28/bushrubsmerke.

Healy, Patrick, and Michael Luo. "$150,000 Wardrobe for Palin May Alter Tailor-Made Image." *New York Times*, October 22, 2008. http://www.nytimes.com/2008/10/23/us/politics/23palin.html.

Henneberger, Melinda. "Rick Santorum: 'The Idea I'm Coming After Your Birth Control Is Absurd.'" *Washington Post*, January 6, 2012. http://www.washingtonpost.com/blogs/she-the-people/post/rick-santorum-the-idea-im-coming-after-your-birth-control-is-absurd/2012/01/06/gIQAOVy0fP_blog.html.

Herstory Lessons. "Bella Abzug." Herstory Network. Accessed September 25, 2015. http://www.herstorynetwork.com/herstory-lessons/bella-abzug.

Huth, Mary. "US Suffrage Movement Timeline, 1792 to Present." Susan B. Anthony Center for Women's Leadership, 1994 and February 1995. https://www.rochester.edu/SBA/suffragetimeline.html.

Jarrett, Christian. "Female Political Role Models Have an Empowering Effect on Women." *British Psychological Society Research Digest*, April 17, 2013. http://digest.bps.org.uk/2013/04/female-political-role-models-have.html.

Kapin, Allyson. "New Poll Reveals Independent Women Voters Are Concerned About Washington's War on Women." *The Blog*, *Huffington Post*, November 2, 2012. http://www.huffingtonpost.com/allyson-kapin/independent-women-voters_b_2061317.html.

Klobuchar, Amy. "Women Are Getting the Job Done." *The Blog*, *Huffington Post*, February 6, 2014. http://www.huffingtonpost.com/sen-amy-klobuchar/women-are-getting-the-job_b_4741106.html.

Lawless, Jennifer, and Richard Fox. *Girls Just Wanna Not Run: The Gender Gap in Young Americans' Political Ambition*. School of Public Affairs, American University, March 2013. http://www.american.edu/spa/wpi/upload/Girls-Just-Wanna-Not-Run_Policy-Report.pdf.

Lawless, Jennifer, Richard Fox, and Gail Baitinger. "Women's Underrepresentation in US Politics: The Enduring Gender Gap in Political Ambition." In *Women and Elective Office: Past, Present, and Future*, 3rd ed., edited by Sue Thomas and Clyde Wilcox, 27–45. New York: Oxford University Press, 2014.

Lee, Brianna. "'Conservative Feminist'? Not Michele Bachmann." *Need to Know on PBS*, PBS, July 13, 2011. http://www.pbs.org/wnet/need-to-know/the-daily-need/conservative-feminist-not-michele-bachmann/10363.

Manning, Jennifer, and Ida Brudnick. *Women in Congress, 1917–2015: Biographical and Committee Assignment Information, and Listings by State and Congress*. Washington, DC: Congressional Research Service, April 27, 2015. http://www.senate.gov/CRS Reports/crs-publish.cfm?pid=%270E%2C*PLS%3D%22 %40%20%20%0A.

McClelland, Edward. "Opinion: Joe Walsh's Manhood Gap." *Ward Room* (blog), *NBC Chicago*, October 15, 2012. http://www.nbcchicago.com/blogs/ward-room/Joe-Walshs-Manhood-Gap-174211941.html.

McGregor, Jena. "More than 100 Women in Congress for the First Time, but Not Much Growth." *Washington Post*, November 5, 2014. https://www.washingtonpost.com/news/on-leadership/wp/2014/11/05/more-than-100-women-in-congress-for-the-first-time-but-not-much-growth.

McKeon, Nancy. "Women in the House Get a Restroom." *Washington Post*, July 28, 2011. https://www.washingtonpost.com/lifestyle/style/women-in-the-house-get-a-restroom/2011/07/28/gIQAFgdwfI_story.html.

Memmot, Mark. "'God Intended' a Pregnancy Caused by Rape, Indiana Candidate Says." NPR, October 24, 2012. http://www.npr.org/sections/thetwo-way/2012/10/24/163529166/god-intended-a-pregnancy-caused-by-rape-indiana-candidate-says.

Miller, Korin. "Politician: Rape Pregnancy Is Like Having Illegitimate Baby." *Cosmopolitan*, August 28, 2012. http://www.cosmopolitan.com/politics/news/a10522/rape-pregnancy-baby-out-of-wedlock.

Millican, Julie. "O'Reilly: Rape, Murder Victim Was 'Wearing a Miniskirt and a Halter Top. ... [E]very Predator in the World Is Gonna Pick That up at 2 in the Morning." Media Matters for America, August 4, 2006. http://mediamatters.org/video/2006/08/04/oreilly-rape-murder-victim-was-wearing-a-minisk/136315.

Moore, Lori. "Rep. Todd Akin: The Statement and the Reaction." New York Times, August 20, 2012. http://www.nytimes.com/2012/08/21/us/politics/rep-todd-akin-legitimate-rape-statement-and-reaction.html?_r=0&mtrref=undefined&gwh=ADDBDE7B45DF7666D99E325A86765D14&gwt=pay.

Moore, Martha. "Focus on Hillary Clinton's Appearance Sparks Criticism." USA Today, May 10, 2012. http://usatoday30.usatoday.com/news/washington/story/2012-05-09/hillary-rodham-clinton/54860282/1.

Napikoski, Linda. "Stop ERA: A Campaign Against the Equal Rights Amendment." About Women's History. Accessed September 25, 2015. http://womenshistory.about.com/od/equalrightsamendment/a/Stop_ERA.htm.

Office of the Secretary of State. "Kansas History." In 2015 Kansas Directory, 21–48. Topeka, KS: Kansas Secretary of State, 2015. https://www.kssos.org/forms/communication/history.pdf.

Palmer, Barbara, and Dennis Michael. Simon. "Understanding the Glass Ceiling: Women and the Competitive Environment." In Breaking the Political Glass Ceiling: Women and Congressional Elections, 127–158. New York: Routledge, 2006.

Parker, David. "Rebecca Latimer Felton (1835–1930)." In New Georgia Encyclopedia. Article updated August 11, 2015. http://www.georgiaencyclopedia.org/articles/history-archaeology/rebecca-latimer-felton-1835-1930.

People for the American Way. "The War on Women: How the War on Women Became Mainstream: Turning Back the Clock on Tea Party America." People for the American Way. Accessed September 25, 2015. http://www.pfaw.org/media-center/publications/war-women.

Pew Research Center. "Section 9: Trends in Party Affiliation." Pew
    Research Center, June 4, 2012. http://www.people-press.
    org/2012/06/04/section-9-trends-in-party-affiliation.

"Shirley Anita Chisholm." National Women's History Museum.
    Accessed September 25, 2015. https://www.nwhm.org/education-
    resources/biography/biographies/shirley-anita-chisholm.

Staff, People for the American Way. "How the War on Women
    Became Mainstream." Truthout, April 18, 2012. http://
    www.truth-out.org/news/item/8603-how-the-war-on-
    women-became-mainstream.

Poston, Dudley L. Jr., and Leon F. Bouvier. "Age and Sex Composition."
    In *Population and Society: An Introduction to Demography*,
    228–264. New York: Cambridge University Press, 2010.
    doi:10.1017/cbo9780511781001.010.

Rad Campaign. "This Is the Modern War on Women." It's A War
    on Women. Accessed September 25, 2015. http://www.
    itsawaronwomen.com.

Rampell, Catherine. "Why Women Are Far More Likely to Vote
    than Men." *Washington Post*, July 17, 2014. https://www.
    washingtonpost.com/opinions/catherine-rampell-why-
    women-are-far-more-likely-to-vote-then-men/2014/07/17/
    b4658192-0de8-11e4-8c9a-923ecc0c7d23_story.html.

Reeve, Elspeth. "The Ghost of Sandra Fluke Is Haunting Rush Limbaugh's
    Mega-Deal." The Wire, May 6, 2013. http://www.thewire.com/
    politics/2013/05/rush-limbaugh-contract-sandra-fluke/64904.

Reuters. "Indiana Republican: When Life Begins from Rape, 'God
    Intended' It." *NBC* News, October 24, 2012. http://nbcpolitics.
    nbcnews.com/_news/2012/10/24/14664931-indiana-
    republican-when-life-begins-from-rape-god-intended-it?lite.

Ryan, Erin Gloria. "Lawmaker Suggests Beaten Ladies Remember
    the Good Times." *Jezebel*, March 14, 2012. http://jezebel.
    com/5893244/lawmaker-suggests-beaten-ladies-remember-
    the-good-times.

Saddleback College. "Media Coverage of Women Leaders." *Women
    Political Leaders and the Media*, 39–53. New York: Palgrave
    Macmillan, 2013. doi:10.1057/9781137295545.0006.

Saner, Emine. "Top 10 Sexist Moments in Politics: Julia Gillard, Hillary Clinton and More." *Guardian*, June 14, 2013. http://www.theguardian.com/politics/2013/jun/14/top-10-sexist-moments-politics.

Sanghani, Radhika. "'Women Shouldn't Laugh in Public': The Dumbest Things Politicians Have Said." *Telegraph*, November 25, 2014. http://www.telegraph.co.uk/women/womens-politics/11252742/Women-shouldnt-laugh-in-public-The-dumbest-things-politicians-have-said.html.

Schlesinger, Robert. "Sarah Palin and the Future of Women in Politics." *US News & World Report*, December 4, 2009. http://www.usnews.com/opinion/articles/2009/12/04/sarah-palin-and-the-future-of-women-in-politics.

Seelye, Katharine Q. "From Congress to Halls of State, in New Hampshire, Women Rule." *New York Times*, January 01, 2013. http://www.nytimes.com/2013/01/02/us/politics/from-congress-to-halls-of-state-in-new-hampshire-women-rule.html

Seltzer, Sarah. "The 10 Dumbest Things Ever Said About Abortion and Women's Rights." *Rolling Stone*, July 15, 2013. http://www.rollingstone.com/politics/news/the-ten-dumbest-things-ever-said-about-abortion-and-womens-rights-20130715.

Simon, Roger. "Hillary Clinton Will Take Only so Much Guff." POLITICO, May 13, 2013. http://www.politico.com/story/2013/05/hillary-will-take-only-so-much-guff-91288_Page2.html.

Somanader, Tanya. "Allen West: Liberal Women Are 'Neutering American Men.'" ThinkProgress, April 25, 2011. http://thinkprogress.org/politics/2011/04/25/161001/allen-west-liberal-women.

Steinhauer, Jennifer. "Senate Races Expose Extent of Republicans' Gender Gap." *New York Times*, November 07, 2012. http://www.nytimes.com/2012/11/08/us/politics/womens-issues-were-a-problem-for-gop.html?_r=0&mtrref=undefined&gwh=FD8A8E83B51E1190C5963290DA3BBC4D&gwt=pay.

Weber, Peter. "Wendy Davis' Stunning Filibuster of a Texas Abortion Bill." *Week*, June 26, 2013. http://theweek.com/articles/462815/wendy-davis-stunning-filibuster-texas-abortion-bill.

Week Staff. "Rush Limbaugh vs. Sandra Fluke: A Timeline." *Week*, March 09, 2012. http://theweek.com/articles/477570/rush-limbaugh-vs-sandra-fluke-timeline.

Wickersham, Joan. "Hillary Clinton's Cookies." *Boston Globe*, January 11, 2013. http://www.bostonglobe.com/opinion/2013/01/11/hillary-clinton-cookies/BQNzDP1QCbIxyQDOwqsLtN/story.html.

Wicks, Buffy. "Why the GOP Has Lost the Women's Vote for 2014 and Beyond." *Daily Beast*, June 21, 2013. http://www.thedailybeast.com/witw/articles/2013/06/21/why-the-gop-has-lost-the-women-s-vote-for-2014-and-beyond.html.

Wing, Nick. "Joe Walsh Hits Tammy Duckworth For 'Picking Out a Dress,' Gets Smacked With Comeback (VIDEO)." *Huffington Post*, October 10, 2012. http://www.huffingtonpost.com/2012/10/10/joe-walsh-hits-tammy-duckworth-debate_n_1955968.html.

"Women in State Legislatures: Statistics." National Women's Political Caucus. Accessed September 25, 2015. http://www.nwpc.org/statistics.

"World Classification." *Women in National Parliaments*, International Parliamentary Union, September 1, 2013. http://www.ipu.org/wmn-e/classif.htm.

Zurbriggen, Eileen, and Aurora Sherman. "Race and Gender in the 2008 U.S. Presidential Election: A Content Analysis of Editorial Cartoons." *Analyses of Social Issues and Public Policy* 10, no. 1 (2010): 1–25. http://people.ucsc.edu/~zurbrigg/pdf/Zurbriggen&Sherman2010.pdf.

CHAPTER 21

Business Wire. "New Survey from Citi and LinkedIn Explores the Factors That Shape Men's and Women's Professional Paths—and Their Varied Definitions of Success." Business Wire,

October 30, 2013. http://www.businesswire.com/news/
home/20131030005200/en/Survey-Citi-LinkedIn-Explores-
Factors-Shape-Men%E2%80%99s#.Vgu3nWRViko.

Goodman, Nadia. "How to Admit When You're Wrong." *Entrepreneur*,
July 18, 2013. http://www.entrepreneur.com/article/227470.

Goodman, Nadia. "How to Train Your Brain to Multitask Effectively."
Entrepreneur, February 25, 2013. http://www.entrepreneur.
com/article/225865.

Llopis, Glenn. "The Most Undervalued Leadership Traits of Women."
Forbes, February 3, 2014. http://www.forbes.com/sites/
glennllopis/2014/02/03/the-most-undervalued-leadership-
traits-of-women.

Miller, George A. "The Magical Number Seven, Plus or Minus Two:
Some Limits on Our Capacity for Processing Information."
Psychological Review 101, no. 2 (1955): 343–352. http://www.
psych.utoronto.ca/users/peterson/psy430s2001/Miller%20
GA%20Magical%20Seven%20Psych%20Review%201955.pdf.

Morgan, James. "Women 'Better at Multitasking' Than Men, Study
Finds." *BBC News*, October 24, 2013. http://www.bbc.com/
news/science-environment-24645100.

Mosbergen, Dominique. "Biological Evidence May Support Idea That
Women Talk More Than Men, Study Says." *Huffington Post*,
February 21, 2013. http://www.huffingtonpost.com/2013/
02/21/women-talk-more-than-men-study_n_2734215.html.

Seidman, Dr. Daniel. "Men and Asking for Help." *The Blog, Huffington
Post*, December 8, 2010. http://www.huffingtonpost.com/
daniel-seidman/men-and-asking-for-help_b_793617.html.

The Muse. "The Right Way to Ask for Help at Work." *Forbes*, September
20, 2012. http://www.forbes.com/sites/dailymuse/2012/09/20/
the-right-way-to-ask-for-help-at-work.

"13 Ways to Be a Better Co-Worker." *Readers Digest*. Accessed
September 25, 2015. http://www.rd.com/advice/work-career/
13-ways-to-be-a-better-coworker.

CHAPTER 22

Bachelet, Michelle. "Removing Barriers to Women's Participation Fuels Economic Development." UN Women, December 4, 2012. http://www.unwomen.org/en/news/stories/2012/12/removing-barriers-to-women-s-participation-fuels-economic-development.

Butler, Bethonie. "Malala Yousafzai, Sheryl Sandberg Promote Girls' Access to Education in Facebook Chat." *Washington Post*, August 8, 2014. http://www.washingtonpost.com/blogs/she-the-people/wp/2014/08/08/malala-yousafzai-sheryl-sandberg-promote-girls-access-to-education-in-facebook-chat.

"Child Marriage." CARE. Accessed September 25, 2015. http://www.care.org/work/womens-empowerment/child-marriage.

Cate, Olle Ten. "Medical Education in the Netherlands." *Medical Teacher* 29, no. 8 (2007): 752–757. http://www.dhpescu.org/media/elip/Medical%20education%20in%20the%20Netherlands.pdf.

Davies, Catriona. "Mideast Women Beat Men in Education, Lose Out at Work." *CNN*, June 6, 2012. http://www.cnn.com/2012/06/01/world/meast/middle-east-women-education.

Equality Now. "Global Sex Trafficking Fact Sheet." Equality Now. Accessed September 25, 2015. http://www.equalitynow.org/node/1010.

"Facts and Figures: Ending Violence against Women." UN Women, October 2014. http://www.unwomen.org/en/what-we-do/ending-violence-against-women/facts-and-figures.

"Facts and Figures: Leadership and Political Participation." UN Women, September 2015. http://www.unwomen.org/en/what-we-do/leadership-and-political-participation/facts-and-figures.

Hausmann, Ricardo, Laura D. Tyson, and Saadia Zahidi. *The Global Gender Gap Report 2011: Rankings and Scores*. Geneva: World Economic Forum, 2011. http://www3.weforum.org/docs/GGGR11/GGGR11_Rankings-Scores.pdf.

"HIV & AIDS in Botswana." AVERT. Accessed September 25, 2015. http://www.avert.org/hiv-aids-botswana.htm.

International Labour Organization. *Global Employment Trends for Women 2012*. Geneva: ILO, 2012. http://www.ilo.org/wcmsp5/groups/public/---dgreports/---dcomm/documents/publication/wcms_195447.pdf.

Italie, Leanne. "New Book on Dating Blames the Numbers _ Not the Women." Associated Press, August 25, 2015. http://bigstory.ap.org/article/3b2d5f5fa78c4bf5851ee69c20122ccc/new-book-dating-blames-numbers-not-women.

Karpf, Ted. "Faith-based Organizations Play a Major Role in HIV/AIDS Care and Treatment in Sub-Saharan Africa." World Health Organization, February 8, 2007. http://www.who.int/mediacentre/news/notes/2007/np05/en.

McDaniel, Anne. *Gender Differences in University Completion Across Europe: The Influence of Family Background and National Context*. Working paper, Institute for Social and Economic Research and Policy, Columbia University, New York, August 15, 2011. http://education.uci.edu/docs/McDaniel_Working%20Paper_Gender%20Gap%20in%20EU.pdf.

Nejad, Maryam Naghsh, and Andrew Young. "Female Brain Drains and Women's Rights Gaps: A Gravity Model Analysis of Bilateral Migration Flows." *IZA Discussion Paper Series*, March 2014. http://ftp.iza.org/dp8067.pdf.

OECD. *Education at a Glance 2012: Highlights*. Paris: OECD Publishing, 2012. http://www.oecd.org/edu/highlights.pdf.

OECD. "Migration and the Brain Drain Phenomenon." OECD. http://www.oecd.org/dev/poverty/migrationandthebraindrainphenomenon.htm

Pintor, Rafael López, Maria Gratschew, Jamal Adimi, Julie Ballington, Craig Brians, Sergei Lounev, Dieter Nohlen, Pippa Norris, Smita Notosusanto, Kate Sullivan, Edmundo Urrutia. *Voter Turnout Since 1945: A Global Report*. Stockholm: International Institute for Democracy and Electoral Assistance, 2002. http://www.idea.int/publications/vt/loader.cfm?csmodule=security/getfile&pageid=4500.

Provost, Claire, and Rich Harris. "Malala Yousafzai and Girls' Access to Education—Get the Data." *Universal Primary*

Education Datablog, Guardian, July 12, 2013. http://www.
theguardian.com/global-development/datablog/2013/jul/12/
malala-yousafzai-girls-access-education-data.

Roudi-Fahimi, Farzaneh, and Valentine Moghadam. "Empowering
Women, Developing Society: Female Education in the Middle
East and North Africa." Population Reference Bureau, 2003.
http://www.prb.org/Publications/Reports/2003/Empowering
WomenDevelopingSocietyFemaleEducationintheMiddle
EastandNorthAfrica.aspx.

Sood, Suemedha. "The Statistics of Studying Abroad." *BBC
Travel,* September 26, 2012. http://www.bbc.com/travel/story/
20120926-the-statistics-of-studying-abroad.

United Nations Educational, Scientific and Cultural Organization
(UNESCO). *Higher Education in Asia: Expanding Out,
Expanding Up.* Montreal: UNESCO Institute for Statistics,
2014. http://www.uis.unesco.org/Library/Documents/higher-
education-asia-graduate-university-research-2014-en.pdf.

United Nations ESCAP. "Statistical Yearbook for Asia and the Pacific
2011." United Nations ESCAP, 2011. http://www.unescap.org/
stat/data/syb2011/I-People/Women-empowerment.asp.

VanderBrug, Jackie. "The Global Rise of Female Entrepreneurs."
Harvard Business Review, September 4, 2013. https://hbr.org/
2013/09/global-rise-of-female-entrepreneurs.

World Economic Forum. *The Global Gender Gap Report: 2013.* Geneva:
World Economic Forum, 2013. http://www3.weforum.org/
docs/WEF_GenderGap_Report_2013.pdf.

CHAPTER 32

Shaitly, Shahesta. "Is China's Mosuo Tribe the World's Last Matriarchy?"
Guardian, December 18, 2010. http://www.theguardian.com/
lifeandstyle/2010/dec/19/china-mosuo-tribe-matriarchy.

Wetzstein, Cheryl. "With 1-Child Policy, China 'Missing' Girls."
Washington Times, January 27, 2010. http://www.washingtontimes
.com/news/2010/jan/27/with-1-child-policy-china-missing-
girls/#ixzz2ZQmhYpfd.

Wickelus, Charles. "The Mosou: A Matriarchal Dream or Aberration of History?" Return of Kings, April 12, 2013. http://www.returnofkings.com/10624/the-mosou-a-matriarchal-dream-or-aberration-of-history.

CHAPTER 33

Ellis, Mark. "An Indelicate Balance." *Kenyon College Alumni Bulletin* 33, no. 2 (Winter 2011). http://bulletin.kenyon.edu/x3514.html.

Jensen, Keld. "Intelligence Is Overrated: What You Really Need To Succeed." *Forbes*, April 12, 2012. http://www.forbes.com/sites/keldjensen/2012/04/12/intelligence-is-overrated-what-you-really-need-to-succeed.

INKSHARES

Inkshares is a crowdfunded book publisher. We democratize publishing by having readers select the books we publish—we edit, design, print, distribute, and market any book that meets a preorder threshold.

Interested in making a book idea come to life? Visit inkshares.com to find new book projects or to start your own.